No More Haunted Dolls

Horror Fiction that Transcends the Tropes

Edited by

Cassandra O'Sullivan Sachar

Series in Critical Media Studies

VERNON PRESS

www.vernonpress.com

In the Americas:
Vernon Press
1000 N West Street, Suite 1200
Wilmington, Delaware, 19801
United States

In the rest of the world:
Vernon Press
C/Sancti Espiritu 17,
Malaga, 29006
Spain

Series in Critical Media Studies

Library of Congress Control Number: 2024935158

ISBN: 979-8-8819-0003-8

Cover design by Vernon Press with elements from Freepik.

Table of Contents

Notes on Contributors

Editor

Cassandra O'Sullivan Sachar, Ed.D., M.F.A., is a horror/suspense writer and associate professor of English at Bloomsburg University of Pennsylvania. She received her Doctorate of Education with a Literacy Specialization from the University of Delaware and her M.F.A. in Creative Writing with a focus on horror fiction from Wilkes University. She also holds a Master of Instruction from the University of Delaware and a Master of Arts in Fiction from Wilkes University. She has chaired panels on and presented horror scholarship at the Northeast Modern Language Association (NeMLA) Convention and the Ann Radcliffe Academic Conference. A member of the Horror Writers Association, her horror stories and essays have appeared in numerous publications, including *The Horror Zine, HorrorAddicts.net. The Angry Gable, The Chamber Magazine,* and *Tales from the Moonlit Path*. Dr. Sachar is the author of the dark suspense novel *Darkness There but Something More* (published by Wicked House Publishing) and the short horror story collection *Keeper of Corpses and Other Dark Tales* (forthcoming from Velox Books). She has additionally served as the fiction editor for *River & South Review* and is the current creative prose editor at *Pennsylvania English*. Furthermore, her research studies and practitioner articles have appeared in diverse educational publications.

Chapter Authors

Zaher Alajlani is a Pushcart-nominated Syrian short story author, editor, researcher, and translator. His work is primarily in English and has been featured in various publications worldwide. He has a Ph.D. from Babes-Bolyai University, an M.A. in Communication from the University of Indianapolis, an M.A. in English Culture, Literature, and Ideology from the National and Kapodistrian University of Athens, and a B.A. in English Literature and Language from Damascus University. He speaks English, Arabic, Romanian, and Greek.

   Priyanka Bharali is a Ph.D. research scholar from the Department of English, Dibrugarh University, Dibrugarh, Assam, India. She has completed her masters and MPhil from the same institution in the years 2018 and 2019, respectively.

   David Edwards, Ph.D., is a lecturer for both the Acting for Stage & Screen B.A. (Hons) and the M.A. in Directing and Theatre Making at the Northern School of Art, UK. He read English at King's College London before training as an actor at the Guildhall School of Music & Drama. He works professionally as an actor and director. Key research areas include mental health in the horror genre, psychophysical performance techniques, and the representation of mental health on stage. He regularly presents at both theatre and film conferences worldwide. His upcoming published works largely focus on mental health representation in various horror subgenres.

Carlos A. González is a scholar and Ph.D. candidate in the Romance Languages and Literatures Department at Harvard University. With a specialized focus on twentieth- and twenty-first-century French and Spanish fiction, and the genres of horror and the fantastic in particular, their expertise extends to Latin American women's neo-Gothic, medieval French narrative, and the exploration of necropoetics in contemporary literature. They reside in Cambridge, Massachusetts, with their spouse, beloved shih tzu, and the creature living under their bed.

Kazım Tolga Gürel received his Ph.D. with his thesis titled "LGBTI+ Representation in Mainstream Newspapers in Turkey." The author of eleven books, seven book chapters, and over 30 articles, he continues his studies on cultural studies, anti-capitalist movements, otherness, gender, and hegemony.

Josh Hanson is a graduate of the University of Montana's Masters Program in literature and creative writing. He is the author of the novels *King's Hill, The Woodcutters,* and *Fortress* (forthcoming), as well as a number of short fiction pieces that have appeared or are forthcoming in a variety of journals and anthologies.

Cass Heid holds a bachelor's degree in Earth and Environmental Science, a Master of Arts in Creative Nonfiction, and an M.F.A. in Creative Writing, all from Wilkes University. In the midst of revising her nonfiction essay collection, *Something's Off,* she is also versed in writing fiction and poetry, most of which is focused on disability activism. Her spoken-word piece "The Four Responses" has a home in the online disability blog *The Handy Uncapped Pen.* She is currently working on her debut horror novel.

Chayyim Holtkamp (she/hers or they/them) is a recent graduate student at the Citadel, having pursued a Master of Education in Higher Education Leadership. She also received a Master of Arts in History from the College of Charleston and the Citadel. She is particularly interested in disability, both contemporary and historically. Her interests include disability history during the Holocaust and medical experimentation. She is interested in disability in video games and representations of disabled characters.

Maria Juko completed her B.A. and M.Ed. in English and Biology for Secondary Education with a focus on Victorian Literature at the University of Hamburg. She is currently reworking her Ph.D. on female self-reliance in late eighteenth to mid-nineteenth-century novels for publication as an independent researcher and teacher in Potsdam. She researches women from these eras, considering novels, conduct books, and self-help literature of the period, and examines adaptations of the period in theme park rides, comics, film, and literature. She also looks at podcasts and graphic novels, especially through the lens of adaptation studies.

Melissa Eriko Poulsen is an assistant professor of English at Menlo College. She received her Ph.D. from the Department of Literature at the University of California Santa Cruz. She specializes in critical mixed-race studies and Asian American literature, with a particular focus on literary and popular culture representations of Asian mixed race in the United States across the twentieth and twenty-first centuries. Her current project examines speculative Asian American literature. Dr. Poulsen's work has been featured in *MELUS*, *Amerasia*, and *Asian American Literature: Discourses and Pedagogies* and is forthcoming in the *Journal of Graphic Novels and Comics*.

Stefan Sonntagbauer is working on his Ph.D. thesis on "Horror and Subjectivity" at the Philosophical Department at the University of Vienna. With his podcast "Dr. Horror," he delivers the most exciting insights from the world of horror science to a broad audience. As an expert on the psychology of fear, he is a regular guest in the media. Most recently, he kicked off a debate about Austrian horror with an essay for Austria's premium newspaper *Der Standard* and accompanied the experimental collective Okabre at their film concerts with lectures on Shinya Tsukamo's *Tetsuo: The Ironman* and George A. Romero's *Night of the Living Dead*.

Andrew Wilczak is an associate professor of criminology and sociology at Wilkes University. He received his Ph.D. in sociology from Bowling Green State University (2011) and his M.F.A. from Wilkes University (2022). His research interests include adolescent violence, the sociology of revolutions, and the intersections between art and justice. He is currently the editor of *Untenured*, a small literary journal that engages in anti-racist, anti- and post-capitalist, and post-gender themes.

Lisa Wood is an award-winning author and screenwriter as well as an educator. She is the recipient of the Golden Stake Award, a MICO Award-winning screenwriter, a two-time Bram Stoker Award® Finalist, a Rhysling nominated poet, and an accomplished essayist. Wood has won over 50 national and international screenplay and film awards. She has penned short fiction that has been published in works including the anthologies *Sycorax's Daughters* and *Slay: Stories of the Vampire Noire*. Her nonfiction has been published in *Nightmare Magazine* and academic textbooks such as the cross-curricular *Conjuring Worlds: An Afrofuturist Textbook*. Her papers are archived as part of the University of Pittsburgh's Horror Studies Collection. Wood is the Vice President of the Horror Writers Association, the founder of the Speculative Fiction Academy, an English and Creative Writing professor, a horror scholar with a Ph.D. in Creative Writing and an M.F.A. in Speculative Fiction, and a frequent contributor to the conversation around the evolution of genre fiction.

Stephan Zguta received a master's in English literature from Westfield State University. His thesis focused on transgressive cinema, a version of which he presented at the Northeast Modern Language Association Conference. Currently, he resides in New York City, where he works in publishing and continues his study of film, literature, and media.

Acknowledgments

I would like to sincerely thank the peer reviewers who dedicated their time and expertise to provide the authors of this volume with thoughtful feedback for enhancing their work:

Frances Auld

Naomi Borwein

Josh Chambers

Valeria Dani

Christina Francis

Jeremy Freeman

Ashlee Harry

Roland Innerhofer

Jamil Mustafa

Andrew Najberg

Cody Parrish

Michael Potts

Melissa Strong

Nicu Szilagyi

Kevin Wetmore

Rebecca Willoughby

Shannon Young

Luca Zanchi

This wonderful assortment includes critics and educators with diverse backgrounds and areas of scholarship. While this group happens to include a few friends, colleagues, and even my brother-in-law, several others listed received an unsolicited email from a complete stranger who spent a lot of time on the internet researching horror scholars. I was fortunate to find peer reviewers whose expertise matched the research areas of the various chapters. I am forever grateful that they were willing to contribute to this book, and hope to return the favor someday through future collaborations.

I would also like to thank the chapter authors for their willingness to endure several rounds of feedback and my seemingly endless questions as we worked together to prepare each chapter for publication. From across the globe, they each somehow found my call for chapter proposals, and I'm so glad they did. I am indebted to them for their tireless dedication to their contributions and for their trust in me as editor.

Introduction

Cassandra O'Sullivan Sachar

Like the final girl who makes it to the end of the novel, thwarting the killer, horror fiction has endured despite obstacles and tired, recycled plotlines. From *The Twilight Zone*'s Talking Tina to *Child's Play's* Chucky or *The Conjuring's* Annabelle, the haunted doll cliché is an example of something that has been done so many times that any new story feels stale. Look at any website of short horror fiction, and you'll find escaped killers, cursed artifacts, and lost ghosts—it's all been done before and *keeps* being done over and over, often with little to differentiate the story from those that have come before.

Horror, like any genre, has its common elements. Rather than the meet-cute in a romance, there's boy meets ghost or girl kills vampire. While certain horror tropes have been reused for centuries, *great* horror writing moves beyond the formula by adding elements that are new and unexpected. We *want* to be terrified, to read something so sinister that we breathe with relief when finished and sigh in contentment as we tuck ourselves in at night, hoping that the creatures about which we read will stay confined to the page rather than reaching out from under our beds. The same old storyline redone with a fresh coat of paint isn't always enough to raise the goosebumps on the backs of our necks.

What makes horror fiction resilient? What breathes new life into a genre that thrives on stereotypes? There's still an enormous audience for horror fiction, but writers and filmmakers must create content that feels unique and exciting. The idea for this book was conceived due to my lifelong love of horror and appreciation for that which is both innovative and entertaining rather than overdone and trite. The title is inspired by a rejection letter I received from an editor after sending him my very own haunted doll story. He complimented my characterization and pacing but said that I didn't offer anything new to the plot with a haunted doll terrorizing a family. He was right, and it got me thinking about horror tropes and how creators use them.

No More Haunted Dolls: Horror Fiction that Transcend the Tropes is a multi-author work united by the common theme of critical analysis of the use of horror tropes in literature, film, and even video games. Tackling issues dealing with gender, race, sexuality, social class, religion, politics, disability, and more in horror, the authors are horror scholars hailing from varied backgrounds and areas of specialty. This book may be used as a resource for classes that study horror or simply as entertainment for horror fans; readers will consider diverse perspectives on the tropes themselves as well as their representation in specific works.

Chapter 1

Disturbed Mask-ulinity: The Mask Motive in the Slasher Film

Stefan Sonntagbauer

Abstract

This chapter shows how the mask of the iconic slasher killer marks a deeply wounded masculinity. While a lot of criticism during the golden age of the genre (1978-1984) dismissed the slasher as misogynistic, Carol Clover saved it by shifting the focus to the female survivor figure, the famous final girl. Just so, comparatively, little has been said of how the slasher reflects on the problems that men face in a patriarchal culture. Examining iconic killers like Michael Myers (*Halloween*), Leatherface (*Texas Chainsaw Massacre*), and Jason Vorhees (*Friday the 13th*), the chapter shows that putting on a mask is a (typically masculine) reaction to the traumatic experience of social exclusion. Hurt boys turn into murderous men when there is no way for them to develop a suitable persona that could guarantee them participation. It is the mask of the killer that makes the man visible in the social sphere and protects him from the pain of not belonging.

Keywords: masked killer, final girl, *Halloween*, *Nightmare on Elm Street*, *Scream*, *American Psycho*

* * *

One of the most common tropes of horror is surely the recurse on the formulaic nature of its subject. Even though all genres, by definition, constitute themselves and evolve in interaction with some never-changing core elements, such as settings, narratives and characters, horror seems to have a special connection with repetitive forms (Grant 9). Certainly, this is linked to its traumatic structure. Horror has always been about the past haunting the present, materializing in unpleasant comebacks—from the ghost of more or less beloved relatives to the undead that come walking (and consuming) amongst the living. Repetition is what marks the haunting as a form of trauma, just as it forms the trope over time. Still, it seems there is another aspect about the ever-recurring tropes of horror, a deeper truth, a bigger "why." Repetition is pressing for resolution. The tropes endure until we are finally able to embrace what they are trying to tell us about ourselves as individuals, as humans, and as a society. Just as the ghosts are condemned to haunt the world of the living until they are "seen" or understood, the tropes keep coming back until we understand them. Only then are they free to go their way, change their form, and take on new meanings.

One such remarkable trope that has stuck around for a while now is the masked killer. No doubt, the mask itself is an "enduring generic motif in horror cinema" (Heller-Nicholas 191). As such, it doesn't only bring up the different philosophical implications of the mask as a *dingsymbol*—a concrete object and highly loaded signifier—but also comments on, criticizes, and revises them. The masked killers that became popular with the slasher in the 1970s and 1980s brought up a discussion on gender-stereotypes. The distribution of the roles— killer and victim—follows a simple recipe: the masked killer is usually a man, while the heroine, i.e., the main victim, is usually a woman.[1] So, it is no wonder that, in the beginning, a lot of criticism dismissed the whole genre as misogynistic.[2] Carol Clover saved the slasher with her legendary 1987 essay "Her Body, Himself" by shifting the focus to the female survivor figure for whom she established the legendary term, the "final girl" (84).

As Clover's theorization became popular—and popularized[3]—a strong focal point for further criticism was set. As a "strong, feminist heroine who turns the

---

[1] In Moore and Heffernan's list of the 15 most iconic masked killers in *Collider Magazine*, the quota of males as killers is 100%.

[2] It all started with Roger Ebert's essay "Why Movie Audiences Aren't Safe Anymore," in which he describes the slasher as an act of masculine revenge on all the women who dared to live out their sexuality, an argument that was gladly taken on by a lot of second wave feminists. From then on, the meta-trope of the misogynistic slasher persisted. Zhou gives an overview over the debate, and Lizardi and Hayt present different takes on the matter, proving at last, that, in terms of the slasher and misogyny, *it's not over yet.*

[3] The popular idea of the final girl as feminist heroine has little to do with Clover's original account. In her essay "Her Body, Himself: Gender in the Slasher Film," she points out similarities between the female protagonists and the killer: "Just as the killer is not fully masculine, she is not fully feminine [...]. Her smartness, gravity, competence in mechanical and other practical matters, and sexual reluctance set her apart from the other girls and ally her [...] with the killer himself" (88). Later on, she makes a clear stance: "To applaud the Final Girl as a feminist development [...] is, in light of her figurative meaning, a particularly grotesque expression of wishful thinking" (100). This concept received some criticism while remaining a central focal point for the debate around the genre. In *Skin Shows: Gothic Horror and the Technology of Monsters,* Jack Halberstam reads Stretch, the final girl of *Texas Chainsaw Massacre 2,* as a representation of the monstrous gender, going beyond the binary matrix, finally turning into "something messier than male or female" (143). Going beyond Clover's theorization, Halberstam pleads to reconfigure gender "not simply through inversion, but by literally creating new categories" (139). Pinedo goes in

knife on the killer," the final girl should very soon become an "interpretative framework that has largely determined the reception" (Paszkiewicz and Rusnak). Meanwhile, the killer himself—as a man with severe problems—somehow got out of sight. Until today, comparatively little has been said of how the slasher reflects on problems that are specifically connected to masculinity. Probably this lack of attention is linked to the specific characteristics of the killer, as he is a man who is just not there. He lacks the human ability to reflect, interact, and negotiate with himself. At the same time, he embodies Žižek's definition of the drive, which cannot be subjected to dialectical mediation (102-03). That is also why it is impossible to get through to him. The killer strikes like a force of nature instead of (inter)acting as a social being. The simultaneity of presence and absence is also reflected in his ontological status. In his interview with Mark Kermode, John Carpenter discusses Michael Myers, the iconic killer of the *Halloween* franchise: "There is a slight supernatural edge to this guy: Sure, he is a person that escapes from a mental institution, [...] but he can't be killed, and there's a certain feeling of, maybe he is not quite a human being." The killer, literally, is larger than life yet still less than a man. Just like that, the slasher reduces the killer to a narrative function.

This is also why viewers often do not see the full picture. The slasher genre typically works with a lot of close-ups of phallic weapons like machetes, knives, or hammers. Just like in mainstream pornography, viewers hardly ever see the male part. The killer appears as an automaton without any individual features; i.e., he is good for exactly one thing. The mask is generic, not at least in this sense, as it dehumanizes the killer. Thereby, it is not just a hide-out but a symbol of a certain kind of masculinity. bell hooks points out the fact that *mask* is literally a part of *mask*-ulinity; this is significant, as men learn from an early age to repress their feelings when they are not compatible with common notions of masculinity (163). In this respect, masculinity means wearing a mask, or even more, masculinity is a mask that is used to hide. Behind every man, there is a *hu*man that, in patriarchy, is prohibited from expressing itself fully. In this sense, becoming a man means to disappear. The killer is not only a perpetrator but also a victim of a certain dynamic. The human whom he once might have been disappears behind the function, which is not exactly an expression of free will but superimposed by parent structures—of the genre, of patriarchal society, or of a troubled psyche.

This chapter provides a new perspective on one of the most influential tropes in horror history, exposing what is behind the mask of the killer. The main objective is to explore the mask-ulinity that is modeled in—or behind—the

---

the same direction, arguing that gender stereotypes get reproduced as "power is coded as masculine, even when embodied in biological females" (81–82).

mask. In addition, the archetypal storyline that the slasher masks behind his extreme aesthetics will be discussed. Thereby, three different types of killers will move into focus:

1. The classic slasher killer: These killers put on their masks as there is no way for them to develop a suitable persona that could guarantee social participation. The mask protects them from the pain of not-belonging. In this case, especially, the mask marks a deeply wounded masculinity.

2. The killer that isn't there: With this type, the mask becomes a signifier for a state of non-being. Understood in a Jungian way as the representation of the social persona, it becomes synonymous with the subject wearing it. It refers to men who are not even (and probably never have been) *there*.

3. The postmodern killer: This type of killer does not deal with individual pathologies or forbidden desires anymore, as he treats his killing spree as a postmodern pastiche project. The postmodern killers are completely dissociated from everything happening around (and because of) them as they frame reality itself as a merely artificial construction.

By going in-depth with the trope of the masked killer, the contribution offers a new perspective on the slasher while exploring horror's ability to reframe and reinvent its tropes time and time again.

Philosophy of the Mask

To get behind the mask of the killer, it's crucial to understand the mask itself. As a *dingsymbol*, it is connected to several different functions and meanings. The following three dimensions are significant here:

The Mask and the Subject: Intra-Subjective Dimension

The mask marks an ambiguous shift in the relationship the subject engages with itself. It shows and hides; it brings forth and makes disappear; it tells the truth and lies. Inner and outer worlds become twisted as the mask brings forth what has been lurking in the subject; it also represents something superimposed on it from the outside. In analytical terms, it is associated with the id as well as with the superego.

The moment the mask is put on marks a visible transition, as explained by Nunley and McCarty: "[M]asks are the most ancient means of changing identity and assuming a new persona [...] Masks symbolize our ability to change, to transform" (15). Joseph Campbell sees the mask as initially expressive, as it brings something forth that has been there all the time. For him, the mask is "the agent of transformation from inner to outer" (Campbell xvii). One of the main functions of the mask is to make something visible that the subject has hidden from itself, often without even knowing it was there. In this sense, the mask is not something coming from the outside but a function—or symptom—of the subject itself. Thereby, it exposes the subject as much as it hides it. On the other hand, the mask can be something superimposed on us. In modern society, putting on a mask can be the price we pay for fitting right in. C. G. Jung established the term *persona*, meaning "a kind of mask, designed on the one hand to make a definite impression upon others, and on the other to conceal the true nature of the individual" (*Collected Works Volume 7* 305). In this often aporetic double function, the mask follows the logic of the double: Mr. Hyde hides Dr. Jekyll, as he could never do the brutal, immoral and deviant acts Hyde commits. At the same time, Hyde is what Jekyll hides from others and even more from himself. Just so, masks are highly ambiguous in their function, "serving simultaneously as tools for disguise and as markers of identity" (Sheppard 25). In action, this leads to another paradox: the mask is only animated by the one who wears it; still, it seems to have a life of its own. In a narrative context, it oscillates between modes of being and modes of representing. The mask is the subject, yet, on the other hand, a representation that is by nature not identical with the "true" subject.

The Mask and the Others: Social Dimension

The mask undermines the social sphere as it makes it hard to connect and communicate with each other. As it renders, hides, and expresses the subject, how can such a subject be addressed? And, much more, how can we be sure that we address the right subject? The iconic *Psycho* evolved around that idea, in the words of author Robert Bloch: "What intrigued me, [...], was how anyone could perpetrate such crimes in such a psychotic state and yet remain undetected for years by his neighbors" (qtd. in Larson 83). The answer is clear: by wearing the mask of a boy who couldn't even harm a fly. Like his psyche, Norman Bates's identity is split up. The mama's boy serves as a disguise for the killer. In the social sphere, the mask marks the difference between the subject and his representation. Doing so radically undermines communication:

> [I]t's not just a deficit of emotion that can add to a mask's horror; it's a false presentation of one. One of the ways humans socialize is via mirroring, mimicking the body language and facial expressions of those around us. Mirror neurons trigger our sense of empathy. Masking breaks

> this connection, making the masked person seem unknowable, perhaps even, in these worst cases, inhuman. (Phillips)

The mask, as a complex function of the subject, makes it difficult to deal with others, as humans simply do not know what is going on inside another person. As it interrupts interaction, the subjects are isolated from each other. The more masks people have around them, the lonelier they get. In the extreme, there are only two ways: staying in the false sense of security of not knowing who the person is or risking a look behind the mask. In Brian Yuzna's *Society*, hero Billy breaks it down, suspecting his parents to be cannibals (which, by the way, they are): "I'm afraid, if I scratch the surface, there'll be something terrible underneath." Unmasking the society in which he grew up costs him his own existence. From E. T.A. Hoffmann's *Der Sandmann* to movies like *The Thing* or *Invasion of the Body Snatchers*, discovering the truth behind the masks of others can be sheer horror.

Another aspect is brought up by Edgar Allan Poe, who was the first to explore the theme in 1840 with *The Man of the Crowd*, who "refuses to be alone," strolling through the city, blending in with changing scenes (515). Here, the persona, as the ability of the subject to adapt to changing environments, allows him to navigate seamlessly through the urban sphere. This comes at a price; after following him through the night, the narrator draws his final conclusion: "[P]erhaps it is but one of the great mercies of God that 'er lasst sich nicht lesen' [German for 'he can't be read']" (515). Poe brings up a new quality—or negativity—of evil. It's not as substantial as, for example, the devil. Instead, it's pure non-being, a lack of substance that comes from never being by and with oneself. As the man of the crowd integrates into the urban sphere, he disintegrates as a consistent, recognizable subject. Again, the reader is confronted with the two-sidedness of the mask: As it points outwards, it also changes what's inside. By putting on a mask, Poe showed that it is not just the others but also the person behind it who gets manipulated.

The Mask and the Ritual: Cultural Dimension

All over the world, masks are used in different rituals, from shamanic healing over different dramatic traditions to modern rituals of putting on masklike 3D glasses in the cinema. As much as rituals may change over time, their basic traits remain the same. The ritual "effects a transition from the everyday life to an alternative context within which the everyday is transformed" (Alexander 139). Thereby, it is set apart from everyday life by alternating rules and behaviors. As a performative gesture, putting on the mask marks the transition, as the Markmans point out: "Whenever and wherever it is used, the ritual mask symbolizes not only particular gods, demons, animal companions, or spiritual states but a particular relationship between matter and spirit, the natural and the supernatural, the visible and the invisible" (XIV). In this sense, the mask not only changes the subject and how it appears to others but evokes a new world. As a ritualistic device, it marks the transition to a new order. Where it is put on, the world turns upside down, new rules are established, and nothing is as it was.

In the slasher, putting on the mask can also mark the transition from one genre to another. Rob Zombie's *Halloween*, as well as Julien Maury and Alexandre Bustillo's *Leatherface*, tell the origin stories of Michael Myers and Leatherface. Both movies take off as social dramas, showing how the two killers had to deal with severe abuse as kids. The scene where they put on their masks marks the transition from drama to horror, drastically altering the rules of the play. In the moment, the movies switch from a more or less realistic mode of narration to the associative mode of the nightmare. At the same time, the mask represents the mythos of death and birth: as the boy dies, the killer is born.

Backstory: A Very Short History of the Slasher

From the beginning on, the movies show that behind the mask of a violent man hides a boy in fear. The iconic thrillers *Peeping Tom* and *Psycho* introduced the motive, linking misogynistic violence to child abuse. What Mark Lewis and Norman Bates do to women is directly linked to what their parents did to them. In addition, these movies establish the main elements of the slasher's psychosexual symbolism—Mark's camera as a materialization of the male gaze and Norman's knife as a rampaging phallus. After that, directors like Mario Bava, Dario Argento, and Sergio Martino came up with the legendary Giallos, the Italian Murder Mysteries, which typically evolve around an anonymous killer and his highly attractive female victims. While still relying on the classical structure of the whodunit, Giallo also sets the tone for the slasher by shifting the focus from "mystery" to "murder." As Lowenstein notes, speaking of Mario Bava's works in the genre, "the multiple murders usually override their narrative significance" (126). Furthermore, many of the Giallos systematically featured subjective camerawork, especially point-of-view shots, that were associated with the killer. In addition while "Peeping Tom" Mark Lewis and "Psycho" Norman Bates hid only behind their more or less harmless everyday identities, the Giallo finally established the motive of the—literally—masked killer. In *Blood and Black Lace*, the killer covers his face with a fedora. In *Strip Nude for Your Killer*, a motorcycle helmet serves as the killer's disguise. *The Devil Has Seven Faces* features a man in a gorilla mask. As such, all the elements were in place for the rise of the slasher.

The golden age of the slasher starts off with John Carpenter's *Halloween*, the film that defined the genre like no other. Rockoff explains:

> It is difficult to overestimate the importance of Halloween. Many of the conventions that have become staples of the slasher—the subjective camera, the Final Girl, the significant date setting—were either pioneered or perfected in the film. It is the blueprint for all slashers and the model against which all subsequent films are judged. Of course, Halloween didn't invent these cinematic devices [...], but it was the first to create a slasher paradigm by bringing them together in a single film. (61)

Many more should follow. After *Halloween* became a great success, over 100 similar films were released over the following six years (Kinch 257). Until today, the genre is associated with three big franchises: *Halloween* with Michael Myers, *Texas Chainsaw Massacre* with Leatherface, and *Friday the 13th* with Jason Vorhees. The infamous terror trio shaped the image of the slasher and brought up the main themes connected with the masked killer. In all three cases, the mask appears as a marker of a deeply wounded masculinity, expressing a definitive break up with society or even reality. Doing so brings up the drama of the outsider: as it hides the man, it makes the killer visible in the social sphere. Masking a traumatic past, the hyper-masculine killer protects the hurt boy inside.

The Killer as Outsider

Even though the drastic aesthetics and exalted plotlines of the slasher can be deceiving, the masked killers of the slasher embody one of the great horror archetypes: the outsider monster. The classic backstory is cultural currency, at least since Mary Shelley's *Frankenstein*. The monster, abandoned by his creator-father, is so ugly that it doesn't stand a chance to have a life, make friends, meet a woman, or even have a family. In a social sense, it is a stillbirth. Still, it's alive. As it is not recognized as the gentle, sensitive and even multilingual being it is, the monster has only two options: lie down to die as a body, just as it is dead as a social being, or be born again as a monster, haunting the normality that exiled him in such a cruel way. In this sense, the monster is not merely out for revenge. To be seen, to exist, it must hide its vulnerability and take on the role of the unscrupulous stalker. This is also where the "slight supernatural edge" of the monster derives (Carpenter): it appears within a certain system as an agent of everything that cannot be contained within this system. No matter what its ontological status is, in one way or another, the monster is just not from this world.

Even though the slasher makes some major adjustments, it follows the traditional outsider plot. Jason Vorhees from the legendary *Friday the 13th* series suffers from a range of deformities. To protect him, his mother hides him from other children. Jason finally gets exposed when she begins to work as a cook at Camp Crystal Lake. Still, he is not seen—as a boy, as a young man, as a human being with human needs. His death as a boy is highly symbolic. Jason drowns in the lake because no one looks after him; the others are away having sex with each other. Jason, metaphorically, drowns in loneliness and sorrow. One of the main themes—being seen—is called out by Mrs. Vorhees, who uses a highly visual vocabulary, for example, in her iconic exclamation: "*Look* what you did to him. *Look* what you did to him!" (emphasis added). Similarly, Leatherface experiences social death by becoming unemployed, as critic Bernard writes: "Job loss and hard economic times have turned the cannibal family to eating human beings" (420). *Texas Chainsaw Massacre*, the same-titled sequel from 2022, works with visibility as a social category: as a man without a perspective, living in the house of his demented mother, viewers only see the character as a shadow lurking somewhere in the periphery. Before putting on the mask, he is nothing, invisible and de-centered. As a victim of gentrification, a cultural reject, and as a person without status, he is just not there. To become visible in the world of the real estate entrepreneurs who want to buy his house, he must put on the mask of the killer. The transition does not go from inside to outside; on the contrary, it is a mere reaction to social exclusion. The mask is put on, and the man just being himself is cast out from the social sphere. Finally, Michael Myers, as the audience learns in Rob Zombie's *Halloween*, is born an outsider since he grows up in a highly abusive family. He never learns what it means to belong. In his first session with Dr. Loomis, Michael explains what the mask really is about: "Because no one sees me." Later on, he tells his mother: "I like the mask because it hides my face. [...] It hides my ugliness." In accordance, the mask has an ambiguous (if not aporetic) double function. On the one hand, it hides the trauma, belonging to the boy. On the other hand, it makes the man visible by turning him into a killer.

In some cases, the face of the killer functions as a highly paradoxical skin-mask, hiding and expressing the killer's hurt at the same time. Frankenstein's creature and Freddy Krueger have their traumas (stemming from the Greek μα for wound) inscribed on their faces. Their wounds, one could say, *serve* as their masks. They carry them openly for everyone to see, not to share their pain but to scare others away. The wound-mask brings up the malaise of masculinity that comes from the desperate wish to be acknowledged and a deep fear of being looked at—the desire for connection and the fear of opening up to others existing simultaneously (hooks 31). That is why looking at the killer is initially dangerous, as the narrator in *Friday the 13th* Part *VII: The New Blood* puts it, talking about Jason: "Few have seen him and lived."

Mask-ulinity: Becoming a Man

Putting on the mask is also a rite of passage gone completely wrong. As Michael, Jason, and Leatherface never had a "real" childhood, the masculinity they represent as grown-ups is deeply disturbed. Instead of men, they become murderers. The narrator in *Friday 13th VII* drops an ambiguous statement talking about the curse of Jason, remarking that "he died as a boy." Thereby, he does not only refer to the event of Jason's death itself but also to the psycho-logic behind it: the boy inside of Jason dying instead of evolving. It fits the picture that the transition from boy to killer takes place in a time that is usually all about separating from the mother while exploring the outer world. Jung explains this phenomenon the following way: "The world comes into being when man discovers it. But he only discovers it when he sacrifices his containment in the primal mother, the original state of the unconscious" (*Collected Works Volume 5* 652). The masked killer literally inverts this process: Jason drowning in the lake is a boy diving into his own subconscious, symbolically becoming one with the mother. Like most of his killer-colleagues— Norman Bates, Leatherface, Ike und Addley from *Mother's Day*, to name a few— Jason is a mama's boy. In Rob Zombie's *Halloween*, security guard Ismael Cruz says to little Michael Myers, dwelling in his cell: "Learn to live inside your head." The moment when the killer withdraws to the inner world is the moment when he stops talking. That is why he is so hard to come by: when the boy is reborn as a killer, he superimposes the logic of the subconscious onto the real world. While his victims are bound to the laws of cause and effect, the killer operates in a dream-like logic. That is where the central paradoxes of the genre stem. Even though Michael Myers prefers to walk, while his victims run in fear, he is much faster than them. He appears and disappears on the scene as he pleases, bending the universal laws of time and place (Florentin 6). In this sense, he represents the subconscious haunting the conscious, the id haunting the ego, the pleasure principle haunting the reality principle. Just so, he disrupts the perception of his victims, invoking trauma as a "breach in the mind's experience of time, self, and the world" (Caruth 4).

The mask of the killer magically protects the hurt boy. The vulnerability of the one is directly related to the hyper-masculinity of the other. Consequently, the killer is stuck in his boyish nightmare, perceiving everyone outside of him as a threat. Rob Zombie's *Halloween* makes a clear stance here. Ronnie, the crippled, deranged, and homophobic friend of his mother, terrorizes Michael from the beginning. When he comes downstairs for breakfast in the opening scene, Ronnie says, "He's gonna end up cutting his dick and balls off and changing his name to Michelle." Later in school, Wesley Rhodes takes over the part of the bully, pushing Michael around: "Hey, ball-licker, check this out. I heard your sister got caught selling blow jobs in the bathroom. I heard they had to pump the cum out of her stomach." It has been noted that shame is one of the key elements for the traumatic perpetuation of the ideology of masculinity. In *Real Boys*, clinical psychologist William Pollack shows that it's the fear of experiencing shame that makes young men resort to anger or violent behavior. Following Pollack, psychologist Ximena E. Mejía links the avoidance of shame to wearing a mask "Boys and men are socialized and taught to avoid shame at all costs, to wear a mask [!!!] of coolness, to act as though everything is under control, even if it is not" (33). Humiliated by his fellow men, Michael uses his mask to ward off his shame, at the same time driving the male ideology into hyper-logic. The killing is, in fact, a defense mechanism. In retrospect, the insults of the bullies function as magic spells, evoking the killer. Taking their words at face value, Michael becoming a killer is just a boy becoming a real man, switching sides from victim to perpetrator. In this sense, the mask is once again highly ambiguous: it hides him, but it also gets him seen for the first time. As Michael cuts open Ronnie's throat, his victim looks at him in astonishment. Just as the mask cuts the killer off from his fellow men, it expresses a radical affirmation of their idea of masculinity.

In Western cultures, becoming a man is often equated to having sex. The exclusion of the killer shows up as the exclusion from sexual activities. Symbolically, this is what makes it impossible for him to break the threshold. Yet another trope of the slasher: Jason dies while his supervisors are having sex with each other. Michael Myers kills his sister Judith while she is having sex with her boyfriend. As the boy goes inwards and the killer appears on the outside, sex and violence become intermingled. In the (bad) dreamlike logic of the killer, one does not only symbolize but acts as a direct metaphor for the other. This is, obviously, a big problem for his victims, who are still living in the real world, where sex is fun and getting stabbed is not. Still, something just as terrible happens on a symbolic level. The sex symbolized in the killing is phallic, mechanical, and brutal. Thereby, the killer takes a symbolic revenge on sex itself. The boy, unable to get 'it," comes back as a raging phallus, or, as we'd say today, a ridiculously big dick. According to *Fandom.com*, Jason's almost super-human size is six foot nine, the same height as Michael Myers. In his groundbreaking essay on *Texas Chainsaw Massacre*, Wood points out the "appalling vitality and the phallic nature of the constantly whirring chainsaw" and calls Leatherface an "embodiment of repressed sexuality returned and uncontrollable" (61). The killer is a phallus *with* a phallus (knife, chainsaw, machete, etc.), while his immortality signifies endless potency. He literally destroys sex by destroying those who have it, acting out his own twisted sexual desires. Thereby, he symbolizes violence as sex and sex as violence. Still, the paradoxical nature of the mask persists: pure phallic sexuality acts as a pretty much foolproof defense mechanism against real sex.

Projection: The Saint and the Killer

The boy turned into a killer superimposes his fears and his powerlessness on his victims. In a way, he acts like the man that C. G. Jung called the saint, who retained his halo by projecting his flaws on his wife. Jung reports the time spent with this man:

> I once made the acquaintance of a very venerable personage - in fact, one might easily call him a saint. I stalked round him for three whole days, but never a mortal failing did I find in him. My feeling of inferiority grew ominous, and I was beginning to think seriously about how I might better myself. Then, on the fourth day, his wife came to consult me ... Well, nothing of the sort has ever happened to me since. But this I did learn: that any man who becomes one with his persona can cheerfully let all disturbances manifest themselves through his wife without her noticing it, though she pays for her self-sacrifice with a bad neurosis. (*Collected Works Volume 7* 306)

The killers behave in the same fashion. What each killer's persona hides is projected on the outside through the mask. As Jason, Michael, and Leatherface conceal their traumas behind their masks, they condemn themselves to reproduce those traumas over and over again. The killer strikes others with the wounds he does not want to feel. This is again deeply connected with the ideology of masculinity. It is widely documented that while women have "higher rates of 'internalizing' disorders like depression and anxiety," men are at an increased risk of "'externalizing' troubles such as aggressive behavior, substance abuse, oppositional defiant disorder" (Smith et al. 78-79). That is also where the narrowness comes from: as he inflicts his pain onto others, the killer himself feels nothing anymore. Rob Zombie's *Halloween* points out that aspect when Dr. Loomis asks Michael an associative question:

> Loomis: "If I say the devil to you [!!!] what do you picture in your head?"
>
> Michael: "Hollowness and blackness and emptiness."
>
> Loomis: "Do you feel that way?" –
>
> Michael: "Sometimes – when I put on my mask."

As such, the killers turn into the living dead. Detached from their own wounds, they feel nothing at all, a state that is also reflected in their physiology. After putting on the mask, Michael and Jason literally stop bleeding. Bloodless, denying their own vulnerability, they also lose their vitality. Killing the others, they superimpose their own state of non-being on them.

The killer embodies the darkest side of patriarchy. The mask constitutes a new subjectivity that gains substance only through subtracting the *hu-* from the man. In this sense, becoming a man means to disappear behind the mask, becoming literally untouchable. Just like that, the killer pays a high price. As he detaches himself from his traumatic wound to never hurt again, he initiates an emotional shutdown. Becoming invulnerable, he is not able to open up to others. Even though he is at the center of attention wherever he goes, he is still not seen. As he mortifies himself to become immortal, he is cut off from the living. Thereby, he reflects another paradox of the ideology of masculinity: when putting on the mask of hyper-masculinity, getting in touch with others leads to a dead end (hooks). I think of this as the Dracula-Dilemma, as the count suffers from the same malaise: he is unable to connect without annihilating the others, whether by incorporating or exploiting them. In the same manner, the killer is not able to get in touch with anybody except by killing them. Freddy Krueger from Wes Craven's *A Nightmare on Elm Street* embodies it in perfection. With his razor-gloves, he literally cannot touch anybody without severely hurting them; even if he'd want to, it's impossible. *Texas Chainsaw Massacre 2* makes an ironic statement here, as Leatherface attempts to (kind of) flirt with the final girl, Stretch, fooling around with his chainsaw. Obviously, she doesn't like it. Life is just not fair in that scene. Why is it always so hard to get a date with a skin-mask on your face and a chainsaw in your hands?

Being Seen: Redemption

Looking behind the mask, seeing the killer as a boy trapped in his own nightmare, undead and isolated, questions arise. Can he be saved by any means? Is redemption possible? And, if yes, how? Once more, the answer lies behind the mask. The killer's energy is initially repulsive, as everything he does serves the purpose of avoiding the traumatic wound. His aggression is, above all else, a defense mechanism. The killer avoids being seen at all costs. At least he knows from his former life that he bears a great risk to show himself to the world. In Rob Zombie's *Halloween*, Michael gets humiliated over and over before he puts on his mask. Likewise, Jason is excluded for his ugliness before he drowns in the lake. Leatherface, meanwhile, is left alone by state institutions as he tries to get away from his crazy cannibal mother. For them, hiding behind the mask is just a logical consequence, as being looked at would bring the pain of the boy back. Still, this is exactly where the answer lies. To find peace, the killer must be seen fully as the hurt boy, as the man he never could be. In order to deconstruct his mask-ulinity, a gaze with specific qualities is needed: a gaze that does not mortify its object by superimposing his own desire on him but reaches beyond the visible; a gaze that doesn't get caught with the appearance but sees right through it, discovering the essence of the boy and the man he could have been.

The man hiding behind the mask of a monster can only be redeemed when he gets seen by a woman. This is usually easier said than done as the killer is full of shame and, therefore meticulously avoids being seen, which he does by just being himself a monster. Still, on the other hand, he longs for love. That is why Eros and Thanatos—sex and violence—get mixed up at this stage. The raging monster can only find peace if someone is able to see the truth beyond the shame, beyond all the monstrous looks and even more monstrous manners. This is a literary trope we know from fairy tales like "Beauty and the Beast." Here, the monster initially is not looking for a woman to marry and live happily ever after; it is instead just waiting for someone who can stand to look at it. Finally, the monster is redeemed by a young woman who is able to see the man behind the beast. While the symbolism in most versions is very subtle— Beauty goes to bed with the Beast just to wake up next to a prince—being seen can absolutely be understood in the sexual sense here (Gehrmann 13)[4]. This is where the union of repulsion (don't look at me) and attraction (I want to be seen/loved) is repealed. The monster learns that touching someone does not have to be a violent act. Another archetypal male monster is Erik, the Phantom of the Opera, from Gaston Leroux's same-titled Gothic romance. Rejected by his own mother because of his ugliness, he terrorizes the Opéra Garnier and its guests in Paris until he falls in love with singer Christine Daaé. The famous monologue of the last chapter shows that it doesn't take much to set the monster free. A look behind the mask is more than enough:

> My mother, daroga, my poor, unhappy mother, would never ... let me kiss her ... She used to run away ... and throw me my mask! ... Nor any other woman ... ever, ever! ... Ah, you can understand, my happiness was so great, I cried. And I fell at her feet, crying ... and I kissed her feet ... her little feet ... crying. [...] and she cried also [...] I felt her tears flow on my forehead ... on mine, mine! ... They were soft ... they were sweet! ... They trickled under my mask ... they mingled with my tears in my eyes ... yes ... they flowed between my lips ... Listen, daroga, listen to what I did ... I tore off my mask so as not to lose one of her tears ... and she did not run away! ... And she did not die! [...] I heard her say, 'Poor, unhappy Erik!' (LeRoux 108)

The scene shows how redemption is possible. A similar ending is featured on *Friday the 13th VIII*. Final girl, Rennie, flees from Jason through the sewers of Manhattan, which are about to get flooded with toxic waste. As Rennie

---

[4] The connection between being seen and having sex dates back to the Bible, where the Hebrew יָדַע for "to know" or "to get to know" is used in such a sense in Genesis 4,1. The English translations often lose this nuance by stating it upfront: "Adam made love to his wife Eve, and she became pregnant and gave birth to Cain." The German translation preserves the original meaning: "Und Adam erkannte seine Frau Eva," literally saying Adam "recognized" Eva.

manages to escape at the last moment, she witnesses Jason getting hit by a big wave of wastewater. This is the moment where it all comes back. Jason's mask melts away, and he begins to vomit water in resemblance to his death as a boy: drowning in the lake with no one looking after him. This is a major shift as he is no longer denying his trauma. Much more, he is flooded by it. In the end, Jason finally finds peace as Rennie sees him as what he really is, not a larger-than-life stalker with a hockey mask but an unconscious, lonely, naked (i.e., innocent) child drowning in sorrow. In this sense, the mask is what keeps the killer alive as it represents the energy that represses the trauma. That is also why the final girl usually cannot set the killer free. By killing him, she affirms and thereby confirms his twisted logic instead of seeing right through it. After getting killed, the undead killer does what undead people always do: he comes back, over and over again. Redemption, not at last, means breaking through the traumatic circle of repetition.

Suspension: *American Psycho*

Mary Harron's *American Psycho*—just like the original novel by Bret Easton Ellis—presents a new take on the slasher killer and his mask. Psycho Patrick Bateman is not exactly hiding behind a mask anymore, simply because there is nothing to hide in the first place. He represents the drama (or anti-drama) of a subject who is stuck in a simulation. Pulling a transparent almond milk face mask off his face, he brings on the famous monologue from the novel:

> ...there is an idea of a Patrick Bateman, some kind of abstraction, but there is no real me, only an entity, something illusory, and though I can hide my cold gaze and you can shake my hand and feel flesh gripping yours and maybe you can even sense our lifestyles are probably comparable: *I simply am not there.* (Ellis 376-77)

Here, Bateman gives a very sophisticated account of what Jung calls the "modern danger," merely that people "become identical with their personas – the professor with his textbook, the tenor with his voice" (Jung, "Concerning Rebirth" 45). In *American Psycho*, it is not what lurks inside of the subject, i.e., behind the mask, but the total narrowness of the whole existence that puts Bateman into crisis. The total dissociation is also doubled in the narrative form as Bateman's voiceover frequently comments on himself from off-screen. Literally standing beside himself, he is radically cut off from his own being. The mode marks an identity that is solely focused on the outside perspective, simulating life instead of actually living it. The transparent mask symbolizes Bateman's mode of being. On one hand, it looks just like him; on the other hand, it is literally nothing. This is the absolutism of non-being. What is behind the mask is not the "real" Bateman (no matter how "psycho") but another mask:

his own face. The twist in *American Psycho* is that there is no trauma behind the mask; instead, the mask itself is the trauma, as it infinitely suspends the subject. Behind the persona, there is no person anymore. The horror of the mask lies in an inversion: it's the lifestyle that executes the person, not the other way around.

Postmodernism: *Scream*

Wes Craven's *Scream* marks a postmodern turn in the genre. The film shows how the slasher, as a cultural form, reformats reality itself. As a movie about murderers who are inspired by murder movies (and bored by reality), killing teenagers who perceive reality only through the lens of movie genres, *Scream* replaces the individual subconscious with pop culture.[5] The famous Ghostface Killers and their victims are not entangled in an oedipal constellation, dealing with individual pathologies or forbidden desires, but much more in a mode of imitation, quotation and reenactment, treating their killing spree as a postmodernist pastiche project. As Ghostface Killer Billy shoots his former buddy Randy, he drops the following line, marking it as a quote: "'We all go a little mad sometimes.' Anthony Perkins, *Psycho*." Then, as he licks fresh blood off his fingers, he adds, "Mhm, corn syrup. Same stuff they used for pig's blood in *Carrie*." Billy's experiences are not masked by trauma but by pop cultural set pieces, rendering reality itself unreal. Just as the reality is medialized, the media itself is realized in the killings. Billy's media-induced psychosis is thereby doubled by the fact that *Scream* is a movie itself. Held against the killers of the first generation, the mask signifies a completely different constellation. While Michael, Jason, and Leatherface are hopelessly immersed in their inner world, Ghostface Killers Billy and Stu are completely dissociated from everything happening around (and because of) them as they frame reality itself as a merely artificial construction. The former are *in too deep*, while the latter have lost contact. Accordingly, the Ghostface Killers don't have a motive that is linked to a deeper truth about them (fear, envy, lust, trauma, whatever). Billy makes a clear stance here, stating, "I don't really believe in motives." *Scream* brings the

---

[5] The substitution of the individual subconscious with pop culture is one of the defining themes of Wes Craven's work. The unique premise of his *A Nightmare on Elm Street* franchise puts it in a nutshell: Freddy, as pop star of evil, is much more than a mere stalker. As he hijacks the dreams of the teenagers, he not only threatens their lives, but also their individuation—their own intimate spaces, where they can get in touch with their deepest fears and desires, symbolizing what they can't tell and work through in their everyday lives—is taken over by his deadly Freddy show. A comical dramatization of this is depicted in the fourth part of the series, *The Dream Master.* As final girl Alice falls asleep, she dreams that she's sneaked out to see a movie. Soon, Krueger sucks her into the screen, and she lands in a rundown diner. Freddy orders a pizza topped with the tormented souls of his victims, dropping one of his iconic one-liners: "I love soul food!"

shadow aspects of an eclectic postmodernist lifestyle to the surface. When life is just a movie, and humans are the directors, it is easy to become lost in dissociation, obsessing with staging instead of living life.

As creators gone wrong, the Ghostface Killers stand in the tradition of mad scientists like Frankenstein or Henry Jekyll, recreating themselves as postmodernist monsters. Doing so, they paved the way for a new kind of killer, one who is much more interested in the construction of reality than in dealing with trauma. One example of this is in *Behind the Mask*, which follows Leslie Vernon, an aspiring serial killer ready to claim his place alongside Jason Voorhees, Michael Myers, and Freddy Krueger. His goal is pretty simple: to become the best in what he does. Likewise, in the post-slasher *Totally Killer*, true crime reporter Chris commits a gruesome murder to fire up his podcast, giving the "being seen" theme a new twist. Overshadowed by his dad, who was a legendary local news reporter, he turns into a killer to finally receive the appreciation for which he always longed. Killing here is nothing personal but a rather reliable strategy to create media value. Besides that, the reflexive slashers also bring up new ethical questions. What happens when killers and their masks turn into top-selling brands? In *Terrifier 2*, heroine Sienna scolds her brother when he wants to dress up as Miles County Clown for Halloween: "Do you have any idea how insensitive that is?" In *Hellfest*, final girl Natalie has big trouble identifying the right masked killer as he hunts her down at a horror theme park, where his appearance naturally matches the overall dress code. In the postmodern slasher, it's not about the past haunting the present; much more, it is about living in a society that is so used to consuming murder as entertainment that it is no longer able to recognize a real murderer.

Conclusion

The horror of the masked killer endures in the present day. This may be due to the dysfunctional coping strategies of the ideology of masculinity. Refusing to feel while hiding behind the mask of hyperbolic hardiness or fitting right in is an experience not exclusively made by male killers with masks but by all sorts of people in our culture. So, while the feminist movement recently changed the storyline mostly for female characters and integrated new archetypes like the girl boss, the drama of the male-monster is yet to be resolved.[6] Consequently, the classical slasher formula is still in use, just as the big franchises keep coming again

---

[6] This references archetypal structures. It is possible, and it happens more and more, that the drama of the male monster is acted out by female protagonists, e.g. in the gender-flipped Netflix remake of Cronenberg's *Dead Ringers*, starring Rachel Weisz as twin gynecologists Beverly and Elliot Mantle, who were portrayed by Jeremy Irons in the 1988 original. Conversely, the new female archetypes can equally empower men to embrace new life forms.

and again.[7] On the other hand, since the end of the golden era, new updates of the slasher are evolving in line with societal changes, bringing forth new aspects of the trope (Sotiris 2).

The mask of the killer is initially connected with troubled mask-ulinity. Carried by the first slasher generation—Jason Vorhees, Leatherface, and Michael Myers—it has an ambiguous double function: protecting the boy inside while making the man visible by turning him into a killer. As the killer hides his traumatic wound, he is unable to get in touch with anybody except by hurting them. That is why the killer cannot effectively be fought with his own weapons. To find peace, he must be seen fully as the hurt boy, as the man he never could be. Then, as the genre evolves, the trope gets transcended. In *American Psycho*, the mask becomes a signifier of a state of non-being by infinitely suspending the subject. Patrick Bateman is executed by his own lifestyle, turning into a pure persona lacking any sense of self. He is a man who is not even (and probably never has been) *there*. Finally, the postmodern killers featured in *Scream* mask themselves under a different premise as they frame reality itself as a merely artificial construction. Killing is not any longer connected to a psyche that is troubled by trauma but to a total dissociation that comes from perceiving life as a mere epiphenomenon of pop culture.

An end for the masked killers is not far in sight. While the trope is evolving, changing, and reflecting on itself, only one thing is for sure: it is on us to take a look behind the mask over and over again.

Works Cited

Alexander, Bobby C. "Ritual and Current Studies of Ritual: Overview." *Anthropology of Religion: A Handbook*, edited by Stephen D. Glazier, Praeger, 1999, pp. 139-160.

American Psycho. Directed by Mary Harron, Edward R. Pressman & Muse Productions, 2000.

Behind the Mask: The Rise of Leslie Vernon. Directed by Scott Glosserman, GlenEcho Entertainment et al., 2006.

Bernard, Mark. "Cannibalism, Class and Power: A Foodways Analysis of the *Texas Chainsaw Massacre* Series." *Food, Culture & Society*, vol. 14, no. 3, 2011, pp. 413-32.

Blood and Black Lace. Directed by Mario Bava, Emmepi Cinematografica et al., 1964.

---

[7] The biggest 2023 releases following the classic formula—or at least playing around with it—are *Thanksgiving, The Island of Doom, Winnie-the-Pooh: Blood and Honey, Natty Knocks*, and *It's a Wonderful Knife*. The classic Franchises (*Halloween, Texas Chainsaw Massacre, Friday the 13th*, and *A Nightmare on Elm Street*) have released 17 movies (including non-licensed fan movies) from 2000 on, while a new *Halloween* reboot has been announced for 2024.

Campbell, Joseph. Introduction. *Masks of the Spirit: Image and Metaphor in Mesoamerica,* by Peter T. Markman and Roberta H. Markman, University of California Press, 1989, pp. xiii-xvii.

Carpenter, John. Interview with Mark Kermode. "The Night He Came Home: John Carpenter's *Halloween.*" *BBC 2,* 1999.

Caruth, Cathy. *Unclaimed Experience: Trauma, Narrative and History.* John Hopkins University Press. 1996.

Clover, Carol J. "Her Body, Himself: Gender in the Slasher Film." *The Dread of Difference,* edited by Barry Keith Grant. 2nd ed., University of Texas Press, 2021, pp. 68–115.

Dead Ringers. Directed by Alice Birch, Astral Projection et al., 2023.

Dead Ringers. Directed by David Cronenberg, Astral Films et al., 1988.

The Devil Has Seven Faces. Directed by Osvaldo Civirani, Variety Distribution, 1971.

Ebert, Roger. "Why Movie Audiences Aren't Safe Anymore." *American Film,* March 1981, 51-56.

Ellis, Bret Easton: *American Psycho.* New York, Vintage, 1991.

Florentin, Groh. "'Experiencing Trauma': Aesthetical, Sensational and Narratological Issues of Traumatic Representations in Slasher Horror Cinema." *Arts,* vol. 12, no. 132, https://doi.org/10.3390/arts12040132.

Friday the 13th. Directed by Sean S. Cunningham, Georgetown Productions Inc., 1980.

Friday the 13th Part VII: The New Blood. Directed by John Carl Buechler, Friday Four, Inc., 1988.

Gehrmann, Daniela. "Die Schöne und das Biest." *Film-Dienst,* vol. 58, no. 24, 2005, pp. 12-14.

Grant, Barry Keith. *Film Genre: From Iconography to Ideology.* Wallflower, 2007.

Halberstam, Judith (Jack). *Skin Shows: Gothic Horror and the Technology of Monsters.* Duke University Press, 1995.

Halloween. Directed by John Carpenter, Compass International Pictures, 1978.

Halloween. Directed by Rob Zombie, Dimension Films et al., 2007.

Hayt, Anthony. "Moving Past the Trauma: Feminist Criticism and Transformations of the Slasher Genre." *The Routledge Companion to Cinema & Gender,* Routledge, 2016, pp. 131-40.

Hellfest. Directed by Gregory Plotkin, CBS Films et al., 2018.

Heller-Nicholas, Alexandra. *Masks in Horror Cinema: Eyes without Faces.* University of Wales Press, 2019.

Hoffmann, E. T.A. *Der Sandmann,* edited by Rudolf Drux. Reclam, 2003.

hooks, bell. *Männer, Männlichkeit und Liebe: Der Wille zur Veränderung.* Translated by Daphne Nechyba, Elisabeth Sandmann Verlag, 2022.

Invasion of the Body Snatchers. Directed by Don Siegel, Allied Artists Pictures, 1956.

Island of Doom. Directed by Keke Soikkeli, Same-eYes & Nordic Films, 2023.

It's a Wonderful Knife. Directed by Tyler MacIntyre, Divide/Conquer, 2023.

"Jason Vorhees." *Fandom,* fictionalserialkiller.fandom.com/wiki/Jason_Voorhees. Accessed 20 Oct. 2023.

Jung, C. G. "Concerning Rebirth." *Jung on Death and Immortality*, edited by Jenny Yates, Princeton University Press, 2000, pp. 36-67.

——. *Collected Works of C.G. Jung, Volume 5: Symbols of Transformation*. Edited and translated by Gerhard Adler and R. F.C. Hull, Princeton University Press, 1967.

——. *Collected Works of C.G. Jung, Volume 7: Two Essays on Analytical Psychology*. Edited and translated by Gerhard Adler and R. F.C. Hull, Princeton University Press, 1967.

Kinch, Erianne. "Scares and Skin: The Golden Age of Slashers." *Voices of USU: An Anthology of Student Writing*, vol. 16., 2023, pp. 252-62.

Larson, Randall D. *Robert Bloch*. Borgo Press, 1986.

Leatherface. Directed by Julien Maury and Alexandre Bustillo, Millennium Media et al., 2017.

Leroux, Gaston. *The Phantom of the Opera*. Charles River Editors, 2018.

Lizardi, Ryan. "'Re-Imagining' Hegemony and Misogyny in the Contemporary Slasher Remake." *Journal of Popular Film and Television*, vol. 38, no. 3, 2010, pp. 113-21.

Lowenstein, Adam. "The Giallo/Slasher Landscape: Ecologia del Delitto, *Friday the 13th* and Subtractive Spectatorship." *Italian Horror Cinema*, edited by Stefano Baschiera and Russ Hunter, Edinburgh University Press, 2016, pp. 127-44.

Markman, Peter T., and Roberta H. Markman. *Masks of the Spirit: Image and Metaphor in Mesoamerica*. University of California Press, 1989.

Mejía, Ximena E. "Gender Matters: Working with Adult Male Survivors of Trauma." *Journal of Counseling & Development*, vol. 83, no. 1, 2005, pp. 29-40.

"Michael Myers." *Fandom*, halloweenmovie.fandom.com/wiki/Michael_Myers. Accessed 20 Oct. 2023.

Moore, Tom, and Ryan Heffernan. "The 15 Most Iconic Masked Killers in Horror Movies, Ranked from Worst to Best." *Collider*, collider.com/the-most-iconic-masked-killers-in-horror-ranked/#michael-myers. Accessed 20 Oct. 2023.

Mother's Day. Directed by Lloyd Kaufmann, Duty Productions & Saga Films A.B. 1980.

Natty Knocks. Directed by Dwight H. Little, Vertical Entertainment, 2023.

A Nightmare on Elm Street. Directed by Wes Craven, New Line Cinema et al., 1984.

A Nightmare on Elm Street 4: The Dream Master. Directed by Renny Harlin, New Line Cinema et al., 2010.

Nunley, John Wallace, and Cara McCarty. "Masks: Faces of Culture." Saint Louis Art Museum, 1999.

Paszkiewicz, Katarzyna, and Stacy Rusnak. "Revisiting the Final Girl: Looking Backwards, Looking Forwards." *Postmodern Culture*, vol. 28, no. 1, 2017. *Project MUSE*, https://doi.org/10.1353/pmc.2017.0009.

Peeping Tom. Directed by Michael Powell, Anglo-Amalgamated Film Distributors, 1960.

Phillips, Maya. "Horror Masks Are Never Just About the Monster." *New York Times*, 31 Oct. 2020, pp. C4-C5.

Pinedo, Isabel Cristina. *Recreational Terror: Women and the Pleasures of Horror Film Viewing*. State UP of New York, 1997.

Poe, Edgar Allan. "The Man in the Crowd." *Collected Works: Tales and Sketches 1831-1842*, edited by Thomas Ollive Mabbot, the Belknap Press of Harvard University Press, 1978, pp. 506-18.

Pollack, William S. *Real Boys: Rescuing Our Sons from the Myths of Boyhood*. Henry Holt, 1998.

Psycho. Directed by Alfred Hitchcock, Shamley Productions, 1960.

Rockoff, Adam. *Going to Pieces: The Rise and Fall of the Slasher Film, 1978-1986*. McFarland, 2002.

Scream. Directed by Wes Craven, Dimension Films, 1996.

Shelley, Mary. *Frankenstein or the Modern Prometheus*, edited by Maurice Hindle. Revised ed., Penguin, 2006.

Sheppard, W. Anthony. *Revealing Masks: Exotic Influences and Ritualized Performance in Modernist Music Theater*. University of California Press, 2001.

Smith, Dena T., et al. "Reviewing the Assumptions about Men's Mental Health: An Exploration of the Gender Binary." *American Journal of Men's Health*, vol. 12, no. 1, 2018, pp. 78–89

Society. Directed by Brian Yuzna, Wild Street Pictures, 1989.

Sotiris, Petridis. *The Anatomy of the Slasher Film: A Theoretical Analysis*. McFarland, 2019.

Stevenson, Robert Louis. *The Strange Case of Dr. Jekyll and Mr. Hyde*, edited by Robert Mighall, Penguin Books, 2002.

Strip Nude for Your Killer. Directed by Andrea Bianchi, Fral Cinematografica, 1975.

Terrifier 2. Directed by Damien Leone, Dark Age Cinema et al., 2022.

Texas Chainsaw Massacre. Directed by David Blue Garcia, Legendary Picture et al., 2022.

Texas Chainsaw Massacre. Directed by Tobe Hooper, Vortex Inc., 1974.

Texas Chainsaw Massacre 2. Directed by Tobe Hooper, The Cannon Group Inc., 1986.

Thanksgiving. Directed by Eli Roth, Spyglass Media Group et al., 2023.

The Thing. Directed by John Carpenter, Universal Pictures, 1982.

Totally Killer. Directed by Nahnatchka Khan, Amazon MGM Studios et al., 2023.

Villeneuve, Gabrielle-Suzanne Barbo de. *The Story of the Beauty and the Beast*. Translated by James Robinson Planche, Create Space, 2014.

Winnie-the-Pooh: Blood and Honey. Directed by Rhys Frake-Waterfield, Jagged Edge Productions, 2023.

Wood, Robin. "Return of the Repressed." *On the Horror Film: Collected Essays and Reviews*, edited by Barry Keith Grant, Wayne State University Press, 2018, pp. 57-63.

Zhou, Maya. *Evolution of the Final Girl: Exploring Feminism and Femininity in Halloween (1978-2018)*. 2019. Scripps College, Senior thesis.

Žižek, Slavoj. *Lacan: Eine Einführung*. Translated by Karen Genschow and Alexander Roesler, Frankfurt a.M. Fischer, 2008.

Chapter 2

*Gore*mands: Human Cannibalism and Eating the Other in Contemporary Fiction

Carlos A. González

Abstract

This chapter discusses the trope of human cannibalism and the act of eating the other in contemporary fiction. It examines the symbolic and cultural significance of cannibalism narratives without deviating from a reading of literal human consumption as meat. The analysis investigates the representation of cannibalism as a subversive act that challenges established norms and hierarchical structures of gender, sexuality, and disability, revealing the ways in which the dehumanized other is made comestible, both to the horror and delight of the reader. Drawing upon Ottessa Moshfegh's *Lapvona*, Sayaka Murata's *Earthlings*, Chelsea G. Summers's *A Certain Hunger*, Agustina Bazterrica's *Tender Is The Flesh*, and Mariana Enríquez's short story "Meat," the chapter examines how the act of eating human flesh serves as a potent tool for a critique of gender dynamics, power imbalances, processes of dehumanization, and the commodification of bodies.

Keywords: cannibalism horror, dehumanization, global literature

* * *

Setting the Table: An Introduction

For most of premodern history, the cannibal was something *out there*, balancing on the edge of the world and just on the periphery of the imaginable (Avramescu 9). When the globe was remapped with the European arrival into the New World, the geography of the cannibal's domain was more clearly drawn, named, and, as much as possible, "civilized." It also meant that the cannibal got just a little closer, now nameable and geographically conceivable, but was still one of *them* trying to eat *us*. Such framings of the cannibal cannot survive without this dichotomy between *us* and *them*, wherein the referential position is always filled by a specifically European or (White) American subject, one that is assumed for the viewer or reader as much as the protagonist or narrator. *We* civilized folks are from *here,* our shared (White, Anglo, Western, Christian, etc.) space, and if we venture too far out *there*, then *they*, the savage inhabitants of uncharted regions of the East and the Global South will have *us* as victims and as food.

Inheriting much from these historical positionings, cannibals find themselves right at home in the horror genre, featuring in many beloved classics. *The Texas Chainsaw Massacre* (1974), *The Hills Have Eyes* (1977), and *Cannibal Holocaust* (1980) represent some of the most successful early forays into cannibal horror. In these films, the man-eating men were not on the edge of the world but just on a road trip or plane flight away, their otherness inscribed onto them through markers of difference like class, education, religion, and disability. Whether still the stereotypical tribe of jungle dwellers or the inbred spawn of working-class mutants, the cannibals were no longer so far out of the imagination that they remained faceless, almost mythical beings like their premodern ancestors. They became human, if even of a lower class. No longer the boogeymen of far-off islands, the cannibals are finally among us. Worse, they *are* us.

The last decade alone offers a smorgasbord of cannibal visual media that captures the popular imagination. From the gorefests offered up in *Bone Tomahawk* (2015), *The Green Inferno* (2016), and *Bones and All* (2022) to subtler renditions of the cannibal like those in *Raw* (French *Grave*, 2016), *Fresh* (2022), and the series *Yellowjackets* (2021-2023), it seems that cannibals are having a cultural moment, both benefiting from and contributing to the horror revival of the last decade or so. Contemporary cannibals don't merely chase us but invite us along for the ride, eager to sit us at their tables to indulge.

Literary horror is no stranger to cannibal fiction and is doing just as much to speak to the anxieties of contemporary society through and within cannibal narratives. Just as the dichotomy between horror and non-horror films has become murkier than ever—which various critics have attempted to ascribe to the advent of a supposed "elevated" horror like *Get Out* (2017), *The Killing of a Sacred Deer* (2017), and *Midsommar* (2019)—the divide between horror and non-horror within fiction (or worse, between "literary" and "popular" horror) seems also to be blurring.[1] In this chapter, I will briefly discuss a set of texts selected not because of their conformity to horror as a genre but because they prominently feature cannibal narratives in new, interesting, and subversive ways. I focus on the depictions of the literal consumption of human meat by other humans, keeping in mind both the motivations and consequences of these acts and why readers consume this material despite the urge to look away. How these encounters between reader and text, reader and narrator, eater and eaten, and other forms of face-to-face encounters are articulated in each

---

[1] For examples, see David Church's *Post-Horror: Art, Genre and Cultural Elevation* and Tom Faber's "From *Suspiria* to *Get Out*—Why Horror Movies Are Having a Moment."

novel—who is the Other, when does the reader or narrator see their face, and how are they rendered comestible?—will be the springboard for explorations of ethical implications present in the narrative.[2] Who eats, who gets eaten, and why will be our analytical framework here, allowing for the metonymy already present in acts of cannibalism to be interpreted and critiqued while never turning away from the material act of eating human meat. This framework will allow me to engage with how the cannibal trope has always been, and in new ways continues to be, a subversive method of considering the other person and the processes, both individual and systematic, of dehumanizing one another, of making human meat (into) matter.

The specific set of texts I bring into conversation with one another are *Lapvona* by Ottessa Moshfegh, *Earthlings* by Sayaka Murata, *A Certain Hunger* by Chelsea G. Summers, *Tender Is the Flesh* (*Cadaver exquísito*) by Agustina Bazterrica, and the short story "Meat" (Spanish "Carne") in Mariana Enríquez's *The Dangers of Smoking in Bed* (*Los peligros de fumar en la cama*). Not all of these titles can be obviously described as horror fiction, and some do not even register as cannibal fiction at first, but my selection process was driven by the specific question of cannibalism instead of the marketability of a title within one or another genre.[3] I also wish to reflect in literary terms the blurred lines previously noted in film between horror and non-horror, or literary versus popular horror, to demonstrate how cultural renditions of the cannibal are transforming across media and not only within one or another kind of product. If a tried (or tired) and true trope like cannibalism continues to be useful and entertaining, it matters why horror producers and consumers across media continue to revisit and redeploy it, exploring what it means and what it does today. We ask ourselves again, each time: Who eats, who gets eaten, how, and why?

Something Horrible Has Happened, My Lord: *Lapvona*

Ottessa Moshfegh is known for her cynical, sometimes comedic, starkness in rendering the human condition (Finch). Though her 2022 novel departs

---

[2] The specific ethical framework employed in this analysis is that proposed by Emmanuel Levinas. While Levinas's ethics underpin this chapter, I chose not to make much overt reference to his writing so as not to draw focus away from the novels themselves as well as to allow a reader unfamiliar with his work to appreciate the ethical concerns brought to the forefront by contemporary cannibal narratives.

[3] The fact that each of these texts is written by a woman is not developed in this chapter but does carry some promising implications. It is no accident that much of classic cannibal media, from *Texas Chainsaw Massacre* to *The Silence of the Lambs*, as well as contemporary renditions like *Yellowjackets* and *Honeydew*, features women in leading roles. For further reading, see Barbara Creed's chapter "Female Cannibalism and Eating the Other: Raw, Trouble Every Day, In My Skin."

significantly from her typical material, the world is just as bleak and lonely as in her other works. *Lapvona*, a sort of dark anti-fairy-tale, tells the story of a handful of characters from the village of Lapvona, set in what is probably medieval Eastern Europe and populated by characters with no redeeming qualities. These characters include the often-violent shepherd Jude, his severely physically disfigured son Marek, the elderly but still lactating wet nurse Ina, and the likely insane lord Villiam. Traces of fabulism that evoke the magic of medieval folklore, like an elderly wet nurse or a corpse that disappears once buried, permeate the world but do nothing to redeem it. In *Lapvona*, life is hard and brutal, and then you die; the lucky ones die quickly. Moshfegh uses a feudal society under a system of fiefs and warlords to criticize contemporary late-stage capitalism, with which it seems to share several features.

The novel wastes no time establishing the human body as, in one way or another, comestible. Grigor, the grandfather of recently slaughtered children, cuts the ear off a captured bandit from the raiding party. He tosses it aside and yells, "For the birds to eat!" (Moshfegh 3). Limbs and other body parts are routinely separated from the person and rendered food. A new mother's placenta is tossed aside and "cooked" over the fire (26); Agata's fetus is literally feeding off her body (197); Villiam's cooks prepare dough for bread in the shape of crosses without washing their hands, bloodied from working with holly (244); Ina is the main food source for village infants as the miraculous elderly wet nurse (36).[4] Meat consumption serves as a class marker; for the villagers, the consumption of meat is considered a sin but is routine in Villiam's lordly hall (20, 91). What *exactly* serves as meat, however, is continually contested. It might seem at moments that meat is simply that which can be killed and consumed, but a network of class-, religion-, and gender-based significations inflect who can and cannot eat, as well as what can and cannot be eaten. These networks are inscribed onto the body in ways that coalesce around physical dis/ability, even as early as when Marek is born, and Jude remarks that the babe, due to his disfigurement, looks "not quite human" (26).

Despite the cannibalistic semantic field, there is really only one overt instance in *Lapvona* where other people eat a person's flesh. During a drought wherein an already suffering population finds itself dying of starvation while Lord Villiam barely looks up from his feasts to notice, an elderly blind man named Klim and his companion dog join the villagers at a nearby lake in a futile attempt to cool off. When Klim is overtaken by heat and collapses, Jude grabs his body while surviving villagers tear into his dog. Ostensibly, he took the body to give it a proper burial, but, as if incapable of stopping himself, he carries the

---

[4] For a detailed treatment of breastfeeding and its relationship to "humanimality," see Peggy McCracken's chapter "Nursing Animals and Cross-Species Intimacy."

fresh corpse to Ina's hut where, at her encouragement, they dismember, cook, and eat portions of Klim's body. Their spartan conversation reveals a great deal:

> "Bring the blind boy and cook him."
>
> … "I won't eat a man, no," Jude said.
>
> "Then cook him for me. I'm hungry." She was serious. "And then I can nurse you, I'm sure."
>
> "What about heaven, Ina? Don't you want to go?"
>
> "It doesn't matter," she said. "I won't know anyone … I'll eat him raw, I'm so hungry. Do it. Now." (Moshfegh 119)

The specific act of cannibalism within *Lapvona* reveals stark class differences between those above and those literally below, but the more interesting and perhaps subtler power imbalance comes from how the (visibly) disabled characters in the novel deal with hunger, meat-eating, and whether the animal in question is a human or not. In *Crip Theory: Cultural Signs of Queerness and Disability*, Robert McRuer theorizes the eponymous term and states that "Everyone is virtually disabled, both in the sense that able-bodied norms are 'intrinsically impossible to embody' fully and in the sense that able-bodied status is always temporary, disability being the one identity category that all people will embody if they live long enough" (30). That one might live long enough is never a given in the village of Lapvona, and the increased exposure to *becoming disabled*, and always in a negative sense, transcends gender, religion, and class, just as hunger transcends these markers of difference. Jude, referencing Ina's failing eyesight, which is restored whenever she nurses, reasons that "Wouldn't God favor a sacrifice to save the life of an old woman? Feed the blind to the blind. It had a certain logic to it" (Moshfegh 125). By a process of dehumanization that begins with affinity between disabilities, he transmutes Klim's body from *that to which I owe a proper burial* to *that which is reasonably sacrificed and eaten.* This dehumanization is reciprocal, paradoxically both restoring[5] the eaters and reducing them to something other than human. Jude, up to this point, had not been marked by any physical disability: "His vision was clear despite the darkness of night—oddly, eating the blind man's body had improved Jude's eyesight … As soon as he'd started eating, he'd turned into a wordless animal, grunting and squatting before the fire,

---

[5] For an analysis on the rhetoric of rehabilitation and restoration in disability discourse, see Robert McRuer's *Crip Theory* and the introduction of Mel Y. Chen's *Animacies: Biopolitics, Racial Mattering, and Queer Affect.*

eating the stump of Klim's leg ... He had blood on his hands, sticky and brown" (130). Jude's normative body is shown to be disabled all along.

Lapvona, in this way, inverts the fairy tale such that physical "wholeness" or capability has no correlation with greater or more whole humanity, and it might even make the claim that disability, in one way or another, creates more affinity between people than conformity to able-bodied myths ever could. Cannibalism in Moshfegh's grim fable crips (to borrow McRuer's term) the perception that the human, or the human body, is by default whole and healthy, succumbing to illness or injury over time and instead places every*body* on a spectrum of deterioration and restoration that is never stable or predictable. Eating a human and eating some other animal is, broadly speaking, cannibalism to the villagers of Lapvona. Eating meat—the meat of any of God's creatures—is a sin because, in so doing, the eater becomes less; even if physically restored, the eater is spiritually deadened by affinity to and by ingestion of the broken, dismembered, masticated body. If you are what you eat, then we are all corpses in waiting.

Always Survive, No Matter What: *Earthlings*

If *Lapvona* is a traumatic anti-fairy-tale, Sayaka Murata's *Earthlings* is an anti-narrative of trauma. The story is set in a Kafkaesque version of Japan where, as far as the protagonist Natsuki is concerned, one is always being watched, always disappointing one's family or employers, always on trial for not meeting societal expectations with no way of defending oneself or ultimately achieving conformity and, thereby, safety. Natsuki's Japan is the "Factory" where earth-bound humans are carefully controlled to better manage their reproductive organs, and only she is cognizant of the encroaching extraterrestrial revolution from planet Popinpobopia which will free her, her asexual husband Tomaya, and her childhood friend Yuu from the constraints of the Factory (Murata 40). Here, a series of traumatic events inevitably leads to the dehumanization of characters who resort to cannibalism, but the dehumanization takes on a decidedly literal sense. Over the course of the novel, Natsuki, Tomaya, and Yuu succumb to greater and greater feelings of alienation to the point of believing they are literal aliens, specifically Popinpobopians, whose job is to break free of human taboos and norms in order to establish an alien community based on logic and security. If initially, this leaves the utopic impression of an innocuous, if delusional, found-family drama, Murata quashes any sense of hopeful transhumanist leaps forward right from the start.

The human body is metaphorically separated into parts throughout Murata's novel before any actual separation of limbs takes place, and this includes the separation between the body and its animating source, the self that Natsuki and the others conceptualize as being their true, alien identities. When the children attend the Obon ceremony in the Akishina mountain dwelling of their extended family, wherein they ritualistically invite and guide the souls of departed loved ones into the home, Natsuki learns of a self that transcends embodiment (23-25). There is immediately this sense that the true, inner reality is not just distinct from the body but totally exterior to it. To Natsuki, the ability to leave her body was granted as a means of defense in the intergalactic battle only she could perceive. She and her young cousin Yuu solidify their bond emotionally by pretending to get married and vowing to "Survive, whatever it takes," and physically by sealing their vows with clumsy, adolescent sex in a barely articulated attempt to wrest control from the Factory over their bodies after which they are caught by their family in a compromising position (30). However, it soon becomes clear to the reader that her ability to, as she calls it, *leave her body* when sensing danger or intense emotion is, in fact, dissociation as a defensive response to sexual abuse by her cram-school teacher, Mr. Igasaki.

Natsuki uses her out-of-body power several times in *Earthlings*. Early on, Mr. Igasaki asks Natsuki to stay after class where he reveals that he has fished her used sanitary napkin out of the garbage and admonishes her for not doing a better job disposing of it. He then forces her to change her current tampon in front of him to ensure it is properly disposable. This ends with a terrified and confused Natsuki promising to meet Mr. Igasaki for further "special lessons" at his home during the summer festival. On the way out, she thinks to herself, "*Magical powers. I have to summon my magical powers … I have to use my magical powers on my whole body before my heart feels anything*" (Murata 51). Later, Mr. Igasaki assaults her by forcing her to perform oral sex on him. At first, Natsuki is totally present and utterly terrified. She describes the assault in spartan, almost clinical prose that attempts to sanitize the situation until she finally states, "Wow, I must have summoned a super strong magical power. I had no idea how … I felt no emotion whatsoever and simply watched my own body in silence from the ceiling … Mr. Igasaki was talking to my body, which was now empty since I was up on the ceiling" (62-63).

This powerful state of dissociation repeats itself not too long after. When Natsuki resolves to defeat the Wicked Witch, she imagines she is possessing Mr. Igasaki and causing him to abuse her. She sneaks into his home at night while he is sleeping. As she approaches him, her perception begins to change, as she narrates here:

> It was the out-of-body power. Before I knew what was happening, I had left my body the way I had the day of the summer festival and was watching myself… My body opened the door and silently went inside. The out-of-body me watched intently as it did so … I was raining down blows [on his head] with the small grass-cutting scythe … I desperately

kept repeating the magic word as Piyyut told me to while sticking the
scythe into the bright blue lump over and over again. (Murata 142-43)

Not realizing what she had done, or at the very least not admitting it to herself,
Natsuki sneaks back home, where she washes up, goes to bed, and is later
shocked when Mr. Igasaki is found dead.

Years later, Natsuki continues to feel increasingly alienated from her
surroundings, including her family, workplace, and society at large. Her
companions are Yuu and Tomoya, essentially husbands of convenience with
whom she has no sexual relationship and who agree they are all aliens who
must do everything they can to rid themselves of residual *humanness*. After
running away together to the now-empty Akishina house, where they become
more isolated and feral as time passes, they are attacked by an elderly couple
in the middle of the night. Natsuki recognizes them from her adolescence
immediately, realizing they have come for revenge since she killed their son,
Mr. Igasaki (232). The group fends off and kills both their attackers. Trapped by
snow after an avalanche and discussing their options for food, Natsuki and her
companions come to a macabre agreement:

"Shall we freeze the Earthling meat while it's still fresh?" Yuu proposed
suddenly.

"Are Earthlings edible?"

"They're animals, aren't they?" ...

"I guess so," I nodded, but in the back of my mind was the thought that
if we did this, we would lose any chance of ever being accepted into the
Earthling fold again... I cowered alone in the room, unmoving. There
was probably still some human left in me. (Murata 234-35)

With barely ten pages left in the book, the Popinpobopians finally shed their
human bodies through successive acts of cannibalism, starting first with Mr.
Igasaki's parents and then, finally, by eating each other alive, seemingly
unaware of any pain or loss this might cause to themselves: "Eventually we
were not satisfied by the surface alone and started in on each other's innards
with our teeth and tongues... That day, my body became completely my own"
(Murata 242). The dichotomy ever-present in the narrative between the *self-as-
body* and the *out-of-body me* feeds into the trauma and alienation from which
the interplanetary trio suffers. If cannibalism is, strictly speaking, the eating of
another member of the same species, then Tomoya's speculation that there are
no Earthlings at all, only brainwashed Popinpobopians, carries heavier ethical
implications than initially glimpsed. Not only does it imply that there is no

possibility to reintegrate into Earthling (that is, human) society, but it carries the potential to normalize destructive defense mechanisms like fugue-state-inducing dissociation and the collapse of taboos like incest or murder. It makes the ingestion of bodies, both one's own and one another's, a liberatory act. One can leave humanity with all its judgments, taboos, and rules behind. One can be free if only one can escape the body, a magical, powerful act. All it takes is a strong stomach.

Eating Gloriously: *A Certain Hunger*

At first glance, Chelsea G. Summers's novel about a food critic-turned-anthropophage seems like a feminist manifesto for #girlboss and #boybbq, having at its center a grocery list of lovers who end up falling out of her bed and onto her plate. Dorothy Daniels is clever, aloof, refined, and hungry, but these are just some of the traits that make her special. Like Lilith or Medusa rising out of the ashes of misogynist myth to become poster children for contemporary bad-girl feminism, Dorothy casts herself as knowing something the rest of us do not, but which she will deign to share anyway. Over the course of the narrative, *what* exactly she knows that we do not is gleaned from her gestures towards personal, nearly esoteric knowledge of human nature, usually along gendered lines.

Far from the confessional feminist manifesto it purports to be, Dorothy's essentialism sabotages her own liberatory project in that she ends up behind bars for murder, but also in the greater sense of ascribing to individuals an inherent generality of what men, women, people, animals, and others *are like*. To her, there are not people but *types* of people, broad categories everyone falls into, which legitimize violence and neglect of one's moral and ethical responsibility to other individuals. I borrow the term *totalization* from Emmanuel Levinas to describe this particular process of dehumanization wherein the height of the other person, their infinite unknowability and alterity as presented in a face-to-face encounter, is denied as the individual is reduced to a set of facts, perceptions, or impressions. What these broad categories, this totalization, require in order to work is a framework of affinity and sameness by which these categories can be placed into a hierarchy. Despite the ways in which Dorothy might claim to be subverting the patriarchy by eating men, she tends to reinforce the heteropatriarchal system, which she uses to constantly dehumanize her victims and render them mere food. To Dorothy, there is no accounting for the person on an individual level; the face of the other is lost among the sea of anonymous meat.

When describing the experience of eating human meat, Dorothy relates, "To eat human is to dine on a chimerical hybrid, a marvelous, mythical meat... To eat people… makes a god out of a woman" (Summers 94). She does not only wax poetic about it, though. In the most distanced language, she says, "The human body holds 66 pounds of comestible meat, on average, more than you might expect. Given how much of humans is inedible... Do a little research and... one could begin to believe it's entirely normal" (89). She follows this with several pages on the various kinds of cannibalism (survival, ritual, metaphoric, etc.) practiced throughout the world. Her use of the term *human* obfuscates one crucial fact: to Dorothy, *men* are comestible. What is more, it was her decision *not* to eat a man that brought about her undoing. When she says "human meat," she is not trying to include all people but is taking for granted the universalization of men as the unmarked subject from whom women deviate.[6] She hints as much when her artist best friend is "...the person whom *Art in America* called 'arguably the greatest American Realism painter working today,' a coup, I pointed out to Emma, because nowhere in the clause did the words 'female,' 'woman,' or 'feminine' appear," just as eating people makes a god, not a goddess, out of a woman, assimilating the unmarked position of the eaten man (125).

A great deal of this worldview has to do with the notion of empathy, which Dorothy only seems to feel for other women but never for men, if she feels it at all. She freely identifies with the term *psychopath*, citing her manipulative and unrestrained behavior (Summers 25, 47). But she is not just a psychopath; she is "a *woman* psychopath, the white tiger of human psychological deviance" (26, emphasis added). She can empathize if empathizing means inferring and emulating another person's interiority, thinking as they would think, but only as far as it achieves her own ends. When she does this, she totalizes the other person, reducing them and denying their infinite interiority.

The only people in the novel with whom she identifies, even in her limited capacity, are women. Speaking of Emma, she says, "Our female friends, the close ones, are the mini-breaks we take from the totalitarian work it requires to keep up the performance of being female... [Emma] was the reflection I saw in the mirror, for true monsters can't see themselves. Without Emma, I was an empty surface" (Summers 214). If empathy is putting yourself in another's place, Dorothy's act of seeing her own face reflected back in Emma is the ultimate empathic act, and it still does not stop her from attempting to kill her in the climax. She is also capable of empathizing with, and assuming the reader can best empathize with, female serial killers as opposed to male:

---

[6] Agender, non-binary, and genderqueer people are not conceivable within the heteropatriarchal imaginary; this lacuna is reflected in Dorothy's conceptualization of the world as male and female—and *only* as male and female—even by omission of any possibility outside this binary.

> We like to think that men kill because they're men—it's as indiscriminate as their wont to procreate… Women, on the other hand, kill for only two reasons… personal financial gain or to escape an abusive relationship. Of course, this binary stereotype is insulting and inaccurate. The truth, whether we want to see it or not, is that women will kill for almost any reason… These are murders that we can imagine with some degree of empathy, if not comfort. (Summers 237-38)

It seems to Dorothy men kill because they are men, and women kill because they are *not* men. If she relates to men at all, it is through a totalization so complete that she can only speak of her victims as part of her *own* identity. Remembering her late lovers and favorite meals, she says, "I am all of them; they are some of me" (Summers 191). Even the imagined reader, to whom Dorothy is narrating her prison memoir, cannot escape her totalizing gaze. To Dorothy, her story is not a means by which another can relate or understand her but is itself an opportunity to indulge in the cannibalistic impulse we all share. This is what she knows that no one else dares to admit: "In sum, you and I are the same. You may not admit it aloud, but I know you will read this book and wonder how your lover would taste sauteed with shallots and mushrooms and deglazed with a little red wine. You read, and you wonder, and you know the answer would be *delicious*" (100).

In collapsing everyone into the Same—same gender, same hunger, same *self*—Summers accomplishes a sleight of hand that too often goes critically unremarked. Far from a feminist call for the upheaval of violent, patriarchal hierarchies for which it is sometimes mistaken, Dorothy's "memoir" is instead the narcissistic musings of a near-total solipsist who sees other women as versions of herself, men as cattle for her own gastronomic and sexual pleasure, and no other possibilities. She props up established binaries and, like the emotions of others that she admits to manipulating for personal gain, treats hierarchies as malleable pathways toward self-empowerment. She *eats* because she can. Men *get eaten* because they should. Simple.

The Meat that Eats Meat: *Tender Is the Flesh*

In Bazterrica's challenging and dark novel, the notion of totalization is expanded to include more and, of course, *less* than individual human beings. Set in a post-pandemic world wherein animal meat has become inedible, the protagonist, Marcos, works as a supplier of "special meat" within this new economy. Through Marcos, whose inner thoughts and tortured conscience betray from the very first page that something is deeply wrong, the reader encounters the new normal of a world after what is referred to as the Transition: "They've normalized cannibalism, he thinks. Cannibalism, another word that could cause him major problems" (4). A whole new meat industry evolved out of the old one in which human meat is regulated, commodified, and legitimized. This legitimization is a direct result of the manipulation and policing of language in the domains of meat, business, and bodies.

On the one hand, Bazterrica creates a linguistic divide between human beings and the "head" of comestible subhuman cattle. The most obvious implementations of this new cannibal necropolitics are the transferal of terms used in the butchering of cows and pigs onto the butchering of people: There are grades of meat quality (24), cuts like "upper extremity" and "lower extremity" instead of hands and feet (35); sex is described in terms of male and female as opposed to man and woman, which can be said to ascribe a sense of personhood; and breeding is done with studs who mount (19). The articulation of the human as *that which is not eatable* that scholar Cora Diamond puts forward collapses under the new linguistic regime meant to render a large portion of the population—the unhoused, Blacks, prisoners, criminals, the disabled—into mere food (470).

On the other hand, it is not just the blurring and redefining of words on the part of the eaters that make meat but also an inherently contradictory policy to keep meat from the capacity for language. Meat is (re)made into that which doesn't talk, both ontologically (meat is that which cannot, does not speak) and physically by cutting the vocal cords (this creature cannot, does not speak) because "No one wants them to talk because meat doesn't talk…" (Bazterrica 20). Evoking the Butlerian proposition that gender is real insofar as it is performative and that sex is not inherently biological but instead the very gendering of the body, Bazterrica calls into question the performative nature of the whole human being—meat does not talk, and therefore we must not let our meat talk, just as boys like guns and trucks and therefore we must not let our sons play with dolls no matter how much they desire it.[7] For example, humans and "heads" are supposed to be ontologically different beings, yet there are laws in place prohibiting reproduction with them as well as punishments for shattering the discursive illusion of difference between them. Just as marriage is *naturally* between one man and one woman but somehow relies on a vast apparatus of legal, social, economic, and cultural circumstances to make sure this remains the case, "heads" are not humans because they are dehumanized within a similar apparatus: "No one can call them humans because that would mean giving them an identity" (Bazterrica 8). The punishment for such a crime, a nightmare rendition of Agamben's *homo sacer*, is equally telling: those found guilty of breaking the law and treating or talking about "head" as humans are arrested and transferred to the Municipal Slaughterhouse, where they are

---

[7] For their exploration on the performativity of gender, see Judith Butler's *Gender Trouble*.

slaughtered, processed, sold, and eaten like any other carcass (157). If the difference between human and nonhuman animals is not biological, social, spiritual, or any one of the popular distinctions commonly supplied but instead is merely the ability to *articulate humanness*, then it is the prerogative of regulatory bodies like the government or the meat industry to decide who does and does not meet the conditions for being meat and who therefore must have their access to and ability for using language policed or removed entirely.

Butler is useful for reading Bazterrica in other ways. In their 2004 book on the making of certain lives grievable during the War on Terror, *Precarious Life: The Powers of Mourning and Justice*, they rework the Levinasian notion of totalization into the more materialist term *derealization*, asking a series of questions from which the problem of grievability springs:

> Who counts as human? Whose lives count as lives? And, finally, What [sic] *makes for a grievable life?* ... How do we understand derealization? It is one thing to argue that first, on the level of discourse, certain lives are not considered lives at all, they cannot be humanized, that they fit no dominant frame for the human, and that their dehumanization comes first, at this level, and that this level then gives rise to physical violence that in some sense delivers the message of dehumanization that is already at work in the culture. It is another thing to say that discourse itself affects violence through omission. (Butler 34)

In other words, derealization is a process—one of totalization—that depends both on the language used to describe, or even shape, the world on the level of discourse and also on the lack of access that dehumanized humans have to language, the ability to grieve or be grieved.

Derealization underpins Marcos's interactions with almost every character, notably the female "head" he is gifted at the beginning of the novel, who supplies the major conflict at the heart of the story, but also others who would be considered human. When Marcos reluctantly attends a dinner at which the game servers are hunted by the participants themselves earlier in the day, he discusses the hunting and devouring of no-longer-human prey—such as Ulises Vox, a formerly famous musician who ran into problems with debt and was being eaten for dinner that night as a result—with the aristocratic and monstrous Urlet. The word "monstrous" is not used here superfluously; Bazterrica uses vampiric terms to describe the big game hunter: "Urlet is drinking wine from a glass that looks like an antique chalice... The man's nails are neat but long... hypnotic and primitive... The man is one of those people who seem to have been part of the world since the beginning... Urlet left Romania after the Transition" (Bazterrica 137-38). If Urlet's name were instead

Vlad Țepeș or Dracula, it would not be any clearer who this character is supposed to evoke. But a vampire is not a human, and few people consider the bloodthirst of this classic monster to be a cannibalistic impulse. The questions arise then who is and who is not the human in this situation, and why? Marcos is surrounded by "head," their slaughter and consumption, every day of his life, yet he feels deeply uncomfortable around Urlet and his practice of hunting his meat. What *makes* him monstrous, Marcos indicates, is his disdain for the language that elides the horror of consumption. His monstrosity does not come from some inner essential difference that is covered up by a human face—as is the case of, say, a vampire, which cannot be a moral agent—but rather from the fact that he is a human-eating another human without recourse to legitimizing linguistic structures and therefore to moral absolution. Urlet discusses this with Marcos, saying,

> "The human being is complex, and I find the vile acts, contradictions, and sublimities characteristic of our condition astonishing. Our existence would be an exasperating shade of gray if we were all flawless."
>
> "But then why do you consider [human behavior] atrocious?"
>
> "Because it is. But that's what's incredible, that we accept our excess, that we normalize them, that we embrace our primitive essence." (Bazterrica 141)

Not *their* condition, existence, excess, or primitive essence, but *ours*. Bazterrica's hypercarnist dystopia feels like science fiction but is closer to real life than anyone would care to admit. As a Texas Lieutenant Governor can suggest that the elderly sacrifice themselves for the good of the economy (Levin), or the CDC Director can state that disabled people lost in disproportionate numbers to the Covid pandemic were "unwell to begin with" (Hill). *Tender Is the Flesh* reveals the ways in which discourse can derealize the suffering of people as a result of policy, culture, and silence. The resultant dehumanization can render lives into little more than bottom lines, statistics, or worse, nothing at all, that which goes totally unspoken, unremarked, ungrieved.

Devotion and Disgust: "Meat"

Until this point, I have discussed cannibalism in varying modes as a form of transgression, either against the self or another. However, cannibalism need not be strictly interpreted in terms of desecration, violence, or a posthumous negation of the other (Burley). If *A Certain Hunger*'s Dorothy eats men to elide their existence as exterior to her own sovereign, somatic experience of pleasure, the protagonists of Enríquez's short story "Meat" ("Carne") eat the dead in order to negate death itself and carry another's life literally in their flesh and blood.

Centered, as so much of Enríquez's fiction is, around a brooding rock star reminiscent of Anne Rices *Prince Lestat* and his obsessed fans (invariably adolescent or teenage girls), *Meat* tells the story of Santiago Espina, colloquially known as El Espina.[8] More accurately, it is the story of his corpse and of the fans who became it. After the release of El Espina's last album, *Meat,* and his subsequent death by suicide, his body is found mutilated; he has skinned his own arms, legs, and stomach, slicing himself to the bone in places before semi-consciously slitting his jugular vein. He has not touched his face. Theatrical as he is, he left a bloodstained note that read, "Meat is food. Meat is death. You all know what the future holds" (Enríquez 101). The protagonists, Julieta and Mariela, react to the death of their star by obsessively listening to the album and hearing in its lyrics a special message, an esoteric truth just for them. The girls marked themselves outwardly[9] as "'Espinosas' (as the press called Santiago's fans, the girls with their eyes lined in mortuary black, cheap feather boas around their necks, and leopard-print pants)" (102). If an outward metonymic joined them to the host of other Espinosas, it seemed natural that they needed something on the inside to join them more forcibly to their hero. The media frenzy was greater than at the time of the artist's death, for "Two teenagers had dug up Santiago Espina's coffin using a shovel and their own hands… But the exhumation was only the beginning. The girls had opened the casket to feed on Espina's remains with devotion and disgust; around the grave, pools of vomit bore witness to their efforts…" (104).

The act of consuming Espina was discussed and interpreted by everyone who heard the story, from journalists and psychologists to Espina's bandmates and family. Most reacted with predictable horror and revulsion, others with highly medicated resignation. His most devoted fans, however, took everyone by surprise:

---

[8] The Spanish *thorn* with the gender changed from female to male is another trademark of Enríquez's many musician androgynes.

[9] It is likely that Enríquez draws inspiration for the story from the disappearance of Manic Street Preachers guitarist Richey Edwards in 1995, alluded to by the similar uniform of sorts worn by fans of the band. There is not enough space in this chapter to discuss either her relationship to fandom or to the notion of disappearance, a common thread throughout her fiction and journalism in her reflections on the Dirty War in Argentina from 1974-1983, though Enríquez has written about her experience specifically dealing with the loss of her favorite band member. See Enríquez's "Rosas de Cristal: La Habana, Cuba."

One of them… cried openly when she was asked what she thought about the girls who had eaten their idol. Defiantly, she shouted, "I envy them! They understood!" And she babbled something about meat and the future, she said that Julieta and Mariela were closer to Espina than any of the rest of them, they had him in their bodies, in their blood…

Meanwhile, all over the country, in every internet café, the Espinosas gathered before computer screens, because the emails had started to come… The emails spoke of two girls who would soon turn eighteen and would be free… to play the songs of *Meat* in basements and garages. They talked about an unstoppable cult, about They Who Have Espina in their bodies. (Enríquez 106)

Far from the total(izing) hunger of starvation or the alienation of dissociative trauma which necessitate survival, cannibalism in "Meat" takes as literally as possible what political theorist Jane Bennett asserts in her book *Vibrant Matter* that food is an "actant inside and alongside intention-forming, morality-(dis)obeying, language-using, reflexivity-wielding, and culture-making human beings, and as an inducer-producer of salient, public effects" (39). In his *The Hungry Soul: Eating and the Perfecting of Our Nature,* Leon Kass says boldly that "we do not become the something that we eat; rather the edible gets assimilated to what we are… the edible object is thoroughly transformed by and re-formed into the eater" (qtd. in Bennett 25-26). In other words, if we are what we eat, we can also be what eats *us*.

In devouring the remains of Santiago Espina, Julieta and Mariela are not mere conduits through which dead, inert matter passes. However abject the process might be from beginning to end (involving a corpse, vomit, feces, blood, perhaps even embalming fluid once made "part of" the body), this is not a story of a corpse being eaten and digested by cannibal fetishists but rather a body being restored to life by an assemblage of living death. The matter that was Espina continues to sing in basements about a future from which it can newly partake. The height of difference between the same and the other collapses in the face of vital materialism that transcends panpsychism or metaphysics centered on a soul or vital force, instead acknowledging matter *in itself* as agential even if inanimate—without breath, unmoving, like a corpse.

Enríquez uses the trope of cannibalism to subvert the idea that death is the end, that to be eaten is to be nullified or silenced. Like a guitar riff on a record that lives in the air as vibrations long after the fingers that strummed it have decayed, a cannibalized body is an immanent soul in "Meat," where "Espina whispers, 'If you are hungry, eat of my flesh. If you are thirsty, drink from my eyes'" while his audience dreams of a future (106).

Sobremsa: A Conclusion

Cannibalism is renewing itself today. If it once reinforced the boundaries of the human body and solidified humans as different from other (i.e., edible) animals,[10] it is today calling into question the very definition of humanness in an effort to reach across the various divides that we find ourselves negotiating in our daily lives. With roots in xenophobia and colonialism, projects that rely on stable and very specific definitions of the human to achieve their ends— racial and social hegemony, the establishment of able-bodied and hetero-patriarchal ideals as the baseline from which *other* bodies deviate, an economy that reinforces and benefits from a single definition of commodifiable concepts like family, souls, (in)edible beings—are subverted by the contemporary cannibal narrative. As a global climate crisis looms and the wave of mass extinctions grows, as fascism returns to the sociopolitical mainstream and formerly full persons with supposed equal rights are threatened, as microplastics and viral pandemics rewrite our very DNA, the cannibalism trope within horror is helping today's audiences negotiate these unstable boundaries and rediscover our responsibilities to all types of Others, reminding us that we can always find affinity, at the very least, in the meat that makes us.

Works Cited

Aaltola, Elisa. "Animal Ethics and the Argument from Absurdity." *Environmental Values*, vol. 19, no. 1, 2010, pp. 79-98.

Agamben, Giorgio. *Homo Sacer: Sovereign Power and Bare Life*. Stanford University Press, 1998.

Avramescu, Cătălin. *An Intellectual History of Cannibalism*. Princeton University Press, 2009.

Bazterrica, Agustina. *Tender Is The Flesh*. Scribner Book Co., 2020.

Bennett, Jane. *Vibrant Matter: A Political Ecology of Things*. Duke University Press, 2010.

Bone Tomahawk. Directed by S. Craig Zahler, RLJ Entertainment, 2015.

Butler, Judith. *Gender Trouble*. New York, Routledge, 1999.

——. *Precarious Life: The Powers of Mourning and Justice*. Verso, 2004.

Burley, Mikel. "Eating Human Beings: Varieties of Cannibalism and the Heterogeneity of Human Life." *Philosophy*, vol. 91, no. 358, 2016, pp. 483-501.

Cannibal Holocaust. Directed by Ruggero Deodato, United Artists Europa, 1980.

Church, David. *Post-Horror: Art, Genre and Cultural Elevation*. Edinburgh University Press, 2021.

---

[10] A large number of articles have since been published in conversation and disagreement with Diamond's definition of the human as *that which is not eatable* (behold, a man!). For examples, see Mikel Burley's "Eating Human Beings: Varieties of Cannibalism and the Heterogeneity of Human Life" and Elisa Aaltola's "Animal Ethics and the Argument from Absurdity."

Chen, Mel Y. *Animacies: Biopolitics, Racial Mattering, and Queer Affect.* Duke University Press, 2012.

Creed, Barbara. "Female Cannibalism and Eating the Other: Raw, Trouble Every Day, In My Skin." *Return of the Monstrous-Feminine,* Routledge, 2022, pp. 127-41.

Diamond, Cora. "Eating Meat and Eating People." *Philosophy,* vol. 53, no. 206, 1978, pp. 465-79.

Enríquez, Mariana. "Meat." *The Dangers of Smoking in Bed,* Hogarth Press, 2022, pp. 99-106.

Enríquez, Mariana. "Rosas de Cristal: La Habana, Cuba." *Alguien camina sobre tu tumba: mis viajes a cementerios.* Editorial Anagrama, 2021.

Faber, Tom. "From *Suspiria* to *Get Out*—Why Horror Movies Are Having a Moment." *Financial Times,* 4 Jan. 2019, www.ft.com/content/98381576-09f0-11e9-a242-6043097d0789.

Finch, Charles. "Book Review: You're Probably Wrong about Ottessa Moshfegh." *Los Angeles Times,* 7 June 2020.

Fresh. Directed by Mimi Cave, Searchlight Pictures, 2022.

Get Out. Directed by Jordan Peele, Universal Pictures, 2017.

The Green Inferno, Directed by Eli Roth, Worldview Entertainment et al., 2016.

Hill, Kayle. "The CDC Thinks Disabled People Like Me Don't Matter." *Teen Vogue,* 13 Jan. 2022, www.teenvogue.com/story/cdc-director-covid-deaths-disabled.

The Hills Have Eyes. Directed by Wes Craven, Vanguard, 1977.

Honeydew. Directed by Devereux Milburn, Dark Star Pictures, 2020.

Kass, Leon. *The Hungry Soul: Eating and the Perfecting of Our Nature.* University of Chicago Press, 1999.

The Killing of a Scared Deer. Yorgos Lanthimos, Film 4 et al., 2017.

Levinas, Emmanuel. *Totality and Infinity: An Essay on Exteriority.* Translated by Alphonso Lingis, Duquesne Press, 1998.

Levin, Bess. "Texas Lt. Governor: Old People Should Volunteer to Die to Save the Economy." *Vanity Fair,* 24 Mar. 2020, www.vanityfair.com/news/2020/03/dan-patrick-coronavirus-grandparents.

Lyle, Ashley, and Bart Nickerson, creators. *Yellowjackets.* Showtime Networks et al., 2021.

McCracken, Peggy. "Nursing Animals and Cross-Species Intimacy." *From Beasts to Souls: Gender and Embodiment in Medieval Europe,* edited by E. Jane Burns and Peggy McCracken, University of Notre Dame Press, 2013, pp. 39-64.

McRuer, Robert. *Crip Theory: Cultural Signs of Queerness and Disability.* NYU Press, 2006.

Midsommar. Directed by Ari Aster, A24, 2019.

Moshfegh, Ottessa. *Lapvona.* Penguin Press, 2022.

Murata, Sayaka. *Earthlings.* Grove Press, 2021.

Raw (French *Grave*). Directed by Julia Ducournau, Petit Film et al., 2016.

Rice, Anne. *Prince Lestat.* Knopf, 2014.

The Silence of the Lambs. Directed by Jonathan Demme, Orion Pictures, 1991.

Summers, Chelsea G. *A Certain Hunger.* Unnamed Press, 2021.

Texas Chainsaw Massacre. Directed by Tobe Hooper, Vortex Inc., 1974.

Chapter 3

Broken Christs and the Advent of Horror: From Shelley's *Frankenstein* to AMC's *The Walking Dead*

Zaher Alajlani

Abstract

By relying on the Christian resurrection narrative as the standard of judgment, this chapter outlines the main attributes of the broken Christ. This trope shares Christ's claim to saviorhood, as depicted in Christian mythology, but lacks His moral fortitude. Horror and tragedy arise from this contradiction. Besides excavating the origins of this subverted messianic figure in Shelley's *Frankenstein*, the chapter focuses on the trope's recurrence in the narrative of AMC's popular series *The Walking Dead*. Since they both possess the core characteristics of the broken Christ, the protagonists, Victor Frankenstein and Rick Grimes, can transcend bland, traditional horror tropes. Such complexity not only pushes the tropological boundaries of the plot but also adds a philosophical and moral depth to the entire narrative.

Keywords: Christian narrative, broken Christ, *Frankenstein*, *The Walking Dead*

* * *

The idea of the dead rising is a master motif that transcends time and culture. Not only can it be found in a myriad of modern video games, films, and fiction, but in one of the most ancient literary works, "The Epic of Gilgamesh." In the Mesopotamian poem, Ishtar threatens to unleash the dead to devour the living. In Abrahamic religions, the idea does not take such a grisly undertone: the dead will simply be resurrected to face God's judgment. But, of all the major Abrahamic religions, Christianity seems to be most reliant on the concept of resurrection, for much of the creed is centered around Christ's coming back from the dead, an act that symbolizes overcoming death and regenerating life.

Against this hopeful representation stands the resurrection of the dead in many horror narratives. For example, in *Frankenstein*, Mary Shelley uses the raising of the dead as a primary plot device and a source of terror. The latter is best embodied by

Frankenstein's creation of the monster. While the Frankensteinian creature and the modern zombie trope differ in various aspects, they still possess the same necrotic essence and macabre literary purpose. The monster is a blend of resurrected corpses that foments death and destruction, just like the zombies in AMC's hit series *The Walking Dead*. In both works, the theme of resurrection facilitates the reader's view of the protagonists as subverted Christ figures. Victor Frankenstein tries to defeat death by bringing a stitched corpse to life, while Rick Grimes battles the emissaries of death (hordes of walkers and other survivors) to ensure his group's survival. Nonetheless, neither of the two can defeat death, sustain life, or attain a savior's glory.

Despite the two centuries between *Frankenstein* and *The Walking Dead*, Victor and Rick still share several traits that make them representations of a failed Messiah or a broken Christ. The latter is a horror trope originating in Shelley's *Frankenstein* that shares with Christ His claim to saviorhood but lacks the needed moral fortitude. While the biblical account of Christ's encounter with the Devil is a tale of moral perfection, a subverted Christ merely suffers from a savior complex. Tragedy and terror stem from this reversal of saviorhood. This chapter approaches the broken Christ figures embodied by the protagonists of *Frankenstein* and *The Walking Dead*, highlighting the similarities between the two despite their differences in time periods. The aim is to investigate this trope, its manifestation, and its role in both narratives, pushing the boundaries of known tropes while using Jesus's resurrection account in The New Testament as a frame of reference.

Unveiling the Broken Christ Trope

The origins of literary narratives and the way tales come into being are fairly obscure. In his memoir *On Writing*, Stephen King makes an insightful remark about the creative process:

> [G]ood story ideas seem to come quite literally from nowhere, sailing at you right out of the empty sky: two previously unrelated ideas come together and make something new under the sun. Your job isn't to find these ideas but to recognize them when they show up. (King 25)

King's assertion certainly holds true in terms of how stories are conceived. Still, their narrative construction—the creation of the connective tissues adjoining such out-of-"nowhere" ideas—relies on discernable master tropes and plot devices extending beyond the confines of time and space, at least in the case of Western literature.

Hence, when examining the macabre landscape, an eerie repetition pattern appears to dominate the genre, and this includes the recurrence of certain tropes and imagery. Many of these timeless building blocks can be traced back to Mary Shelley's 1818 masterpiece, which, in various ways, constitutes a landmark in the literary history of the West. Brian Aldiss, a foremost British science fiction author and historian, believes the novel represents the genesis of science fiction and provides the first model of the mad scientist prototype (Goodrich 71). The novel's importance was also recognized by H. P. Lovecraft, the father of cosmic horror, whose work influenced modern masters of the macabre, such as Stephen King and Clive Barker. In *Supernatural Horror in Literature*, Lovecraft stipulates that *Frankenstein* possesses the "true touch of cosmic fear" (39).

The novel's protagonist, Victor Frankenstein, has a prominent place in the pantheon of literary tropes. His influence on many important works of fiction is indisputable. These include Stevenson's 1886 *Strange Case of Dr. Jekyll and Mr. Hyde*, Wells's 1896 *The Island of Doctor Moreau*, Verne's 1892 *The Carpathian Castle*, and Lovecraft's 1922 "Herbert West–Reanimator." Confirming this, Aldiss and Wingrove write, "Jekyll is one in the line of meddling savants from Frankenstein to Wells's Moreau and Griffin and so on to yesterday's 'mad scientist' and today's horribly sane ones" (139).

In *Frankenstein*, we encounter Victor as an aspiring scientist who aims to overcome death. One of his early declarations strikes the reader as a fit of megalomania:

> No one can conceive the variety of feelings that bore me onwards, like a hurricane, in the first enthusiasm of success. Life and death appeared to me ideal bounds, which I should first break through and pour a torrent of light into our dark world. A new species would bless me as its creator and source; many happy and excellent natures would owe their being to me. No father could claim the gratitude of his child so completely as I should deserve theirs. (Shelley, ch. 4).

This passage is the onset of Victor's process of self-deification. Much like the death-conquering Christ, he blurs the lines between life and death and even echoes the famous biblical passage, "Then God said, 'Let there be light'" (Genesis 1:3, *New King James Version*), as he wants to "pour a torrent of light into our dark world." The difference between what the Western mind perceives (at least, figuratively) as a divine act of creation, on the one hand, and Victor's "pour[ing]" of light is authenticity.

The biblical phenomenon of creation is preceded by nothing that existed, which means that God made all things and beings, including humans, ex nihilo. The Christian creed stipulates that the eternal God (embodied in the Holy Trinity of the Father, the Son/Jesus, and the Holy Spirit) is the origin of everything. Jesus, as the pre-incarnate God, is the orchestrator of creation. In Colossians 1:16, Saint Paul tells early Christians that "[a]ll things were created through [Jesus] and for Him," echoing the statement in John 1:3 that "[a]ll things were made through Him, and without Him nothing was made that was made" (*New King James Version*). The Christian narrative alludes to a genuine act of creation from absolute nothingness. In the case of Victor, the antecedent of his creation is an original, enduring one to which he belongs as merely a created being and which he corrupts by forming the monster. The seeds of subverting Christhood are rooted in this contradiction.

Another relevant paradox is the cadaverous nature of the monster, which Victor describes as a "catastrophe" (Shelley ch.5). This reflects the corruption within Victor himself. Martin Tropp argues that all "monster[s]" are mirror images of their makers' true beings (16). Such impressions are molded upon challenging God and come into being as the desired victory turns into a tragic defeat (Tropp 16). Victor uses dead body parts to generate life, one that eventually begets death and destruction (Alajlani 235). In this context, "the meaning of life and death" is subverted (Alajlani 235).

The very name of *Frankenstein*'s protagonist may entail another contradiction. The name Victor means conqueror (Hanks and Hodges 330)—someone who overcomes his adversary (*Merriam-Webster Dictionary*). In Christianity, Jesus triumphed against death and sin, thus deserving the title of Christ. Victor is one of the oldest Christian names and is closely associated with Christ's said victory (Hanks and Hodges 330). Nevertheless, in Frankenstein's case, there is virtually no victory or overcoming death. His attempt at becoming God fails and leaves him terrified and sick. His very own creation ends up harvesting the lives of his loved ones. Finally, he perishes in the Arctic while pursuing the monster without redeeming himself and ridding the world of the evil he unleashed. Again, one can see Victor as a distorted image of Christ. In Romans 6:9, Saint Paul preaches that "Christ, having been raised from the dead, dies no more. Death no longer has dominion over Him" (*New King James Version*). In contrast, Victor is repeatedly defeated by death. This devastating series of failures begins when he "announces" in an ironically "triumphant religious tone" his "coming … as a new God and creator" (Alajlani 203). His proclamation incites in the reader's mind a sense of adventure. Ultimately, however, Victor's pseudo-Christological announcements merely pave the way for tragedy.

Regarding moral responsibility, Victor displays utter failure despite the grandiose claims. When his eyes first fall upon the monster, he runs away. A morally responsible character would attempt to rectify his mistake "either by improving the monster or euthanizing it," but Victor, in the beginning, casts away what he created, simply wishing that he would no longer encounter it (Alajlani 233). His fruitless efforts to avenge the death of his loved ones and end the monster's reign of terror come too late (Alajlani 233). In contrast, Jesus's ethical and moral fortitude is repeatedly shown in The New Testament. For example, what Jesus exhibits when He encounters the "tempter" in Mathew 4:1-11 is precisely what Victor lacks; Shelley's protagonist fails to carry a genuine claim of divinity that comes with moral duties. This represents another point of contrast that gives Victor an anti-Christ-like dimension, which is amplified when considering that he compares himself to Lucifer, a fallen angel: "All my speculations and hopes are as nothing; and, like the archangel who aspired to omnipotence, I am chained in an eternal hell" (Shelley ch. 7).

Thus, one can single out several core elements of a broken Christ figure as originated in Shelley's novel: 1) a grandiose claim, 2) a proclamation of advent, 3) horror and tragedy following such proclamation, 4) moral failure, and 5) subverted saviorhood. Such traits cluster around the broken Christ prototype and are essential to any narrative featuring such a figure. In the case of Western horror, they often contrast the Christian master narrative of the resurrection.

Master narratives, as Mclean and Syed stipulate, are "culturally shared stories that guide thoughts, beliefs, values, and behaviors" (qtd. in Syed et al. 504). They are, thus, timely and spatially expansive, though they share some cultural specificity. That is, a master narrative offers a narrational framework for tales about belonging to a certain culture (Syed et al. 504). This is definitely the case with the Christian story of the resurrection, so much so that Saint Paul's statement that "if Christ be not risen, then is our preaching vain" (Corinthian 15:14, *New King James Version*) still sets the cultural undertones in the West and defines belonging to it. In this chapter, neither the veracity nor the historicity of the resurrection narrative (or Christian scriptures) matters. Instead, the focus is on this narrative's function, role as a myth, universality, timelessness, and ability to generate meaning and affect artistic creation.

One must distinguish here between fiction and myth, especially religious mythologies. While it undoubtedly contains archetypal and mythological elements, fiction is exceptionally multipurpose. It entertains, offers an escape, incites feelings, and deals with philosophical, social, and moral questions. Myth, however, encapsulates values that guide cultures, acting as an enduring master narrative that gives meaning. Carl Jung believes that "myth" and "fiction" are not the same (220). He brilliantly surmises that the "religious myth is one of man's greatest and most significant achievements, giving him the security and inner strength not to be crushed by the monstrousness of the universe" (qtd. in Segal 19). Not only this, but Jung also theorizes that "facts" are the threads making up the fabric of "myth" and that these "facts" occur in a loop and are subject to constant investigation (Jung 220). Hence, given its prominence in Western culture and its ability to generate meaning, whether historical or not, the resurrection narrative is a master myth that possesses a pervasive influence and provides a continuing sense of safety (as opposed to fear). To subvert the resurrection's symbolism is to both subvert its influence and produce terror—precisely what a broken Christ does.

Lovecraft remarks that the terror in *Frankenstein* is cosmic in nature (39). He begins *Supernatural Horror in Literature* by explaining how this primordial fear is passed on from one generation to another and what it entails: "The oldest and strongest emotion of mankind is fear, and the oldest and strongest kind of fear is fear of the unknown" (Lovecraft 12). The "fear of the unknown" is the root of all horror in broken Christ narratives. In *Frankenstein*, the primary agent of terror—the monster—is associated with the unknown. First, it is made up of nameless corpses. Second, the very essence of existence, a living cadaver, is incongruent with human reason. Third, it has a pervasive, insidious presence: it appears out of nowhere to cause death and destruction. It is, therefore, the perfect manifestation of the unknown, and the fear it stirs is, by default, cosmic.

Locating Subverted Messianic Elements in *The Walking Dead*

A reasonable question follows: how can all of this manifest in AMC's *The Walking Dead*? The answer is through this type of cosmic fear brought about by the broken Christ traits specified above. Fear and unknowability are the core of the zombies, which are referred to as "walkers" in the series. The nature and whole being of these anonymous corpses are incompatible with human logic (walking/acting dead bodies). They permeate the protagonist's world and are the source of inevitable havoc and demise. Additionally, the narrative adopted by the series, which differs from that of the comics, does not explain the outbreak. From the onset, viewers are exposed to a dystopian, post-apocalyptic world that is unexplained. This obscurity embodies cosmic dread where man is constantly under the threat of extinction in a vast, unforgiving universe. For instance, Rick tries to talk to the walkers in the first episode, showing that, even when one is face to face with such sanity-defying creatures, human reason cannot immediately grasp the situation. In other words, the protagonist seems unable to instantly fathom the possibility of a living dead.

Following his killing of his best friend Shane ("Better Angels"), Rick makes his first unprecedented grandiose claim, which is the first characteristic of a broken Christ. After a series of events that forces Rick and his group to camp in the wild, a dispute breaks out over whether they should leave or not. Rick then assumes control, saying that he is "keeping the group together, alive" ("Beside the Dying Fire"). He says he did not "ask" to be the leader, offers his fellow survivors the option to leave, and then tells them: "If you're staying, this isn't a democracy anymore" ("Beside the Dying Fire"). Interestingly, this proclamation is preceded by Rick's telling the group that he killed Shane for them. One gets the impression here that Rick's establishment of himself as the group's savior and dictator is preconditioned upon this gruesome, albeit justified, act.

Rick exhibits a compromised sense of morality evident in his overconfidence, mainly due to his claim to be the sole reason the group is alive. This proclamation fulfills the second criterion, evoking a sense of advent or a second coming. Rick's assumption of the role of the sole leader implies that a new reign is about to come. From then on, the fulfillment of the third broken Christ criterion (horror and tragedy) begins. Rick becomes entangled in a continuous struggle with various surviving groups to the point that the viewer ceases to see the living dead as the main antagonists. In the third season, we are introduced to Woodbury, another surviving community. Governed by Philip Blake (often referred to as the Governor), Woodbury is depicted in a dualistic manner. On the surface, it seems to be an ideal place, but underneath that façade, brutality is the glue binding the community together. The Governor is shown as a charismatic, charming dictator with psychopathic tendencies. Despite being nemeses, the same can be said of Rick. The only difference is that we see the events from Rick's perspective, and therefore, we tend to empathize with him. Probably, this is the series creator's (Robert Kirkman's) intention. In an interview with Adam Kepler for *The New York Times*, he says that he views Rick and the Governor as "two sides of the same coin," adding that "if Rick had gone down a certain path, he could have ended up exactly like that guy … [who turned into] that bad of a person."

This brings us to the fourth broken Christ criterion, moral failure. Rick's morally questionable decisions lead to the untimely death of many characters he is supposed to keep alive. Throughout the series, we see Rick making one risky decision after another and displaying a hawkish attitude. The most flagrant instance comes in episode twelve of season six, titled "Not Tomorrow Yet." Rick, against the advice of his trusted companion Morgan and in a groupthink moment, decides to launch a preemptive attack on the Saviors (a group led by the brutal dictator Negan), saying that they should simply "kill them all" ("Not Tomorrow Yet"). The Saviors retaliate, killing several of Rick's friends and subjugating the whole group.

Albeit the brief periods of success and stability, Rick's behavior tends to beget death and destruction, making the macabre aspect of *The Walking Dead* pulsating. If there is any doubt in the viewer's mind about Rick's inadequate imitation of Christ, "What Comes After," the episode in which he exits the show, is enough to quell such uncertainty. The reference frame for sketching the figure of the broken Christ is The New Testament's resurrection narrative: Jesus is tortured, crucified, and raised from the dead before ascending to the heavens. This narrative stands for achieving victory and overcoming death. In John 19:34, "one of the soldiers pierced Jesus' side with a spear, bringing a sudden flow of blood and water" (*New King James Version*). Rick's departure from the show mirrors this account. After defeating Negan and the Saviors, under Rick's supervision, a massive herd of walkers attacks survivors while reconstructing a bridge. In a desperate attempt to lead them away, Rick is caught in an explosion and believed to be dead. However, Jadis (the leader of a group called the Scavengers) rescues the dying Rick and asks a mysterious helicopter pilot to rescue them. The latter airlifts them, leaving both the survivors and the audience waiting for Rick's return—or second coming. Before getting spirited away, Rick falls off his horse, and a rebar penetrates his side. This is a stark reminder of the piercing of Jesus's side in John 19:34. After his disappearance, the survivors and the viewers alike are left with the impression that Rick has sacrificed himself for the sake of others and is bound to come back.

Despite these messianic undertones, the fifth criterion is met: subverted saviorhood. Rick's exit does not offer redemption, unity, or relief. It aggravates the misery of the rest of the survivors and results in a division among his former followers. If the building blocks of Christ's crucifixion and resurrection are suffering, piercing of the side, death, and ascension to the sky, then Rick's exit possesses them. In this sense, Rick is a Christ-like figure but also a broken savior absent of all the glory of overcoming death and tragedy.

Reimagining Protagonists as Broken Christs

Two major counterpoints can be made against this argument: anachronism and conflation of concepts. First, though one may argue that the difference of nearly two centuries between the two works is sufficient to warrant anachronism, the focus has not been on era-specific concepts in this research. That is to say, the broken Christ figure is approached as a universal archetype. What was precisely investigated is the trope's building blocks and how they have been used in two culture-shaping fictional narratives. Second, Victor remains a mad scientist with a strong Romantic and Gothic undertone. The novel's narrative may strike the modern reader as restrained, slow, and somewhat archaic. In contrast, Rick is a modern horror protagonist belonging to American pop culture. The series' storyline is unrestrained, energetic, and saturated with sudden changes. Considering all that, it is better to think of Rick and Victor as having common narrational traits, as the former fulfills the five criteria originating in the latter but remains distinct. The attributes the two protagonists share enable each of them to transcend the limits of ordinary horror tropes. Victor is thus no longer simply a mad scientist, and Rick is no longer a pop-culture protagonist. They are ethically and psychologically intricate as they stand in opposition to some of Jesus's messianic qualities, projecting a false sense of advent, moral deficiency, and inability to defeat death despite their initial belief otherwise.

Through their failure, we witness horror and death. As for Shelley's masterpiece, one may be tempted to consider raising the dead (symbolized by the monster) as a sign of success, but neither Victor's viewpoint nor the sequence of actions attests to this conclusion. Instead, Victor views the fruit of his experiment as a disaster, and the novel concludes with his death, which is preceded by that of his loved ones. In this sense, Victor's role in the narrative is the catalyst for horror. He intends to become God, only to be crushed. The same goes for Rick. Despite his group's reverence for him, Rick makes disastrous decisions. His early claim that he kept them alive and his assumption of the role of the leader afterward prove to be warning signs of what is to come: utter failure.

Just like *Frankenstein* is a timeless piece that can stir dread in the readers' hearts, even after two centuries, *The Walking Dead* series will be appreciated by many future generations as such. One of the principal reasons is their protagonists' resemblance to a broken version of Christ, a figure of undebatable influence in terms of adding narrational and tropological depth. In both *Frankenstein* and *The Walking Dead*, the subverted messianic dimension enables the protagonists to transcend the boundaries of a traditional trope. In *Frankenstein*, Victor is multifaceted and compound. His savior-like aspirations give his character a moral complexity and address issues that are still very relevant today, from dangerous knowledge and the limitations of humanity to the importance of moral caution. As for Rick Grimes, these complexities enable him to surpass what we anticipate from the stiff representative of bygone law and order and become a failed redeemer who, by falling short, makes us reflect upon existential issues, such as the ethics of conflict and the futility of a life whose main purpose is survival. Hence, broken Christs ultimately push the conventional confines of horror tropes beyond their standard thresholds.

Works Cited

Alajlani, Zaher. *Harbingers of Doom: Mad Science and the Death of Meaning.* 2023. Babeş-Bolyai University, Ph.D. dissertation.

Aldiss, Brian W., and David Wingrove. *Trillion Years Spree: The History of Science Fiction.* Paladin Grafton Books, 1988.

"Beside the Dying Fire." *The Walking Dead*, season 2, episode 13, AMC, 18 Mar. 2012.

"Better Angels." *The Walking Dead*, season 2, episode 12, AMC, 11 Mar. 2012.

Goodrich, Peter H. "The Lineage of Mad Scientists: Anti-Types of Merlin." *Dionysus in Literature: Essays on Literary Madness*, edited by Branimir M. Rieger, Green University Press, 1994, pp. 71–88.

Hanks, Patrick, and Flavia Hodges. *A Dictionary of First Names.* Oxford University Press, 1995

Jung, Carl G. *Encountering Jung: On Mythology*, edited by Robert A. Segal, Princeton University Press, 1998.

Kepler, Adam W. "For 'Walking Dead' Creator, It Takes a Novel to Explain What Spawned 'The Governor.'" *The New York Times*, 14 Oct. 2011, archive.ny times.com/artsbeat.blogs.nytimes.com/2011/10/14/for-walking-dead-creat or-it-takes-a-novel-to-explain-what-spawned-the-governor/.

King, Stephen. *On Writing: A Memoir of the Craft*. Pocket Books, 2002.

Lovecraft, H. P. "Herbert West — Reanimator." *The Complete Works of H. P. Lovecraft*, Kindle ed., Sanage Publishing, 2021.

——. *Supernatural Horror in Literature*. Dover Publications, 1973.

"Not Tomorrow Yet." *The Walking Dead*, season 6, episode 12, AMC, 15 Mar. 2016.

Segal, Robert A. Introduction. *Encountering Jung: Jung on Mythology*, by Carl G. Jung, Princeton University Press, 1998, pp. 3–45.

Shelley, Mary. *Frankenstein*. Kindle ed., HarperCollins Publishers, 2010.

Stevenson, Robert Louis. *The Strange Case of Dr. Jekyll and Mr. Hyde*. Kindle ed., Grapevine India, 2018.

Syed, Moin et al. "Master Narratives, Ethics, and Morality." *The Oxford Handbook of Moral Development: An Interdisciplinary Perspective*, edited by Lene Arnett Jensen, Oxford University Press, 2020, pp. 500-15.

The Epic of Gilgamesh. Translated by Andrew George, Penguin Classics, 1999.

The Holy Bible: The New King James Version. Thomas Nelson, 1982.

Tropp, Martin. "The Monster." *Mary Shelley's Frankenstein*, edited by Harold Bloom, Updated ed., Infobase Publishing, 2007, pp. 13–28.

Verne, Jules. *Castle of the Carpathians with a Critical Introduction by Ace G. Pilkington*. Kindle ed., Forest Tsar Press, 2010.

"Victor." *Merriam-Webster.com Dictionary*, 2023, www.merriamwebster.com/dictionary/ victor. Accessed 24 Oct. 2023.

Wells, H. G. *The Island of Dr. Moreau*. Kindle ed., OPU, 2018.

"What Comes After." *The Walking Dead*, season 9, episode 5, AMC, 4 Nov. 2018

Chapter 4

Conjured Others and Exorcized Bodies: Reimagining the Horror of Possession in Alice Sola Kim's "Mothers Lock Up Your Daughters Because They Are Terrifying"

Melissa Eriko Poulsen

Abstract

This chapter argues that Alice Sola Kim's short story, "Mothers, Lock Up Your Daughters Because They Are Terrifying," deploys the genre of horror in order to elucidate the experiences of transracial Korean adoptees. Resignifying common horror tropes and narratives of demonic possession, the story draws attention to adoptee experiences of dislocation against the backdrop of Asian American women's hypersexualization in popular culture. Kim's work thus brings race, gender, and sexuality to the forefront, using horror tropes to both estrange and refocus representations of Asian American women and transracial Korean adoptees. In doing so, "Mothers" breathes new life and possibilities into the genre, becoming emblematic of recent horror writing that refracts traditional conventions in order to draw attention to racialized and gendered representations—and question the potential of and paths for self-determination and agency.

Keywords: Asian American literature, transnational Korean adoption, Asian American women, exorcism

* * *

At the beginning of Alice Sola Kim's short story, "Mothers, Lock Up Your Daughters Because They Are Terrifying" (referred to henceforth as "Mothers"), three teenage girls attempt to summon the souls of their dead mothers in a Staples parking lot using an X-Acto knife, lard, and a spell pulled up on their phones. Caroline, Mini, and Ronnie are deceptively irreverent about summoning the dead, egging each other on after weeks of half-serious discussion, cobbling together supplies from around their houses, and declaring the whole idea dumb when no motherly spirits appear. Their seemingly failed summoning—and all that comes after—is a familiar enactment of horror tropes, from guileless teens who flirt with the occult in eerie settings to grotesquely contorted bodies and lurking demons. Yet the clichéd tale of possession by a vengeful spirit who calls herself Mom is nonetheless chilling.

Locating Kim's story within a larger collection of twenty-first-century U.S. horror writing and reading it through the lens of Asian American racialization and transnational adoption histories in the United States, this chapter will analyze how "Mothers" unexpectedly deploys the genre of horror in order to elucidate experiences of transnational, transracial Korean adoptees. By resignifying common horror tropes and narratives of demonic possession, the story draws attention to adoptee experiences of dislocation against the backdrop of the racialization and hypersexualization of Asian American women in popular culture. As "Mothers" traces the effect of possession on each girl—including the transformation of their relationships with their adopted families and the dissolution of their friendships with each other—the story invites readers to grapple with the true terrors at its heart. Kim's work thus brings race, gender, and family to the forefront, using horror tropes to both estrange and refocus representations of Asian American women and transnational Korean adoptees.

In doing so, "Mothers" joins the proliferation of horror texts in our current moment, a so-called new "golden age" of horror (Shapiro and Storey 10).[1] Responding to the unsettling and horrific realities of our contemporary moment— where the international struggles of war, disease, and climate change are met with the domestic struggles of political and economic polarization, increasingly vocalized hate rhetoric, and ongoing violence against people of color— contemporary horror texts express, question, and sometimes transform these realities. Authors and artists, from Jordan Peele in film to Carmen Maria Machado in literature to Marjorie Liu in comics, create horror as a form of critique and resistance.[2] Kim's work—of which screen rights were acquired in 2018 (Fleming)—is demonstrative of this ongoing trend, offering a fascinating case study of the genre's transformative potential *and* its limitations.

Possessed Adoptees

"Mothers" follows transnational adoptees Caroline, Mini, and Ronnie on a teenage romp with the occult. The girls initially meet at a Korean adoptee event

---

[1] Shapiro and Storey's introduction to *The Cambridge Companion to American Horror* offers a helpful historicization of contemporary horror, tracing its distinctive traits as well as its continuity with earlier American horror. Russell Meeuf, in *White Terror: The Horror Film from Obama to Trump*, pp. 3-4, summarizes a bevy of popular culture proclamations that we have entered a horror golden age.

[2] See, for example, Jordan Peele's *Get Out* (2017); Carmen Maria Machado's *Her Body and Other Parties*; and Marjorie Liu and Sana Takeda's *Monstress* series.

and, despite their very different personalities, bond over their experiences as transnational, transracial adoptees in the United States. The girls unite over the struggle to find belonging with their adoptive families: Caroline contorts herself for parents who expect a high-achieving, stereotypically feminine daughter; Mini rebels to hide her dismay at her parents' looming divorce and what that means for her place in the family; and Ronnie agonizes over her sexual attraction to her adoptive brother, Alex. The girls' desire for a more secure and clear sense of familial belonging comes to a head when Mini finds a spell to summon the ghosts of their presumably dead Korean mothers. Instead of their mothers, they summon a spirit that calls itself "Mom" and inhabits each of their bodies in ongoing rotation. While Ronnie resists possession because she fears, Mom will discover her incestuous relationship with Alex, Caroline and Mini grow to appreciate Mom's performance of "motherly" duties—feeding, praising, beautifying, and occasionally harshly criticizing her daughters. Mom, for example, sings a lullaby in Korean to Caroline and helps her finally dance ballet with grace and poise; she coaxes Mini, prone to eating frozen egg rolls and Jell-O, to cook a nourishing meal brimming with vegetables. For a while, Mom gives Caroline and Mini the attention and care they desire. However, when Mom discovers the messy realities of her "daughters"—not only Ronnie's affair with her brother but also the teenage rebellion, adolescent impulses, and budding sexuality of all three—she threatens to kill them. To save Caroline and Mini, Ronnie sacrifices herself, inviting Mom to permanently share her body. By the end of the story, Ronnie remains possessed, and all three girls have drifted apart.

Alongside contemporary progressive horror, "Mothers" is fruitfully read as part of a growing collection of Asian American horror texts, a subset of Asian American cultural production that has yet to be fully examined.[3] Much like the genre as a whole, Asian American horror writing is currently proliferating. In addition to Kim, a recipient of the 2016 Whiting Award who has published several well-regarded speculative short stories, including the oft-discussed "Hwang's Billion Brilliant Daughters," writers like Angela Yuriko Smith, Alma Katsu, and Julie Kagawa, along with filmmakers like Karen Kusama and Iris Shim, all explore Asian American horror. These creators, in turn, are part of a long tradition of ghostly, haunting presences in Asian American literature, perhaps most famously featured in texts ranging from Maxine Hong Kingston's *The Woman Warrior* to Lan Samantha Chang's *Hunger* to Shawna Yang Ryan's *Water Ghosts*. While the focus of this chapter is not to define or theorize Asian American horror, the subgenre should be distinguished from the more frequently discussed and commercially-popular category of Asian horror. This

---

[3] See Stephen Hong Sohn's 'Defining and Exploring Asian American Speculative Fiction" for an initial exploration of horror in Asian American literature.

does not foreclose the possibility of interconnections and overlap but instead emphasizes Asian American horror as grounded in the specific histories of Asians in the United States, even as that reading necessarily considers U.S. imperial presence in Asia. "Mothers," for example, can be read in the context of transnational Korean adoption and U.S. militarization in Korea, as well as the racialization of Asian American women in the United States.

While ostensibly centered around the demonic possession of Ronnie, Mini, and Caroline, the catalysts for that possession—indeed, for the girls' friendship at all—are their experiences as transnational and transracial adoptees. Though often framed as a twentieth-century emergence so it "parallels movements toward racial integration in the United States" (Jerng xxxvi), transracial adoption has a longer history in the United States, particularly during the "large-scale national traumas…[of] Native American removal; slavery and emancipation; the height of Jim Crow/segregation; and the Korean and Vietnam wars" (xii). Early examples of transracial adoption include the "forcible removal of children from Native American reservations" as well as "early twentieth century Catholic Charities' placing of Irish orphans from the New York Foundling Hospital with Mexican mineworker families" (Jerng 103). In these and other historical cases, orphaned children were not always voluntarily placed with adoptive families.

Transracial adoption became more formalized—and codified as humanitarian— in the mid-twentieth century with the advent of modern transnational adoption. After the Korean War, international charities began facilitating the adoption of South Korean children by primarily white families in the United States, Western Europe, Canada, and Australia. Several major adoption "operations" quickly followed, including the long-running Hong Kong Project from the 1950s-1960s, Operation Pedro Pan in Cuba in the early 1960s, and Operation Babylift in Vietnam in 1975.[4] A formalized network of transnational adoption from additional nations, including China, India, and the Philippines, emerged throughout the second half of the twentieth century, most often modeled after what had been established in South Korea (Choy, "Adoption" 7). These adoptions from non-white sending nations to Western receiving nations were understood as humanitarian and were frequently closed, proxy, and/or social adoptions.[5]

---

[4] See, for example, Jenny Heijun Wills's "Asian North American Adoption Narratives" for discussion of Operation Babylift and Catherine Ceniza Choy's *Global Families: A History of Asian International Adoption in America* for discussion of the Hong Kong Project.
[5] Wills discusses the view of transnational adoption as humanitarian. For histories of closed, proxy, and social Korean transnational adoption, see examples in Choy's *Global Families* as well as Deann Borshay Liem's *Geographies of Kinship*.

In one reading, "Mothers" activates horror tropes to draw attention to the underlying horror of the normalized structures of transnational adoption. At its heart, "Mothers" is a search narrative gone wrong. Search narratives, stories about seeking one's biological family, are necessitated by the initial institutionalization of closed transnational adoptions.[6] The idea of children going to the extremes of summoning to find mothers who might not even be dead emphasizes the damage of such legal and familial silences. The whole-hearted embrace of and longing for Mom—"a ghost that couldn't even tell different Asian girls apart to recognize its own daughter' (Kim 26), a ghost who claims them each as "THE MOST BEAUTIFUL GIRL IN THE WORLD" (19)—echoes the early practice of proxy adoptions while also countering celebratory narratives of adoptee rescue and assimilation as it reveals the depths of the girls' desire for a semblance of familial belonging.

Simultaneously, writing a search narrative through demonic possession allows readers to viscerally experience the way the girls become racialized Others and sexualized objects as adoptees. Stories of demonic possession—which more often than not center on possessed girls—dwell in the increasingly shocking (if generically predictable) sexualized behavior of the possessed.[7] They revel in imagining a perceived innocent whose deviance can be blamed on a demon, and their shock and catharsis lie in the questioning and eventual triumph of heteropatriarchal institutions usually represented by a priest.[8] "Mothers" uses these aspects of possession narratives to instead trace the failures and fallibilities of these institutions as well as the lasting impact they leave on Caroline, Mini, and Ronnie.

To this end, Kim's reliance on horror tropes long before Mom's arrival frames the girls' institutional experiences as horrific. Caroline, Mini, and Ronnie find themselves in a horror story from the moment they meet each other at an event meant to bring together Korean adoptees. This meeting is described as a site of terror, taking place at "a low-ceilinged…community center" that is "catered with the stinkiest food possible," including "a giant cut-glass bowl full of kimchi" that "emitted a vinegar-poop-death stench" and "looked exactly like a big wet pile

---

[6] See Jerng and Wills for further discussion of the prevalence of search narratives in adoptee literature as a result of closed adoptions.

[7] Many scholars have observed the tendency for possession narratives to focus on possessed women and girls who are saved by a male exorcist; see, for example, Carol Clover's *Men, Women, and Chain Saws: Gender in the Modern Horror Film*; Barbara Creed's *The Monstrous-Feminine: Film, Feminism, Psychoanalysis*; and Russell Meeuf's *White Terror: The Horror Film from Obama to Trump*.

[8] See Meeuf, who explores this *and* the recent shift in possession films of the exorcist "reject[ing] official knowledge and institutions in order to reclaim patriarchal authority" (80).

of fresh guts" (12-13). The proliferation of eerie, grotesque descriptions transforms an event ostensibly created to give adoptees a sense of shared identity via Korean culture into a place that, in typical horror stories, readers would futilely tell protagonists *not* to enter. Kim's use of generic conventions highlights the violence Caroline, Mini, and Ronnie experience as they are expected to identify with the notion of Korean and adoptee identity presented at this event they have been forced to attend. For example, the description of Korean food as abject and the intimation of cannibalism capture the experience of being perceived as the Other through the reminder of the historical tendency to label Asian food as abnormal *and* how often people of color have been cast as the "monster" in horror stories.

"Mothers" then uses the language of demonic possession to consider how the required event has stripped the girls of their agency. Though still weeks from summoning Mom, both Ronnie and Mini appear physically inhabited. Resentful of having to make friends and feeling socially awkward, Ronnie "experience[s] split consciousness" (Kim 13). Meanwhile, Mini imagines telling her "real" friends about the party later, so she appears possessed or haunted as she "smiles [s] condescendingly at an imaginary person to her left" (14). The potential interpretations of these moments of possession are many: a comment on parental control, a comment on the social expectations we place on teenage girls, and a comment on the assumptions about culture and identity on which these events rest. Perhaps most prominently, however, is its comment on internalized racism.

The girls' internalized racism, suggested even in their collective narration of the food, comes to a head when Caroline tells Mini and Ronnie a racist joke about Koreans. Their reaction, rendered through the imagery of demonic possession, suggests that such racism is a form of possession, a stripping away of one's sense of self. All three girls lose bodily control in this moment, passing "alarmingly substantial" burps and gas so loud "it was like the fart had bent [Caroline], had then jet-packed her into the air and crumpled her into the ground" (Kim 14). They then begin "puking laughter," which is described as "a thick brambly painful rope being pulled out of their faces" (14). Though no demon possesses the girls yet, they are already performing the bodily deviance of exorcism stories. Their bodies—their identities—are not their own in the confluence of self-othering, enforced community, and assumed heritage evoked by the adoptee event. The joke, the racism, is the demon ravaging their bodies.

These scenes of possession at the party also reveal that the girls have learned to see *themselves* as demons. Ronnie imagines herself, for example, as "the sole foreign element and corrupting influence in this household of Scandinavian blondes" (Kim 25). The girls collectively recount something like demonic possession when they look at themselves in a photo or a mirror and see "someone else…kapow boom sizzle, you got slapped upside the head with the Korean wand" (15). Such moments of identification and disidentification are the result of being constantly surrounded by their white family and friends in a society that privileges whiteness. While this experience is eventually paralleled to demonic possession—in one scene with Mom, Mini notices her reflection in unset Jell-O and sees "the face of another" who "was on Mini, made up of the Mini material but everything tweaked and adjusted" (23)—Mom is merely reenacting the differences, the othering and self-othering, the girls already experience.

Possessed Daughters

Alongside a consideration of racialized identity, possession tropes in "Mothers" highlight the revealing but under-discussed aspect of gender in transnational Korean adoption. Kim's story draws upon the tradition of using possession narratives to police female sexuality and pathologize female coming of age. As Barbara Creed famously traces in her analysis of *The Exorcist* (1973), the horror of demonic possession arises because the possessed "woman has broken with her proper feminine role. .[and] put her unsocialized body on display" (42). Horror deepens because this reveals "the inability of the male order to control the woman whose perversity is expressed through her rebellious body" (Creed 34). "Mothers" uses this familiar aspect of demonic possession to trace the ways Caroline, Mini, and Ronnie become disciplined, socialized Asian American women rather than unruly girls laughing uncontrollably in public at each other's jokes and bodily functions.

Kim writes the body horror typical of demonic possession to highlight the horror of the girls' adoptive families' insistence upon cisgender, heteropatriarchal sexuality. In one instance, Mom's invasion of Caroline's body appears to cause aches "from [Caroline's] toenails to her temples" (20). These aches, however, are revealed as preexisting muscle pain from the ballet Caroline's parents force on her, including the summer "pointe intensive that made her feet twinge like loose teeth" (20). Caroline's parents are willing to ignore their daughter's pain not because they like ballet but because they believe ballet will ensure their daughter will "be skinny and not a lesbian" (20). They are as guilty as Mom in seeking to control Caroline's body, and their form of possession *also* results in bodily pain and transformation.

In a departure from typical iterations of possession narratives, where the demon revels in the aberrant, Mom aligns with the girls' adoptive parents and wants them to conform. Mom helps Caroline dance beautifully, "arranging her daughter like a flower, a sleek and sinuous flower that would be admired until it died and even afterward" (Kim 21) and sets the girls' hair while they sleep in "complicated little tiny braids" (24). Mom later asserts that she and Ronnie "are every magazine clipping on how to charm and beautify, the tickle of mascara wand on a tear duct, the burn of a waxed armpit" (31). The terrifying language in each of these examples—the objectification, the death, the admiration of a corpse, the burns, the non-consensual alteration of the body—renders the beauty rituals passed from mothers to daughters, the "socialized" female body as horrific. Mom's departure from other demonic possessors lays bare the way stories of possession are most often used to punish blossoming daughters and their wayward mothers in order to reinvigorate and empower aging fathers.

The focus on beauty and female sexuality in "Mothers," however, is particularized, drawing attention to the role of Asian women in U.S. society and under U.S. imperialism—including the interrelated, under-analyzed aspect of gender in transnational Asian adoption. Asian women in U.S. popular culture are often hypersexualized as either the passive, subservient china doll/lotus blossom or the sexually aggressive, dangerous dragon lady.[9] Mom's molding of Caroline into a "sleek and sinuous flower" recalls the objectification of Asian women for (white) men's viewing pleasure; the "true terror" of Ronnie's multidimensional beauty after she merges with the demon recalls the titillating danger of the dragon lady (Kim 21, 31). Yet Mom's horror at any *actual* sexual acts—the way Mom condemns Caroline for her sexual thoughts and Ronnie for her incestuous relationship (26-27)—echoes the seemingly contradictory perception of East Asian women in the United States as maternal model minorities. Though long enforced through immigration laws that preferenced female East Asian immigrants as wives and mothers, East Asian women became understood as potential saviors of the nuclear family and traditional gender roles during and after the Cold War when the American family was perceived as under threat from working white mothers on the one hand and single Black motherhood on the other.[10] Mom's possession of the girls and Kim's revision of possession conventions highlight the gendered and racialized expectations that Caroline, Mini, and Ronnie face as they mature.

Kim's focus on the girls' transformations from adopted children to sexualized Asian American women also brings a different lens to transnational adoption. Because most transnational adoptees are girls, some scholars argue we must understand adoption in a larger market of Asian female bodies. Notably,

---

[9] Many scholars have discussed these portrayals; see, for example, Deborah Gee's documentary *Slaying the Dragon* (1988) and its update, Elaine H. Kim's *Slaying the Dragon: Reloaded* (2011), as well as Celine Parreñas Shimizu's *The Hypersexuality of Race: Performing Asian/American Women on Screen and Scene.*
[10] See Pamela Thoma's discussion of the maternal model minority in *Asian American Women's Popular Literature*; see Koshy's *Sexual Naturalization*, Marchetti's *Romance and the Yellow Peril*, and Nishime's *Undercover Asian* for more discussion of the triangulation of Asian American, white, and Black motherhood.

transnational Korean adoption began at the same time as "the historical emergence of war brides, mail-order brides, comfort women, and sex workers" because of the U.S. military presence in Asia (Eng 105). These seemingly different characterizations of Asian women demonstrate both the idealized sexuality of the domesticated maternal model minority *and* the hyper-sexualization of the extraterritorial China doll/lotus blossom and dragon lady. Both bride and sex worker reveal "the commodification of Third World female bodies for First World male consumption and pleasure" (Eng 105). Ignoring this "historical and economic legacy…obscures an understanding of [transnational adoption] as one of the more recent embodiments of gendered commodification" (Eng 105). Just as—or perhaps because—East Asian women have been used to shore up the heteropatriarchal nuclear U.S. family in the second half of the twentieth century, so too do transnational Korean adoptees "consolidate the *affective* boundaries of the white, heteronormative middle-class nuclear family" (Eng 109) faced with declining birth rates and a dearth of white children (Choy, "Adoption" 8; Eng 108). Attending to this history, then, reveals the adoptees' labor and gendered racialization within the family. Ronnie's affair with her adoptive brother becomes a particularly apt demonstration of this. The affair, seen by Mom, Ronnie herself, and potentially readers as deviant because it is incestuous or, conversely, because it is a reminder of difference, surfaces the occluded histories of war, imperialism, and Asian women's commodification. By activating horror tropes alongside (but not always simultaneously with) a story of demonic possession, "Mothers" draws attention to these less frequently voiced, even rejected narratives about transnational adoption.

Narrating Transnational Adoption

Exploring Caroline, Mini, and Ronnie's experiences through horror thus offers a significant and revealing intervention in the kinds of stories told about transnational Korean adoption. Transnational adoptees have so often been the objects of discussion, written about by adoption organizations and adoptive parents as a way to frame a positive narrative of humanitarian relief and successful adoptee assimilation.[11] These accounts avoid considering the role of U.S. militarism in transnational adoption, including the booming, exploitative sex trade as it met the stigmatization of single mothers.[12] More recently, they

---

[11] See works including Wills's "Asian American Adoption Narratives" and Soojin Pate's *From Orphan to Adoptee: U.S. Empire and Genealogies of Korean Adoption* for further discussion of these two strands of discourse.

[12] See Choy (*Global Families*), Jerng, Pate, Wills, and Eng for further discussion of how militarism in Asia created the conditions for transnational adoption.

have been supplemented by stories told by transnational adoptees representing their own experiences and often questioning the accounts of their parents and adoption charities.[13]

"Mothers" joins such narratives by using horror to surface what is often silenced in celebratory accounts of transnational adoption. The specific choice of demonic possession also emphasizes the strain *between* celebratory stories told about adoption and the more nuanced stories told by adoptees themselves. For example, when Ronnie resists Mom's invasion of her body, the demon uses a familiar parental refrain, albeit usually indicating a different kind of privacy invasion that insists on the authority of the parent and the parent's "right" to define the child's life: "I Am Going To Knock First—...And Then I'm Coming In" (Kim 25). Even Mom's penchant for speaking first loudly in all-caps and then, after the girls' request, just with first letters capitalized, emphasizes the primacy of the parent: the demon's words are *all* capitalized as if they were proper nouns or the first word of a sentence. Similarly, when Mom speaks through the girls, their jaws become unusable; their self-expression is prevented by Mom's need to be heard.[14] Here, the supernatural reflects the actual as the girls find themselves restricting their self-expression around their adoptive parents because of their status as adopted daughters. The story describes how they morph into "perfect and PG-rated" daughters, "never asking for anything, never complaining" (19) so that they might "earn [their] places in [their] homes" (12). Both Mom's bodily invasion and the self-censorship the girls engage in embodies the tension between the narratives told about transnational adoption—as represented by Mom and by the parental expectations assumed by Caroline, Mini, and Ronnie—and those told by Korean adoptees, as represented when Caroline, Mini, and Ronnie reflect on their own experiences.

Arguably, however, the text is more invested in drawing attention to the difficult positionality of adoptees and adoptive parents than in demonizing either or both. The differences in the discussions of adoption reflect "the competing demands for recognition made by parents and children on each other," especially as adoptive parents' constructions of themselves as parents meet the adopted child's sense of self (Jerng 171-73). This is demonstrated by the tug and pull of possession. The way the girls call Mom into being and (mostly) willingly allow the spirit to inhabit their bodies reminds readers of the complicated process of identification. Individuals "are constructed, legitimized, and regulated through different acts of claiming, attachments, and demands" (Jerng xxi-xxii). As a result, narrating one's identity is not about simply "communicat[ing] 'my story' to another, as in some reciprocal exchange...[but] is marked by what you demand

[13] See Wills and Jerng for further discussion of texts written by transnational adoptees.
[14] For example scenes of the slack jaw, see Kim, 18, 23, and 28.

of me, what I project onto you, what we desire of each other, in the act of narration" (Jerng 179). "Mothers" activates demonic possession to underscore this relationality, simultaneously problematizing and embracing the process of co-creation, while its ongoing illustration of racial othering and gendered objectification emphasizes how this co-creation takes place in a larger context.

Reimagining Horror

The complex engagement with transnational adoption stories in "Mothers," of course, only becomes visible *because* of audience fluency in the language of horror stories—*because* horror relies on generic conventions. Possession narratives beginning with *The Exorcist* and extending into the present are about the deviant behavior of the possessed, blamed on the possessor; they feature demons who challenge religious mores in grotesque, unsettling ways; and, while shifting with some more recent texts, they center fathers—both religious and biological—who tame and recover unruly daughters. Readers understand the impact of "Mothers" because of its reversals of these expectations: a *possessor* who insists on heteropatriarchal constructions of womanhood and policed female sexuality in a story essentially devoid of father figures. Again, "Mothers" here is demonstrative, rather than unique, in its reversals, pointing to one reason why horror might be, to use the words of film critic Justin Chang, "the signature genre of the present moment."

Contemporary American horror, though, is merely part of a much longer U.S. tradition of deploying fictional horror to express real-life horror. The history of the United States is shadowed by the "American Nightmare" (Stephen and Storey 9)—the violent realities of "American exceptionalism and the social and environmental consequences of its imperialist projects" (Huang 169). Articulations of fictional horror in the United States have thus tended to center on "Atlantic slavery and its residues; Native American dispossession and genocide; violent conflict (both rural and urban) over class, immigration, and rights; and matters of gender, sexuality, and ability" (Shapiro and Storey 9). Past and present horror writing, of course, does not always offer critique of or resistance to the ideologies undergirding the American Nightmare. Horror frequently bolsters "the core fear of the powerful: that Others are lurking around every corner, attempting to dismantle traditional institutions" (Meeuf 5). Horror reinforces *and* subverts, questions *and* affirms, often simultaneously.

Initially published by *Tin House* in 2014 and anthologized in Rowan Hisayo Buchanan's *Go Home!* in 2018, "Mothers" demonstrates this vacillation and ambiguity. The story's publication history spans two distinctive periods of twenty-first-century horror. "Mothers" was written during the Obama administration, a time when mainstream horror films—if not other textual forms of horror—tended to dwell on "the anxieties of White Americans struggling with a perceived loss of social and economic standing in a post-recession America overseen by a Black president" (Meeuf 5).[15] Exorcism films, in particular, increased drastically and were often revised from the 1970s tradition initiated by *The Exorcist* to express the (white male) desire in the late aughts and early 2010s to "reject official knowledge and institutions in order to reclaim patriarchal authority" (Meeuf 80).[16] By the time "Mothers" was anthologized, though, the Trump era had ushered in a wave of economically successful horror films that "tackled issues of race, social justice, and the corruption of the powerful…[taking] the horror genre in sometimes radical new directions" (Meeuf 179).[17] "Mothers," then, is both part of the Obama era increase in often reactionary exorcism texts *and* of the Trump era's mainstream embrace of more progressive horror narratives.

A close reading of "Mothers," however, reveals the text's refusal to produce static meaning and clear messages. Kim's work *resists* interpretation in important ways. The story's full title—"Mothers Lock Up Your Daughters Because They Are Terrifying"—is a case in point. Which mothers? Biological, adoptive, demonic, readers? Which daughters? Caroline, Mini, and/or Ronnie, the demon (maybe someone's daughter, at some point), adoptive mother, or the reader? And where, as suggested by the story of possession, does a mother end and a daughter begin? "Mothers" deepens these questions and the resulting resistance to interpretation through the use of pronouns in its final paragraphs. The story moves from the assumed collective "we" of Caroline, Mini, and Ronnie to instead introduce the "I" and "her" of Ronnie, the "they" of Caroline and Mini, and the "we" of Mom/Ronnie. This sudden shift in perspectives is a formal enactment of possession, inviting the reader to consider who has been narrating the story. Rather than from the perspective of the girls, "Mothers" is instead told from the perspective of Mom/Ronnie. Yet the final three sentences of the story resist even that interpretation: "We both felt a moment of regret. She once loved them too, you know. Then her mother turned our head and we walked away" (Kim 31). Every attempt to understand the subject of these sentences is foiled; if "we" is Mom/Ronnie, then who is "her mother"? If "we" is Caroline and Mini, are they also the "them" of the next sentence? Is the "she" who has forsaken whoever "they" are Ronnie or Mom or Caroline or Mini? Or perhaps a biological or adoptive mother?

---

[15] Examples of horror films during this time include *Halloween* (2007) and *Insidious* (2010). For discussions of the most common types of horror film during this period, see Meeuf, p. 17.

[16] Examples of exorcist films during Barack Obama's presidency, as explored by Meeuf, include *The Last Exorcism* (2010) and *The Possession* (2012).

[17] Meeuf points to transformative *and* profitable media including the television series *The Terror: Infamy* (2019) and *Lovecraft Country* (2020), pp. 179-81.

In one reading, this ambiguity plays upon a typical interpretation of adoptee identity. Adoptee search narratives, as well as contemporary discussions of transnational, transracial adoption, frequently end by "emphasiz[ing] the inability to locate oneself within a specific national or racial framework" before "valorizing the necessity to reconcile these differences and to 'embrace both'" (Jerng xxxvii). "Mothers" enacts these conclusions uneasily, embracing "both" through demonic possession and the final use of pronouns. A simplistic reading might see Ronnie's merging with Mom as pathologizing the desire for multiple identifications. Yet "Mothers" also emphasizes how Ronnie's merging with Mom is empowering, helping her feel guided and focused while giving her the confidence to stand up to the sexual advances of her brother. Ronnie is otherworldly, almost divine, because of Mom, and as a result, becomes dazzlingly popular and a source of "true terror" (Kim 31). This, of course, comes at a clear cost—not only of sharing consciousness and body but of adopting damaging societal standards of beauty, isolating herself from her adoptive parents, and rejecting old friends.

As a result, "Mothers" refuses any specific outcome of embracing both, celebratory or otherwise—just as its narrative refuses to valorize or demonize the stories told by adoptive parents or adoptive children. Instead, the text dwells on indeterminacy and resists the trap of dichotomies. Often, the rhetoric of "embracing both" is framed through "understandings of identity formation within adoption as a profoundly personal struggle to reconcile extreme differences" (Jerng xxxviii). Such thinking proliferates in—perhaps is even foundational to—discussions of adoption as "the language of choice and free will, as well as the rhetoric of donation and gift…serve to cover up and cover over the inexorable disparities in a global system of gendered commodification and exchange that cannot be equalized" (Eng 106). "Mothers" thus comments on the valorization of individual action as a solution as it asks readers to question the apparently simple and teleological act of "embracing both" as well as its opposite, the pathologizing of multiple identifications. In the process, "Mothers" begins to suggest the important work of horror in our contemporary moment.

In their consideration of American horror, Shapiro and Storey suggest that horror's "intellectual sidelining," even in a moment of increased popularity, is due in part to "its resistance to institutionalized protocols of interpretation" (5). Horror readily offers up a seemingly simplistic meaning *or* holds no clear meaning at all. Its reliance on consistent tropes to the point of cliché compounds and illustrates—rather than contradicts—this problem of interpretation: the legibility of demonic possession, violated bodies, eerie spaces, and more to an audience fluent in the language of horror hold obvious, already-known meaning and therefore, to an extent, becomes devoid of meaning. Yet this resistance to interpretation might also be one of the genre's strongest suits—and one of the reasons it can be so transformative.

Certainly, a "new" horror can and is using the old to reveal what has too often been obscured, what we've allowed to become the quotidian.[18] But, perhaps more crucially, in a moment of such extreme polarization, a new horror will resist and foil our attempts at interpretation, meaning, and certainty. Kim's "Mothers" is exemplary of this important work of horror and the centrality of generic conventions in performing that work. Even as readers are left terrified and disoriented by the story, the *illegibility* of Caroline, Mini, and Ronnie's legibility becomes a powerful, horrific testament to the difficult path of self-expression and agency when one is always also determined by others. In the end, horror's resistance to interpretation and certainty, to meaning and progress, is its ultimate terror and ultimate transformative power.

Works Cited

Borshay Liem, Deann. *Geographies of Kinship*. Mu Films et al., 2019.

Chang, Justin. "Has Horror Become the Movie Genre of the Trump Era?" *Los Angeles Times*, 13 Oct. 2017, www.latimes.com/entertainment/movies/la-ca-mn-horror-movies-trump-20171013-story.html. Accessed 27 Oct. 2023.

Chang, Lan Samantha. *Hunger*. W. W. Norton, 1998.

Choy, Catherine Ceniza. "Adoption." *Keywords for Asian American Studies*, edited by Cathy J. Schulund-Vials et al., New York University Press, 2015, pp. 7-13.

——. *Global Families: A History of Asian International Adoption in America*. New York University Press, 2013.

Clover, Carol. *Men, Women, and Chain Saws: Gender in the Modern Horror Film—Updated Edition*. Princeton University Press, 2015.

Creed, Barbara. *The Monstrous-Feminine: Film, Feminism, Psychoanalysis*. Routledge, 1993.

Eng, David. *The Feeling of Kinship: Queer Liberalism and the Racialization of Intimacy*. Duke University Press, 2010.

The Exorcist. Directed by William Friedkin, Warner Brothers, 1973.

Fleming, Ian, Jr.. "Fox 2000, 21 Laps Win Screen Auction to 'Mothers, Lock Up Your Daughters Because They Are Terrifying.'" *Deadline*, 10 Dec. 2018, deadline.com/2018/12/Fox-2000-21-laps-movie-auction-to-mothers-lock-up-your-daughters-because-they-are-terifying-1202517496/.

Get Out. Directed by Jordan Peele, Universal Pictures, 2017.

Green, Misha, creator. *Lovecraft Country*. Warner Bros. Television Studios et al., 2020.

Halloween. Directed by Rob Zombie, MGM Distribution Company, 2007.

Huang, Betsy. "SF and the Weird." *The Cambridge Companion to American Horror*, edited by Stephen Shapiro and Mark Storey, Cambridge University Press, 2022, pp. 169-82.

---

[18] See Dawn Keetley's discussion of "the monsters of normality" in "Monsters and Monstrosity," p. 191.

Insidious. Directed by James Wan, FilmDistrict, 2011.

Jerng, Mark C. *Claiming Others: Transracial Adoption and National Belonging*. University of Minnesota Press, 2010.

Keetley, Dawn. "Monsters and Monstrosity." *The Cambridge Companion to American Horror*, edited by Stephen Shapiro and Mark Storey, Cambridge University Press, 2022, pp. 183-97.

Kim, Alice Sola. "Hwang's Billion Brilliant Daughters." *Lightspeed*, Nov. 2010, www.lightspeedmagazine.com/fiction/hwangs-billion-brilliant-daughters/.

——. "Mothers, Lock Up Your Daughters Because They Are Terrifying." *Go Home!*, edited by Rowan Hisayo Buchanan, The Feminist Press, 2018, pp. 9-31.

Kingston, Maxine Hong *The Woman Warrior*. Alfred A. Knopf, 1976.

Koshy, Susan. *Sexual Naturalization: Asian Americans and Miscegenation*. Stanford UP, 2004.

The Last Exorcism. Directed by Daniel Stamm, Lionsgate, 2010.

Liu, Marjorie. *Monstress*. Illustrated by Sana Takeda, vol. 1-7, Image Comics, 2016-2022.

Machado, Carmen Maria. *Her Body and Other Parties*. Graywolf Press, 2017.

Marchetti, Gina. *Romance and the "Yellow Peril": Race, Sex, and Discursive Strategies in*
Hollywood Fiction. University of California Press, 1993.

Meeuf, Russell. *White Terror: The Horror Film from Obama to Trump*. Indiana University Press, 2022.

Nishime, LeiLani. *Undercover Asian: Multiracial Asian Americans in Visual Culture*. University of Illinois Press, 2014.

Pate, Soojin. *From Orphan to Adoptee: U.S. Empire and Genealogies of Korean Adoption*. University of Minnesota Press, 2014.

The Possession. Directed by Ole Bornedal, Lionsgate Films, 2012.

Ryan, Shawna Yang. *Water Ghosts*. Penguin, 2007.

Shapiro, Stephen, and Mark Storey. "American Horror: Genre & History." *The Cambridge Companion to American Horror*, edited by Stephen Shapiro and Mark Storey, Cambridge University Press, 2022, pp. 1-11.

Shimizu, Celine Parreñas. *The Hypersexuality of Race: Performing Asian/American Women on Screen and Scene*. Duke University Press, 2007.

Slaying the Dragon. Directed by Deobrah Gee, National Asian Women United, 1988.

Slaying the Dragon: Reloaded. Directed by Elaine H. Kim, Asian Women United of California, 2011.

Sohn, Stephen Hong. "Defining and Exploring Asian American Speculative Fiction." *The Oxford Encyclopedia of Asian American Literature and Culture*, edited by Josephine Lee, Oxford University Press, 2019.

Thoma, Pamela. *Asian American Women's Popular Literature: Feminizing Genres and Neoliberal Belonging*. Temple University Press, 2013.

Wills, Jenny Heijun. "Asian North American Adoption Narratives." *The Oxford Encyclopedia of Asian American Literature and Culture*, edited by Josephine Lee, Oxford University Press, 2018.

The Horror of Adolescence: Coming of Age Tropes in Horror Cinema

Andrew Wilczak

Abstract

Adolescence is one of the most tumultuous periods in the life course. Adolescents are marginalized; so-called "coming of age" stories exhibit this marginalization as characters navigate the many trials of this period of life—identity, emerging sexuality, puberty, delinquency, shifting relations with authority, etc. In horror, coming-of-age stories are especially powerful, arguably more so than non-horror or otherwise non-genre-related storytelling. Coming of age in horror presents the audience with an exaggerated view of the oppression young people experience daily, as the main characters in many of these films become responsible for saving themselves when none of the adults around them are willing or capable of supporting them. Coming-of-age horror and the tropes contained therein remain powerfully important tools for adolescents to see themselves in the world.

Keywords: adolescence, slasher films, life course, sociology

* * *

The Sociology of Adolescence

Horror cinema centered on the lives of adolescents—especially slasher films—may be among the most trope-ridden of the genre. Ultra-hormonal high school students in some isolated setting are picked off one by one by some unknown, unstoppable killing machine that seems to be targeting them strictly because of their age and vanishing innocence until the final survivor—usually a girl, often the least likely person from the cast to have the capacity for the levels of violence and physical resilience needed to survive—are still able to defy the odds and defeat the monster(s) attacking her. The tropes in these slasher films have become so pronounced that they have launched at least two iconic film franchises satirizing them—*Scream* (1996) and *Scary Movie* (2000)—while the newest generation of slasher screenwriters and directors continue to trade on these well-worn clichés

Drawing on the life course perspective in sociology developed by Glen Elder, Jr., the purpose of this chapter is to explore the continued utility of these tropes in adolescent-focused horror cinema. The continued presence of these tropes suggests they serve some purpose for the audience—what, then, is that purpose, and how does it relate to arguably the most tumultuous time in our social and biological development?

Defining Adolescence

Adolescence is a difficult stage to formally define and a relatively new concept. Susan Sawyer et al. outline the different chronological definitions of adolescence that have emerged over the last century, highlighting just how difficult it is to reach an agreed-upon definition of this stage in the life course. Adolescence as a stage in the life course is a result of child labor laws in the early twentieth century. Removing children from the workforce and putting them into a mandatory public education system carved out a new period in the life course. Adolescence is entirely socially constructed.

It is easy to think of adolescents as young people in their teenage years, but it is not always true that this specific age range means adolescence. For example, young people who are victimized may experience what some criminologists call an early exit from adolescence or a premature entry into adulthood (Haynie et al.). These young people may chronologically appear to be in the adolescent stage but have the roles, responsibilities, and behaviors of someone older. Second, there is the issue of brain development. The human brain is not fully developed until around 25 years old (Arain et al.). Further, the average age at first marriage in the U.S. is just over 30 years old for men and 28 years old for women ("Decennial Censuses"), while a high percentage of people in the 18-29 range still live at home (Napolitano) and may not be working full-time ("Employment Rate by Age Group").

Theoretical Perspective

The life course perspective is extraordinarily useful in understanding how horror tropes speak to adolescent development because no other sociological perspective so fully captures the complete adolescent picture. Elder identifies four main points to this perspective: lives in historical times, human agency, linked lives, and the timing of lives (5). Each relates to how time structures our lives—how it affects our perception of ourselves and the world around us, forcing us into a normative set of behaviors.

First, lives in historical times speak to time at a macro level. Each of us is affected by the circumstances of the era in which we live (Elder 5). For example, at the time of this writing, the world is still experiencing the aftershocks of the

Covid-19 pandemic. While this is not the first pandemic in human history, it is the first of the twenty-first century and the first in human history where much (but not all) of the world has access to instantaneous communication, allowing many people to compare and contrast the reaction of their government to the pandemic to others around the world. Beyond Covid-19, our lives today are undeniably affected by the cascading effects of climate change, the gradual decline of capitalism, neo-liberalism, the war in Ukraine, protests in the United States, China, and the Middle East, and so on.

Human agency refers to how we perceive the options available to us at any given time (Elder 6). This is especially important when considering adolescents, as they do not possess the same agency as adults. By definition, they have less life experience than adults and do not have fully developed brains; thus, their problem-solving abilities are not on the level of an adult.

Linked lives refer to the relationships we forge; the term considers how embedded and interconnected we become with others and how these relationships can have long-lasting effects, both positive and negative, over our individual lives and across generations (Elder 6). Like human agency, the idea of linked lives is vital to understanding what horror has to say about adolescent life.

Lastly, the timing of lives speaks to the multitude of transitions we make across the life course (Elder 3). The onset of puberty, for example, is a life course transition that everyone experiences but not necessarily at the same time. Conversely, high school graduation is a transition that happens to the majority of adolescents at the same time within a school and around the same time of year in any given society (i.e., in the United States, the overwhelming majority of high school students graduate in June).

Lives in Historical Times

The idea that we are all at the mercy of the historical epoch into which we are born does not necessarily have immediate or obvious application to horror tropes but is still worth exploring. Thinking of horror cinema broadly and those franchises that have spanned multiple decades, it is apparent how the horrors visited upon so many young people on screen may have been the result of the time in which they have lived. For example, the *Friday the 13th* films provide a number of excellent examples of experiences that may have felt normal to teen audiences at the time but do not necessarily apply to the lives of young people today, namely, being alone at summer camp without adult supervision, either through direct contact or through constant technological contact. The original *Halloween* revolves around Michael Myers preying on unguarded and unmonitored babysitters, who may also feel unfamiliar without the constant intrusion of technology.

The use of technology—and technological changes—is a central part of the *Scream* franchise which has allowed these films to remain relevant during the franchise's nearly 30-year existence. In the original, the Ghostface Killer taunts Sidney Prescott, played by Neve Campbell, and her friends by landline. In *Scream 2* (1997), Jada Pinkett Smith's character Maureen, while watching the in-universe retelling of the original movie retitled *Stab*, shouts in a movie theater that a character on the screen should use *69 to call the Ghostface Killer back to discover who he is. Today, landline telephones feel as archaic as a telegram to many young people, and the concept of using *69 to identify someone is a cultural artifact that feels increasingly anachronistic. In the recent *Scream* films, however, the widespread use of smartphone technology that has happened since the release of the original film has become a central part of the story. The most recent film as of this writing, *Scream 6* (2023), includes a scene where the Ghostface Killer calls Sam Carpenter using the number from the now-deceased killer from the previous film. This storytelling mechanism simply would not have been possible in 1996, and it speaks to how technological growth over nearly three decades has been incorporated into the story.

One way to think about life course is the timelessness of horror in general and of adolescent slashers in particular. In the larger scheme of things, *how* technology changes is not central to the story. That said, the ways writers and directors have been able to adapt the basic premise of these films across generations while the classic films maintain their position in the larger horror zeitgeist shows how timeless these stories really are.

Human Agency

On the subject of decision-making and linked lives, one of the most interesting ways the life course perspective applies to adolescent horror films is in terms of human agency. Human agency refers to the options people perceive as available at any given time. It is how we respond when faced with a problem: the ability to mentally run through the list of possible solutions, weigh the pros and cons of each, and then proceed with whatever we believe to be the best choice(s). For adolescents, human agency is tricky for a couple of reasons. Although adolescents are not necessarily incapable of making the same decisions or arriving at the same conclusions as adults, the paths they take to arrive at those conclusions may be more circuitous due to brain development. This is especially useful in storytelling and may contribute to the phenomenon of audience members yelling at the screen when the character—oftentimes in mortal danger—makes snap decisions that may not appear to make logical sense. Second, adolescents, by definition, lack the life experience of adults, so problems may feel monumentally larger to them, yet they do not possess the level of coping skills adults have.

The obvious trope around human agency is that characters in horror movies, especially ones that focus on young people, often make completely wrong decisions, and these mistakes often lead to their deaths—either immediately or in the long term. The film *Happy Death Day* (2017) is ripe with this trope. Jessica Rothe's character, Tree Gelbman, is stuck in a time loop where she repeatedly dies and comes back to life. Prior to Tree's realization that she cannot truly die, the ways she meets her demise fall into this "bad decision" trope: she doubles back into a tunnel where the killer awaits her, she hooks up with a sketchy guy at a frat party when the killer is waiting in his bedroom, etc. Ironically, it is her bad decision-making that ultimately leads her to find out who the killer is; she repeatedly rudely turns down a poisoned birthday cupcake from her secretly jealous roommate.

The agency—or lack thereof—exhibited by young people in films may seem ridiculous to adult audiences, but it reflects the adolescent decision-making process quite well. In *A Nightmare on Elm Street* (1984), Nancy Thompson, played by Heather Langenkamp, plans to go into her dreams to pull Freddy Kruger into the real world is ludicrous when spoken aloud. The idea is that she and Glen Lantz, played by Johnny Depp, will stay up late to fight Freddy from their separate bedrooms (as their parents have grounded them), and Glen will stay awake so he can call Nancy to wake her up on time, feels overly complicated and very dangerous. Clearly, the plan used by adults in later films (especially 2003's *Freddy vs Jason*) to medicate everyone so they can't dream while doing everything in their power to eradicate the legend of Freddy Krueger makes much more sense, at least from an adult perspective.

Linked Lives

The idea of linked lives refers to the various ways our individual decisions can affect people around us and how interconnected our lives truly are. In no other film series is the concept of linked lives more apparent than in *A Nightmare on Elm Street*. Arguably, the films do not exist without this concept. Through flashbacks across different films, the parents of Elm Street take it upon themselves to act as judge, jury, and executioners of accused pedophile Freddy Krueger, burning him alive in the school basement. The film (and its sequels and remake) brings us into Elm Street once their children are in late adolescence and Freddy is back from the dead, killing the teens of Elm Street in their dreams. The characters in *Nightmare* and its sequels are only in danger because of a decision their parents made collectively.

To continue the focus on Wes Craven, the *Scream* franchise also showcases the role of linked lives, arguably to the point of absurdity. With each successive *Scream* film, the ways the various Ghostface Killers related to either protagonists Sidney Prescott and Samantha Carpenter or to each other shows how the entire ordeal—so many people killed over the span of six films—was caused by the various toxic or codependent relationships people had with each other (with just a hint of sociopathy baked in). In the original film, Sidney is tormented by Billy and Stu, who take their inspiration from the horror films with which they're obsessed. In *Scream 2*, Billy's mother seeks revenge. In *Scream 3* (2000), it's her estranged half-brother; in *Scream 4* (2011), her jealous cousin. The ripple effects of Sidney's initial victimization spread further and further out as the films progress to the point where, even though she does not appear in *Scream 6*, having passed the torch on to Melissa Barrera's Sam Carpenter, we still hear that Sidney has gone into hiding in response to the most recent Ghostface Killer appearance. Even off-screen and away from the story, she's not safe because of how entrenched her life has become in this madness.

Admittedly, the application of linked lives to horror may be more of a sociological description rather than an exploration of any one particular trope. We all have a profound ability to make each other's lives better or worse at both the macro- or micro-level, in Earth-shattering ways or otherwise. In each of the aforementioned films, the engine of the plot is ignited by the choice made by one character. The Ghostface Killer murders Drew Barrymore's character, Casey and then chooses to hunt Sidney. Because Sidney chooses to fight back, the story progresses.

In the original *Halloween*, the hospital staff's inability to contain Michael Myers, coupled with Dr. Loomis's (debatable) incompetence regarding his patient, inexorably alters Jamie Lee Curtis's character Laurie Strode's entire life. Bad—though seemingly innocuous—decisions made by one person drag an entire community into chaos. Perhaps, then, there is a trope here so obvious that it is hiding in plain sight: a friend, parent, or neighbor makes one bad decision, and all hell breaks loose. This is something we can all relate to but is especially salient for young people whose lives often feel like hellish rollercoasters. The idea that one rash or impulsive decision can lead to the slaughter of their entire friend group is something that speaks to the lives of young people in a way that it does not for adults.

The Timing of Lives

Just as the life course perspective focuses on the role of time, several films follow the same protagonist(s) over a long period of time: the Sidney Prescotts, Laurie Strodes, Ellen Ripleys, Tommy Jarvises, and Nancy Thompsons of the world who are dealing with the same kind of violence over and over again. This may be our most cynical trope: just when our hero thinks they have survived the day, the great evil killing machine is back from the dead. What is the function of these sorts of long-form stories?

Violent victimization is brutally hard, especially in a culture that frequently expects victims to move on with their lives. In *Halloween: H2O* (1998), Laurie Strode, having survived the attack by Michael Myers in the original *Halloween* (1978), has changed her name to Keri Tate and becomes headmistress at a private school. Laurie/Keri is a barely functional alcoholic, the trauma she experienced in the first two *Halloween* films clearly having wreaked havoc on her life. In the reboot trilogy *Halloween* (2018), *Halloween Kills* (2021), and *Halloween Ends* (2022), Laurie, grizzled like a war vet, is hypervigilant for any signs of a threat to her family. In the *Scream* sequels, Sidney Prescott goes through her own transformations as a crisis hotline counselor for women in danger, as an author taking power back and telling her story in her own way, and finally (evidently) as a stay-at-home mom. Here, Sidney's reactions to her trauma are subtler than Laurie Strode's, but this doesn't make them any less realistic.

These sequels resonate with audiences because trauma is not something anyone can move on from immediately, and many people are haunted by the very real ghosts of their past for a long time. Victimization in adolescence can lead to a variety of negative outcomes in adulthood, including lower socioeconomic attainment (Macmillan), an onset of depressive symptoms, suicidality, substance use disorders (Haynie et al.), and risk of future offending behaviors (Lauritsen et al.). The gulf between Sidney's and Laurie's adaptations to their trauma speaks to the variety of ways victims of violence cope with it in the aftermath.

Transitioning to Independence

Of the life course transitions the majority of people experience, horror cinema involving adolescents focuses on the transition to independence above all else. This can include independence from parental/adult control and independence in terms of increased human agency. These transitions can be both terrifying and exhilarating for young people, making them ripe for adolescent horror films. Typically, this transition to independence is reflected on the screen as a conflict between our main character(s) and their parents, who are either absent, negligent, abusive, or just don't believe that their children are in any kind of danger. This conflict with authority at home represents the first step into independence and all that that represents, as our main character(s) must figure out a solution to their problem without any adult guidance.

One of the best examples of young people gaining independence from the authority figures in their lives happens in the original *A Nightmare on Elm Street*. Nancy Thompson must solve the mystery of Freddy Krueger as her friends are picked off by Freddy one by one. Nancy's father, a police lieutenant played by John Saxon, not only disbelieves Nancy's claim that Freddy is behind the murders but goes so far as to bar the windows and lock Nancy in, leaving her defenseless against Freddy's final attack. The complete refusal of Lt.

Thompson and the other adults to believe that Freddy is responsible for the terror being visited upon their children, while crucial to the narrative of the film, represents a larger problem adolescents face. The problems experienced by so many young people are frequently downplayed by the adults in their lives as trivial, unimportant, or just part of life. While this often ultimately proves to be true to young people at the moment, being told that a problem that feels all-consuming to them is just a trivial bump in the road can be immensely frustrating. Taken to the extreme—Nancy and her friends were being menaced by a serial killer in their dreams—and then to the same logical conclusions most parents would reach, creates a story that has resonated with generations of adolescent horror fans.

The use of this particular trope—parents downplaying and disbelieving their teens' concerns—was done so well by the original *Nightmare* that almost all of the sequels utilize it to varying degrees of success. Heather Langenkamp reprises her role as Nancy in *A Nightmare on Elm Street 3: Dream Warriors* (1987) as an intern on her way to becoming a therapist. She is the only adult directly in the lives of the new cast of teenage victims to truly grasp the severity of the situation, and she dies because of it. Again, while this works for the narrative of this particular sequel, the larger message—the one adult who truly understands the teens' problem dies—arguably speaks to the transition into adulthood we all make. Put differently, Nancy's death represents the crossing of the adolescence-to-adulthood bridge. She was an adult who cared. She shouldn't have.

A similar use of this trope is evident in the recent *Fear Street* trilogy (2021). Here, our core cast must navigate a crisis wherein they're being stalked by multiple monstrous serial killers simultaneously with minimal adult guidance. Our main characters never interact with their parents, lending to the archetype that they are lower- or working-class kids from the "bad" school left to raise themselves. The two adults with whom they *do* interact—a survivor of a previous attack and a police officer—are useless, as one is traumatized beyond repair, and the other is responsible for all of the violence in the first place.

Viewers see a twist on the disbelieving authority figures trope in the 1998 cult hit *The Faculty*. Here, the characters have to contend with the reality that the teachers and staff in their high school have been replaced by an invading alien species. The crisis in *The Faculty* represents not only a break with disbelieving pseudo-parental figures but with authority itself. Since the evil in *The Faculty* is coming directly from the faculty themselves, our heroes battling against them represent teenage rebellion. Similar to *A Nightmare on Elm Street*, the filmmakers took a traditional part of the life course—burgeoning independence from and rebellion against authority—and then dropped it into a horror film, taking it to its logical conclusion. Because rebellion against authority has become a ubiquitous part of adolescence, *The Faculty* remains a timeless and eternally relatable film for young people, so long as public education is mandatory. Where the premise of *The Faculty* really takes things to the next level is in the reveal that the source of the alien invasion is a new girl in class who has infiltrated the thrown-together friend group of main characters. Adolescent life in the late twentieth and early twenty-first century is often defined by rigid in-group and out-group dynamics, an intractable and impenetrable hierarchy that is the source of so much drama and discontent in their social lives; Peggy C. Giordano provides an example of this in "The Wider Circle of Friends in Adolescence." The facts that the characters allow the *new girl* into their group and that she is the source of the invasion speak to the realities of adolescent social dynamics.

Fear of Sexuality

One of the most popular tropes in slasher films of the 1970s and 1980s, especially through the *Friday the 13th* films, is that sexuality equals death; consequently, emerging sexuality is akin to having a death wish. Of all of the life course transitions young people make—first job, learning to drive, high school and potentially college graduation—their sexual debut is possibly rifest with tension, anxiety, and potential embarrassment. Boys in high school locker rooms are not posturing about how good they are at their first jobs or talking about how excited they are to one day pay income taxes for a reason.

The cult-classic *Jennifer's Body* (2009) takes on the "sex equals death" trope in a fascinating way, certainly one that makes it stand out among its peers. Megan Fox plays Jennifer, a version of the classic hyper-sexualized and aggressively-sexual high school girl. Jennifer and her best friend, Needy, played by Amanda Seyfried, go to a local bar to see an indie band playing. Jennifer wants to hook up with the lead singer, and after the bar accidentally burns down (such is small-town horror life), the band abducts Jennifer and leaves Needy behind. When Jennifer returns, she has taken on a monstrous form—and attitude. We learn that Jennifer has been possessed by a demon, that the band mistook her for a virgin and tried to sacrifice her to Satan. But, because she was no longer virginal, the ritual didn't work out exactly as planned. The intricacies and logic of the lore aside, the utility of *Jennifer's Body* is how aggressively sexual Jennifer is and how that translates to the broader adolescent fear and/or struggle with emerging sexuality. By contrast, Needy, a typical teenager in a sexually active monogamous relationship. is much more of a conformist than Jennifer. When boys in their school start turning up dead—brutally murdered, in fact—the discovery that Jennifer is behind it is too much for Needy to take. The power of *Jennifer's Body* is its willingness to engage with the trope that sex equals death and its choice to flip the trope on its head, making the killer a conventionally attractive woman and making all the victims men.

In the lexicon of horror films centered on the lives of young people, *Black Christmas* (1974) is either the most realistic or the least sensational. Here, sex isn't so much a central piece of the film as is its consequence: Jess, played by Olivia Hussey, is pregnant and wants to get an abortion. For context, *Black Christmas* was released one year after *Roe v. Wade* was passed, and access to abortion was legalized at the federal level. Here, sexuality is not an exploitative part of the film but rather presented in a very pragmatic, antiseptic way. That Jess is the survivor—possibly, anyway, given the twist at the end of the film—means that the single, pregnant young woman with intentions to abort her pregnancy is the hero of the film. The use of Jess's pregnancy as a central part of the human element of *Black Christmas*, along with displaying her conflict with her boyfriend, Peter, played by Keir Dullea, shows adolescent audiences an aspect of their fear around their own sexuality—the risk of pregnancy—in a much more realistic way than other films. Moreover, this is interesting in contrast to later films where the idea that sex equals death frames sexuality in terms of rampant promiscuity; here, Jess and Peter are a couple at a significant crossroads in their relationship. Unlike Jason Voorhees in the *Friday the 13th* series, the killer isn't targeting Jess because of her sexuality but because she is a woman in this particular sorority house. How this trope is deployed in the *Friday the 13th* films becomes part of the fun of the films, as evidenced by 2001's *Jason X*'s self-referential humor in a scene where Jason is taunted by two holographic campers about their plans to get high and have sex, whereas *Black Christmas* grounds it in more serious terms. Arguably, *Black Christmas* is subverting the idea that sex leads to death, as Jess is alive at the end of the film, while also communicating the audience's fear of their own emerging sexuality.

Rebellion

Rebellion against authority is a key part of adolescence that arguably touches on each component of the life course perspective in some way. It is through rebelling against authority—parents, school, the law, and society in general— that young people establish their own adult identity. Moffitt discusses this in terms of the maturity gap young people experience: biologically, they are adults, but socially, they are children, and this cognitive dissonance can lead to delinquency, which is itself a kind of rebellion given that much involves status offenses (curfew, underage drinking, etc.) that speak to the maturity gap in which young people find themselves stuck (687).

Rebellion in horror also isn't necessarily the same as being disobedient towards authority. Nancy Thompson, in the original *A Nightmare on Elm Street*, isn't being rebellious when she goes against her father's wishes and continues to investigate Freddy Krueger; instead, she is exercising her own agency and being disobedient. Nothing about her outward personality changes otherwise.

Rebels in these films tend towards one of two tropes: either their nonconformity gives them some perspective or insight on how to survive, or their nonconformity is the direct cause of their own death, if not the death of others around them. In *The Faculty*, mirroring Moffit's typology of adolescent-limited versus life-course-persistent offenders, the main characters turn to bad boy Zeke Tyler, played by Josh Hartnett. After all, if the teachers have become monsters, who better to turn to than the kid who has been fighting them his entire life? Zeke's rebelliousness naturally makes him a drug dealer, and though all he is dealing with is caffeine, the message that drug use is going to save the day still comes across loud and clear.

The character Tommy Jarvis in the three *Friday the 13th* films is an example of how rebellion works and changes as we age. In *Friday the 13th: The Final Chapter* (1984), Tommy, here played by Corey Feldman, is a boy obsessed with making his own monster masks. While this isn't rebellious on its own, it certainly marks Tommy as deviant—he's a weird kid. In *Friday the 13th: A New Beginning* (1985), Tommy is a patient in a sort of halfway house for people with a history of mental health problems. Tommy is haunted by hallucinations of Jason Voorhees, and as his fellow patients begin dying off, he learns these aren't actually hallucinations and that Jason appears to be back from the dead. When Tommy confronts and kills him, discovering that it was a copycat and not the actual Jason Voorhees, his mental health completely destabilizes, and viewers are left with the image of him wearing the copycat Jason's hockey mask. The deviance that protected Tommy as a child has morphed into something more dangerous: he is now *unacceptably* deviant, and his nonconformity is turning him into the thing he hates most. Viewers can interpret this in a few different ways. On the one hand, cynically, the film seems to be telling the audience something along the lines of "deviance in moderation." Tommy's trauma gave him the capacity for violence necessary to save the day, but he clearly went too far. On the other hand, perhaps more cynically, the film may be telling the audience that there is no coming back from the kind of trauma Tommy experienced as a child.

In *Friday the 13th: Jason Lives* (1986), Tommy, apparently having undergone extensive therapy off-screen, is now a (mostly) rational adult who really just needs to confirm Jason is dead so he can move on with his life. After exhuming Jason's corpse from his grave, the body is struck by lightning, and Jason Voorhees is resurrected, now a near-invincible zombie/Frankenstein's monster sort of hybrid. Tommy does everything in his power to alert the authorities but is locked up for being a general pest, so he must spend the film trying to evade both the police and the monster he unleashed. Here, Tommy's deviance—incarcerated in a town jail cell reminiscent of simpler, less carceral times—is a gigantic step backward from the dangerous proto-monster he became at the end of the previous film. It has been whitewashed. He is the misguided and misunderstood soul. Nevertheless, as vanilla and sanitized as his rebellion may be, it is still rebellious in the context of the film. Rebelliousness saves the day again.

Conclusion

Horror films involving adolescents, especially slasher films, are ripe with tropes that have become genre standards over the past several decades. Young people rebelling through sex and drugs are picked off one at a time by some unstoppable force that their parents have no regard for. While these tropes may seem two-dimensional at first blush, in actuality, they do much to convey the very real fear and confusion that adolescence brings.

The idea of "coming of age" is frequently romanticized in American culture, and many of the tropes discussed here are also evident in non-horror coming-of-age cinema, much of which centers on the synthesis of an intense desire and fear of becoming an adult. Finishing school, becoming responsible, navigating an emerging sexual identity, and rebelling against authority are necessary steps young people take in the process of becoming fully formed adults. The tropes in horror cinema provide a sort of catharsis for the audience, externalizing their fears about growing up and transforming them into some unstoppable killing machine, whether the invincible Jason Voorhees, the slapstick-esque Ghostface Killer, or something in between. By using these villains as a representation of the inherent tension of adolescence and seeing them bested by a young person—especially one whose vulnerability is on display, who seems the least likely to emerge as the hero but can rise and conquer the day, navigating the myriad tropes present in these films—the message to young people in the audience is clear. You, too, will grow up, and everything will be alright.

Works Cited

Arain, Mariam, et al. "Maturation of the Adolescent Brain." *Neuropsychiatric Disease and Treatment*, vol. 9, 2013, pp. 449-61.

Black Christmas. Directed by Bob Clark, August Films, 1974.

"Decennial Censuses, 1890 to 1940, and Current Population Survey, Annual Social and Economic Supplements, 1947 to 2023." *United States Census Bureau*, www.census.gov/content/dam/Census/library/visualizations/time-series/demo/families-and-households/ms-2.pdf. Accessed 25 Jan. 2024.

Elder, Glen, Jr. "Time, Human Agency, and Social Change: Perspectives on the Life Course." *Social Psychology Quarterly*, vol. 57, no. 1, 1994, pp. 4-15.

"Employment Rate by Age Group." *OECD*, data.oecd.org/emp/employment-rate-by-age-group.htm#indicator-chart. Accessed 30 Jan. 2024.

The Faculty. Directed by Robert Rodriguez, Dimension Films, 1998.

Fear Street Part One: 1994. Directed by Leigh Janiak, Netflix, 2021.

Fear Street Part Two: 1978. Directed by Leigh Janiak, Netflix, 2021.

Fear Street Part Three: 1666. Directed by Leigh Janiak, Netflix, 2021.

Freddy vs Jason. Directed by Ronny Yu, New Line Cinema, 2003.

Friday the 13th: A New Beginning. Directed by Danny Steinmann, Georgetown Productions Inc. and Paramount Pictures, 1985.

Friday the 13th: The Final Chapter. Directed by Joseph Zito, Paramount Pictures, 1984.

Friday the 13th: Jason Lives Directed by Tom McLoughlin, Paramount Pictures, 1986.

Giordano, Peggy C. "The Wider Circle of Friends in Adolescence." *American Journal of Sociology,* vol. 101, no. 3, 1995, pp. 661-97.

Halloween. Directed by John Carpenter, Compass International Pictures, 1978.

Halloween. Directed by David Gordon Green, Blumhouse Productions, 2018.

Halloween Ends. Directed by David Gordon Green, Blumhouse Productions, 2022.

Halloween H20: 20 Years Later. Directed by Steve Miner, Dimension Films, 1998.

Halloween Kills. Directed by David Gordon Green, Blumhouse Productions, 2021.

Happy Death Day. Directed by Christopher Landon, Universal Pictures and Blumhouse Productions, 2017.

Haynie, Dana L., et al. "Exposure to Violence in Adolescence and Precocious Role Exits." *Journal of Youth and Adolescence,* vol. 38, 2009, 269-86.

Jason X. Directed by Jim Isaac, New Line Cinema, 2001.

Jennifer's Body. Directed by Karyn Kusama, Fox Atomic, 2009.

Lauritsen, Janet L., et al. "The Link between Offending and Victimization among Adolescents." *Criminology,* vol. 29, no. 2, 1991, pp. 265-92.

Macmillan, Ross. "Adolescent Victimization and Income Deficits in Adulthood: Rethinking the Costs of Criminal Violence from a Life-Course Perspective." *Criminology,* vol. 38, no. 2, 2000, pp. 553-88.

Moffitt, Terrie E. "Adolescence-Limited and Life-Course Persistent Antisocial Behavior: A Developmental Taxonomy." *Psychological Review,* vol. 100, no. 4, 1993, pp. 674-701.

Napolitano, Elizabeth. "More Young Adults Are Living at Home across the U.S. Here's Why." *CBS News,* www.cbsnews.com/news/gen-z-millennials-living-at-home-harris-poll/. Accessed 30 Jan. 2024.

A Nightmare on Elm Street. Directed by Wes Craven, New Line Cinema, 1984.

A Nightmare on Elm Street 3: Dream Warriors. Directed by Chuck Russell, New Line Cinema, 1987.

Sawyer, Susan M., et al. "The Age of Adolescence." *The Lancet Child & Adolescent Health,* vol. 2, no. 3, 2018, pp. 223-28.

Scary Movie. Directed by Keenen Ivory Wayans, Dimension Films, 2000.

Scream. Directed by Wes Craven, Dimension Films, 1996.

Scream 2. Directed by Wes Craven, Dimension Films, 1997.

Scream 3. Directed by Wes Craven, Dimension Films, 2000.

Scream 4. Directed by Wes Craven, Dimension Films, 2011.

Scream 6. Directed by Matt Bettinelli-Olpin and Tyler Gillett, Paramount Pictures, 2023.

Chapter 6

"It's What You Can't See…That's What Matters": A Re-Evaluation of the Human Monster

David Edwards

Abstract

Throughout the 1970s and 1980s, rather than exploring emotional psychology or motives, the human monster in horror was considered to be a two-dimensional cipher for violence and murder. However, due to contemporary developments in the area of mental health and the impact tragic events can have on the self, this trope can now be viewed through a very different lens. Taking the specific case studies of Joseph Ruben's *The Stepfather* (1987) and Peter Weir's *The Plumber* (1979), this chapter re-examines these characteristics. This re-evaluation of the human monster trope will discuss the developments of psycho-emotional research and then consider a new understanding of these complex characters.

Keywords: human monster, emotional psychology, extant studies, *The Stepfather, The Plumber*

* * *

Throughout the 1970s and 1980s, the human monster in horror was largely considered to be a two-dimensional cipher for violence and murder. These films, largely from the slasher subgenre, didn't focus on a considered evaluation of the emotional psychology or motives of the killer but simply portrayed them as outlines of bloodlust. The Oxford English Dictionary defines a "monster" as those who are "repulsively unnatural of character, or (exhibit) such extreme cruelty or wickedness (so) as to appear inhuman" (*OED* 2023). This definition can clearly be seen in multiple genre entries such as Jason Voorhees in the *Friday the 13th* franchise (1980 to present), Madman Marz in *Madman* (1981), and the maniac in *Don't Go in the Woods… Alone!* (1981), where the killers are hulking, disfigured brutes.

Often, but not always, some form of motive is given in these films. For example, the abusive Cropsy is accidentally set alight by summer campers in

The Burning (1981), and Peter hates sexually promiscuous women in *The New York Ripper* (1982). There is little depth to these psychological catalysts, however, and they merely act as a basic *reason* for the murder as opposed to any considered performative nuance. It could be argued that John Carpenter's *Halloween* (1978) deliberately uses the motiveless trope as a considered, terrifying cue as Michael Myers disappears at the end of the film, his breathing still audible, as he morphs into the anonymous Shape, "a shape of evil rather than a distinct individual…the haunting appearance of the unmarked everyman…a blank…(canvas) on which it is possible to project any fear" (101). The Shape is striking in this subgenre because of how far Michael is departed from the usual slasher killer trope. He is deliberately anonymous and could be hiding anywhere, similar to Billy in *Black Christmas* (1974) and Pamela Voorhees in the original *Friday the 13th* (1980), albeit Michael acquires a more mystical elevation on his fall from the balcony.

When examining the slasher subgenre in more depth, there are a number of films that differentiate themselves from the hack-and-slash formula and yet utilize the same tropes. This could be seen from the late 1980s and beyond with non-horror films such as *Fatal Attraction* (1987), *Pacific Heights* (1990) and *Single White Female* (1992). Here, due to larger budgets, Hollywood casting profiles, and named directors, these films and many others of what has been commonly termed as the "yuppie horror film" became box-office hits. What is of note is that the killer character was significantly fleshed out to account for the actors now playing them. Glenn Close as Alex Forrest, Michael Keaton playing Carter Hayes, and Jennifer Jason Leigh's portrayal of Hedra Carlson all gained plaudits for their troubled, murderous characterizations. Cyclically, it could be argued this attention to character moved back into the horror genre as Anthony Hopkins won an Oscar playing Hannibal Lecter in *The Silence of the Lambs*, the *Scream* franchise broke box-office records, and mainstay monsters Jason, Michael, and Leatherface mounted multiple comebacks.

Two films that are not often discussed in this latter area are Peter Weir's *The Plumber* (1979) and Joseph Ruben's *The Stepfather* (1987). Both focus on troubled individuals who feel an ever-burgeoning resentment at the cards life has handed them. These two films utilized the slasher tropes but placed them in films that actually disturbed on a more social, familial level. Similar to Michael Myers's transformation into The Shape, these films utilized the ideas of the *human* monster, one who could actually be your neighbor, father, or husband. Whereas Weir's film supplants his interest in Australian rural terrors to the suburban for the first time in his career, Ruben uses Hitchcockian tensions to amplify the residential anxieties of Reagan's America in the late 1980s. What becomes of interest, though, is how these two films use, and often subvert, the generic conventions of the slasher genre. To that end, distinct tropes must be considered.

The slasher genre itself contains many well-recognized tropes which aim to divert attention away from the shallow killer. Graphic violence is a clear indicator due to the development of practical special effects as well as the audience's desire for the extreme. This genre works similarly to comedy: set-up and punchline. Here, the set-up involves building tension through image and sound, with the punchline being a graphic kill. It is comedy yet also a rollercoaster: fun but terrifying, perfect for Friday night cinema audiences.

From a textual point of view, the tropes are identified in the characters—the recognizable archetypes with which we immediately identify so as to save on specific character building where the runtime is short: the final girl (the antithesis of the killer), the alpha male, the insatiable sexual couple as they arrive at a location specific to the requirements of the film (a summer camp in *Friday the 13th*; a sorority house in *Black Christmas*; a train station in *Terror Train* (1980)).

Further recognized tropes to the subgenre include a specific or seasonal setting, sexual relations and/or nudity (again following the comedic set-up and gratifying pay-off mechanism), and, as discussed in the meta-movement of the 1990s, a series of life-saving rules, as spelled out by cinephile Randy in Wes Craven's slasher reinvention *Scream* (1996):

> Number one, you can never have sex. Big no–no, big no–no...sex equals death, okay? Number two, you can never drink or do drugs. No sin factor. This is sin. It's an extension of number one. Number three, never, never ever under any circumstances do you ever say "I'll be right back" cause you won't be back. (Craven)

When considering *The Plumber* and *The Stepfather*, one can recognize many of these aforementioned tropes, but their titular characters can now be read differently. The slasher genre, long the cinematic outcast but also the unloved reprobate of horror, has been given a refocus through a contemporary lens. If writers and audiences can consider a recontextualization of these films and many of their tropes, then the killer is long overdue for a reassessment.

Current developments in the areas of mental health and post-traumatic stress disorder (PTSD) allow the viewers of these films to re-evaluate the impact that tragic effects can have on the self. The tabula-rasa killer trope can thus begin to be viewed from a very different perspective. Through a review of the extant data and contemporary considerations of both mental health and theories of the self, the case studies of *The Plumber* and *The Stepfather* presented in this chapter will examine and challenge the trope of the monstrous male. These case studies will not seek to validate in any way the killers' physical violence but will aim to find a psychological reason for their actions. Navigation of these films will explore how they can transgress the subgenre and be considered more focused works in the current climate.

"It's what you *can't* see that counts in plumbing. Always remember that" (*The Plumber*)

The Plumber, Australian director Peter Weir's fifth film, was initially only a television production for the South Australian Film Corporation. It has largely been forgotten by mainstream audiences when placed alongside either Weir's independent Australian work, such as the horror comedy *The Cars That Ate Paris* (1974) or his more prominent Hollywood movies. The film follows many of Weir's thematic considerations, such as a strong focus on an outcast on the periphery of societal constructs, never truly accepted, often due to being forcibly placed into these social roles.

On an initial viewing, *The Plumber* leans heavily into the slasher tropes of the time, even though it is bloodless and short on kills. The brooding score, the apparently frail final girl, and a home invasion plot place it in the "yuppie" area of horror films. What Weir constructs here, though, and this is clearly due to a release of the studio structure and the comparative freedom of 1970s television, is a manipulation of the tropes. Contextually, the slasher genre was gathering pace but was not yet in its heyday. However, the cinematic language was mainstream enough to be recognizable.

In the titular plumber, Max, Weir constructs his proto-bloodless slasher character. Nesseth states that "the monster…must obviously be a monster, whether it's based on a historically or culturally familiar threat…that said, the monster always represents a threat of some form, whether it's a literal threat to the personal body or a figurative threat to social norms" (93). Although Max can be considered as a classist metaphor, it is his human form that terrifies—that and his apparently random decision to persecute the Cowpers of Floor 9, Apartment 15c.

Jill allows Max into her residence on the pretense that he is the plumber for the apartment complex, something she doesn't even question. Interestingly, the occupation of plumber is one that Weir regards as almost anonymous; for example, when considering his casting of Harrison Ford in *Witness*, he stated, "If he'd been a plumber and came to fix your tap, he's a person you'd notice." The innocuous "checking of the pipes" rapidly descends into a full demolition and restructuring job, which leaves the bathroom broken down and useless. Weir's decision to center his film on the bathroom focuses the action on perhaps the most intimate place in one's home, and this is clearly deliberate.

The bathroom is generally considered a secure space in one's home, a place of clean, solitary safety:

> There is nothing fearful or unreasoning in our dirt-avoidance: it is a creative movement, an attempt to relate form to function, to make unity of experience. If this is so with our separating, tidying and purifying, we should interpret primitive purification and prophylaxis in the same light...rituals of purity and impurity create unity in experience. (Douglas 2)

What we see here is a violent reclamation of this safe space, which in itself can find a reference point back to *Psycho* (1960) as Marion Crane showers in a locked hotel room, washing away her crimes, deciding to return the money she stole two days prior. One may question how familial this space is, though, in Weir's film. Jill and her husband, Dr. Brian Cowper, have only been in the apartment for three months, moving from Melbourne to Adelaide, an area Jill dislikes. The Cowpers are perceived as elitist and different from Max, and this appears to fuel his actions even more. Brian is never present at the same time as Max, leading him to be distant when Max's actions become increasingly problematic. The Cowpers appear emotionally distant from each other, and this can be juxtaposed with their careers: Brian is engaged in academic dialogue with the World Health Organization (WHO), and Jill is an early-career academic in anthropology. It is clear that Brian is too blinded by his work to even remotely consider that his wife might be in any form of jeopardy, whereas Jill's research in cultural and societal studies still leaves her thoughtlessly fearful of the "other," whether an indigenous Papuan man when in New Guinea, or Max, the working-class manual laborer. It is Jill's inherent classism that causes her to mistrust Max from the moment she mistakenly allows him into the apartment, with Weir here playing on the "audience's biases about the working class and (invoking) a sense of dread about the less educated" (Blick).

Max's actions become increasingly nightmarish as, within moments, he slams the door on Jill and takes a shower. This continues in the film's later moments, as Jill believes Max has spied on her getting changed to the dramatic moment a few scenes later where he crashes through the bathroom ceiling, ridiculing her instruction that he comes through the "tradesman's entrance." This all develops the suburban power struggle, but it is taking place in Jill's own dwelling, her safe space. This common trope, the innocent location (i.e., a summer camp), is heightened here by her total loss of control. Her journey is almost Kafkaesque in its absurdity: the understanding that the world is "out of accord with reason or propriety; illogical" (Esslin 23). This harkens back to Kafka's *The Metamorphosis* (1915): "We can't all work as hard as we have to and then come home to be tortured like this, we can't endure it" (III). What is clear, however, is that Max is representative of the working-class element of a society that views them suspiciously; he is Kafka's "vermin." The film never seeks to identify Max as the protagonist, and his apparent random singling out of the apartment is a core modern fear: random acts of violence. What viewers *do* feel through Max is his anger at a system that has placed him at the bottom of class structure with no way of escape. As he says to Jill, "Some people treat you like a real peasant. You're just a mere tradesman. You know? Some people still have the sign on the gate, 'Tradesman's Entrance.' Talk about discrimination against the blacks! They're still allowed to flog those signs in hardware shops."

Max becomes a physical manifestation of class anxiety and anger. His heroes are the political folk singers of the 1960s and 1970s, and this juxtaposes him with the Cowpers, who understand anthropology from an academic level but cannot equate it to events happening in their own homes. Max is deliberately attacking the very world he despises. He takes privacy away from the Cowpers when he renders their bathroom unusable and dangerous for the visiting WHO dignitaries and his actions become increasingly malicious. Again, Max is a signifier of the working class and the way the academic elite perceive them: "Bloody plumber," Jill calls him. Blick explains the film's societal implications:

> At the time this film was made, there was a push to make public universities in Australia more accessible to working and middle-class families. Max is an individual who has no upward social mobility. He lacks both intelligence and the talent to transcend his position. While the film never outlines the exact motive for Max's malicious and obsessive behavior, this frustrated classism may offer some insight into the position.

Through social inequality, increased worldwide poverty, and burgeoning unemployment rates, we can see Max's anger in countries beyond Australia. Not only is the dialogue of the film relevant, it remains contemporary. Through the inevitable cyclical nature of political societies, it is a sad trope of the socio-political world that Max's actions are as relevant now as they were almost 50 years ago.

"Father knows best" (*The Stepfather*)

Joseph Ruben's *The Stepfather* is another film that places its monster in a very precise societal construct. The film seeks to examine the lines between familial happiness and the potential loneliness one can feel even within the socially accepted norms of a "traditional life." That said, though, the film has long been considered a generic slasher containing many of the tropes previously discussed: teens in peril, shower scenes, and murders committed via a butcher's knife. As Roger Ebert said at the time, "[The film has] a plot that has too many distracting loose ends and oversights, avoidable errors and Idiot Plot mistakes." However, unlike many other 1980s slashers, the interest here lies in what we *don't* know about Jerry Blake, the titular stepfather, and it is this that requires further investigation.

The film is based, in the first instance, on the case of "John E. List, who escaped his drab existence as a failed New Jersey accountant by killing his family in 1971, disappearing and building a new life far away" (Stout). List had lost his job as vice president of a New Jersey bank but continued to go to work every day. According to reports, his wife, Helen, was an increasingly unstable alcoholic. List claimed his religion drove him to complete the acts in the hope that the family would be assured a place in heaven. He shot his wife and mother and then waited for two of his children to return home, shooting them as soon as they entered the house. He then made himself lunch before closing the bank accounts of his adult victims and traveling to watch his eldest son in a soccer match. They then drove home before List completed the massacre by shooting his son repeatedly. He placed the bodies in sleeping bags in the loft and then cleaned the house, removed his picture from all family photographs, and left. The bodies were not discovered for over a month. In the meantime, List had moved to Colorado, changed his name to Bob Clark, and remarried. It wasn't until a 1989 episode of *America's Most Wanted* that List's crimes became current again, and, through an age-progressed bust, he was arrested just two weeks later (Stout).

The narrative of *The Stepfather* largely follows these beats but, in keeping with the low-budget slasher tropes, ups the ante by making the titular character a multiple-family murderer, thus completing the journey from mass murderer to the far more cinematically fashionable serial killer. Although largely discarded at the time as a yuppie slasher beneath *Fatal Attraction* et al., it gained a cult following due to both Terry O'Quinn's lauded performance and director Ruben's Hitchcock influences. When recontextualizing the character of Jerry Blake, one must consider both psychological and societal pressures. Although a psychiatrist at John List's trial stated that he had been undergoing a "midlife crisis" (Stout), it appears Blake has a desire for familial perfection and life satisfaction, which is intrinsically linked to a suburbanized ideal of the American Dream.

The term "life satisfaction" is generally considered a concept to mean "employed in philosophical and psychological accounts of happiness and well-being" (Hall 3599). Life satisfaction is perhaps harder to pin down as a simple definition; not only will it differentiate around the globe, but it can also concern class, economics, and sociological constructs of the self. According to the Office for National Statistics, the concept of life satisfaction is connected to three key areas: health, employment, and relationship status. To further examine this third area, living alone is negatively related to our personal well-being, regardless of relationship status. All household types where two or more people live together to give higher ratings for "worthwhile" and "life satisfaction" than those living alone (Office for National Statistics). Again, the happiness quotient is juxtaposed between those single and living alone to those married and cohabiting. This also rises when combined with employment status and dependent children. Blunt as it is, according to this recent research, one is happier when in a good job and married with children. Add to that a friendship, which could be defined as a two-way relationship where mutual emotions are found between each other, and it begins to feel that society hasn't moved on from the early twentieth-century definition of the "nuclear family": two heterosexual parents and one or more children typically living in a one home residence. Obviously, this definition of the family has changed immeasurably, but when examining how "life satisfaction" is measured, there are still some clear throughlines.

Even without the contextual knowledge of John List, it becomes apparent early on that Blake has a fixed idea of his identity as a "father" and what a family should be in Oak Ridge, Washington. Although little is known of Blake's past—he says to his new wife, Susan, that "it didn't exist until I met you"—his stepdaughter, Stephanie's psychiatrist, says that he is a "real cheerleader for the old traditional values." The patriarchal attitudes continue when Blake accosts Stephanie and her high school suitor Paul as they are about to kiss and accuses him of trying to rape his stepdaughter. This links back to when John List collected his daughter from a police station, and, on returning home, beat both her and his wife, calling them "sluts" (Stout). These dated, narrow-minded ideals run through Blake, from the traditional Thanksgiving dinner to the woodworking hobby of building traditional family houses, or the American Dream, as he calls them. Indeed, Stephanie even compares him to Ward Cleaver, the patriarch from the 1950s American sitcom *Leave it to Beaver*.

This traditionalism also feeds into the "why" of Jerry Blake's motives (beyond finding links to List's murders). There are several moments in the film where Blake is alone. Yes, he has all of the elements that should enhance his life satisfaction: his wife, (step)daughter, John Hughes-esque family home, and a job at the center of the community as a real estate agent. Ruben, however, includes many moments of Blake alone or being detached from society. The clearest of these is the moment when, just as his family is breaking down, he watches the family to whom he had earlier sold a house embrace as the father returns from work. Though the slow-motion, dreamy aesthetic is lacking in subtlety, it is Blake's sadness at his realization that he could never be farther from this middle-class, Western perception of happiness that genuinely draws the viewer in. When contextualizing the "self" at this moment, Blake's thought processes are being altered through the image he sees before him, and it is this that becomes the catalyst for moving on from his current adopted family. His comparator systems experience contradictory information between his current life and the American ideal. His self-reflection led him to resolve that it is time to move on again violently, and this form of comparative reflection is a part of the way we all function in society. Zahavi explains this concept as follows:

> In order to obtain proper knowledge about one's experiences, something more than pre-reflective self-consciousness is indeed needed. Reflection does not simply reproduce the lived experiences unaltered; rather, the experiences reflected upon are transformed in the process to various degrees and in various manners, depending on the type of reflection at work. This transformation is precisely what makes reflection cognitively valuable. (37)

Blake reflects and compares his life satisfaction with the stereotype, the prescribed manner in which the U.S. middle class should live their lives. By juxtaposing it with such a perfect ideal, however, he will always fail in his pursuit of the "American Dream" because most families *do* have a problematic child, money worries, or moments of tension with partners. Due to Jerry's firmly conservative ideals, he is always destined to fail.

Interestingly, both Ruben and screenwriter Donald E. Westlake play a very specific game with the audience that can be traced back through a variety of texts. Viewers begin to feel sympathy for the monster as his home life crumbles, often in areas he seemingly can't control, such as his stepdaughter's behavior at school. "Neurotic characters…feel helpless (but despite this) they consider themselves as the master of any situation because to feel helpless for them, is unbearable" (Baral 43). Viewers want his search for happiness to succeed, even if it is only for that moment. A clear psychological precursor to this can be found in John Fowles's 1963 novel *The Collector*, the text of which Baral was previously discussing. Here, briefly, a lonely man called Frederick Clegg kidnaps a young art student, Miranda Grey, and holds her captive in the cellar of his farmhouse. Brilliantly, the novel is told from the viewpoints of both characters and, to that end, a genuine sympathy is exhumed for Clegg after all he has done. After agreeing to treat her with "every respect" and attempting to cultivate a relationship, Miranda verbally destroys him. Again, without context, it is ridiculous to feel any sympathy for Clegg, a psychopath who has kidnapped a girl much younger than him, but within the world of the novel, readers are forced to explore the emotions and motivations of both characters. Fowles makes a point of highlighting Miranda's higher class and her later attempts to seduce him, even though Clegg has stated that he's not interested in that element of a relationship. Her fantasies about murdering Clegg muddy the water further, but, again, Fowles brilliantly dissects the readers' viewpoint, making them reconsider what were thought to be standard norms.

Despite the audience's knowledge of Jerry's transgressions, from the murders he commits at the beginning of the film to his vicious bludgeoning of Dr. Bondurant, Stephanie's psychiatrist, Jerry begins to question the viability of his current family. These often-silent moments reveal an inherent sadness for him, prompting a surprising level of empathy. This is a man who is alone and feels like he can never attain the family perfection that others achieve. As Newell says in his essay on the film, "*The Stepfather* is somewhat more unsettling compared to other slasher-styled horrors due to how real Jerry is as a character." *The Stepfather* explores how societal pressures can break the family unit. Again, this comes from the perspective of a pro-conservative 1980s slasher containing the stock, crowd-pleasing tropes of the genre. Contextually, however, the world Blake inhabits is full of the pressures of attaining positive life satisfaction.

It would be remiss not to consider Blake's chosen victims in this film: his wife, Susan, and teenage stepdaughter, Stephanie. Susan validates the role of the powerful mother figure and embodies the ideal of female bonding between mothers and daughters. Often, the role of the mother in films of this period is authenticated by the presence of a heterosexual partner, but this is not the case here. Viewers never learn the circumstances of how Blake and Susan meet but do see how Blake courts his next partner in his new identity as Bill Hodgkins, playing the affable, unassuming new neighbor to Dorothy Rinehard. Both Susan and Dorothy are widows and are part of a traditional family unit without a patriarchal figure. Again, the conservative model of the family places pressure on the single mothers in this film, something of which Blake takes advantage. It has only been a year since the passing of Susan's husband; to that end, Stephanie is still in the process of mourning. What is significant in the final moments of the film, as Blake attempts to murder his failed family unit, is that Stephanie and Susan join forces to take down the patriarch. Although the ending could be accused of falling into slasher tropes of the final girl(s), it is this mother/daughter relationship that eradicates the abusive male figure, thus transcending the usual slasher finale. The sequence—from Blake's stabbing through the heart to the final, symbolic chopping down of the perfect home birdhouse at the film's finale—finally ends the murderous cycles of Jerry Blake until, of course, that generic slasher trope, the inevitable sequel. Feminist horror critic Barbara Creed states,

> The heroine of the slasher film is…represented as a castrating figure – a crucial point that is largely ignored in critical discussions of the genre. Clover emphasizes the savage nature of her revenge. In dispatching the killer, the heroine frequently engages in castration, symbolic or literal. (135)

The film's tagline of "Who am I here?" can now begin to be redefined in a contemporary context. As many discovered during the coronavirus pandemic beginning in 2019 and the subsequent social lockdowns, we are constantly forced to (re)consider our placement in a society that still emphasizes conservative family values even though the "traditional" family unit is slowly being statistically overtaken by, as some commentators call, non-formal units. In a particularly cold take from the Office for National Statistics, "a single person can be categorized as a family unit, but they are not considered a family."

The pressure that is placed on individuals, even in this ever-changing post-lockdown world, can be seen in Jerry Blake. The conservative ideals by which he has clearly been raised mean that the chance for familial failure will always be high. Again, the audience almost wishes the family to succeed for Jerry because we know the probable outcome is death, and this creates a refocus on the titular character. Indeed, from a metaphorical point of view, as Newell says, "he is the man who wants a loving, perfect family so bad that he'll kill for it. The entire movie is one big allegory about suburban America, how it's saccharine and loveable on the outside (and yet, at its core), it's hideous and putrid." Of note is that *The Stepfather* was released several months after David Lynch's similar dissection of the American Dream in *Blue Velvet*. Here, the rotten underbelly is immediately symbolized through the camera's journey of the perfectly kept lush lawn down to the swarming nest of insects underneath.

It, therefore, could be argued that, ironically, for a real estate agent, Jerry has been mis-sold the American Dream to which he aspires. Perhaps the strongest moment of this dichotomy is found in the doubly upsetting BBQ scene. Here, Jerry, on a small stage with his wife and stepdaughter, states, "This is as good as it gets. I sell houses, that's my job, but sometimes, but I truly believe, I sell the American Dream. You can call me sentimental; I don't care. When I came here, I was a stranger, but I've never felt more at home anywhere in my life. I have beautiful friends, a wonderful new family…have a good time." Only minutes later, though, a recently published article on the murders committed by Henry Morrison sends Jerry into the basement and a terrifying explosion of rage, watched by a hidden Stephanie, as he exclaims, "All we need is a little order here." It is also chilling to note that he says of the murders that maybe the family "disappointed him."

Jerry just wants to make his life work according to the prescribed rules that have been imprinted on him. By striving for perfection, though, Jerry condemns himself to a life of loneliness The beauty of life is that it is imperfect, but Jerry has been brought up to believe that "tradition is important." Even in his last moments, beaten, shot, and stabbed, he looks directly at his stepdaughter and whispers, "I love you." At this moment, an element of sympathy underscores

Jerry's apparent death because it feels like he genuinely means it. As Jerry smilingly says to his "perfect" family, "Father knows best."

Conclusion

Although one must always consider the historical context of when a film was made, *The Plumber* and the political ideologies of class in Australia in the 1970s, for instance, inevitably, the political cycle comes back around. The Indigenous Voice Referendum of 2023 sought only to highlight the political and classist divide still apparent in Australia ("Referendum on an Aboriginal and Torres Strait Islander Voice"). Similarly, the Covid-19 pandemic has sought only to refocus the lens on a loneliness epidemic that has long gone undiagnosed by the political classes. Society's recent shift into even more individualistic thoughts when considering the concept of life satisfaction has only exacerbated this, as seen in *The Stepfather*.

It is in the tropes of these characters that a further emphasis should be applied. The aggressive males, in an attempt to replace violence with happiness, refocus their wiles on finding a satisfactory place in society. They are as intelligent as their final girl opposites and genuinely have motives that are only seen once the audience allows their psychological constructs to develop *after* the film has concluded, the schlock tropes being replaced by a true consideration of Max's and Blake's motives.

In this now-developed trope of the sympathetic slasher, viewers not only see re-contextualization but also developments beyond the genre. One can reconsider Pamela Voorhees as a single mother whose mental health has deteriorated to such a point that she will do anything to stop the re-opening of Camp Crystal Lake, Axel, in *My Bloody Valentine* (1981), who has schizophrenia following the murder of his father, and Billy Chapman—the Santa Claus killer of *Silent Night, Deadly Night* (1984)—as one who has not only watched the murder of his parents but also has endured abuse when in the orphanage. The acts are not to be commended, but the motives, in any other genre, would be more highly considered. Hence, a reconsideration of these murderers must be further developed. As opposed to looking at the diagnosed as the "villain," perhaps the recontextualized cinematic trope should look at the personal circumstances of these individuals and the members of society who have abused them to the point of creating multiple personalities. The catalytic abusers are the real villains in these pieces, and one can see the lineage in Max and Jerry.

For many of these characters, there is a simple desire for acceptance: to find a place in society and be heard. Viewers see this in Max, a man who, while personable enough, lacks the basic social cues needed when developing relationships. In Jerry, viewers find a man who cannot fulfill the shared tropes designated by a society raised on the American Dream. If these societies had sought to help as opposed to attack, then the events within these basic slashers would have been averted; a sympathetic support system would have sought to help these characters through these troubling life events. As it is, to some, they remain the monster, the *other*, but surely it is scarier to think of these characters as just like us, finding their way in a world that seeks to brand them at every turn, where the monsters are, in fact, the shadows in their memories who made them this way.

Works Cited

Baral, Raj Kumar. "View of Repression: A Road to Neurosis in John Fowles' *The Collector*." *International Journal of Linguistics, Literature and Translation*, vol. 2, no. 5, 2019, pp. 42-46, al-kindipublisher.com/index.php/ijllt/article/view/562/492.

Black Christmas. Directed by Bob Clark, Ambassador Film Distributors, 1974.

Blick, William "Bill." "Stopping up the Works: Weir's *The Plumber* and Social Class Conflict." *Senses of Cinema*, Nov. 2017, www.sensesofcinema.com/2017/feature-articles/peter-weirs-the-plumber/. Accessed 19 Oct. 2023.

Blue Velvet. Directed by David Lynch, De Laurentiis Entertainment Group, 1986.

The Burning. Directed by Tony Maylam, Filmways Pictures, 1981.

The Cars that Ate Paris. Directed by Peter Weir, British Empire Films, 1974.

Creed, Barbara. *The Monstrous Feminine: Film, Feminism, Psychoanalysis (Second Edition)*. Routledge, 2024.

Don't Go in the Woods… Alone! Directed by James Bryan, Seymour Borde & Associates, 1981.

Douglas, Mary. *Purity and Danger: An Analysis of the Concepts of Pollution and Taboo*. Routledge, 1966.

Ebert, Roger. "The Stepfather: Review." 1987. *RogerEbert.com*, www.rogerebert.com/reviews/the-stepfather-1987. Accessed 15 Oct. 2023.

Esslin, Martin. *The Theatre of the Absurd*. Anchor Books, 1969.

Fatal Attraction. Directed by Adrian Lyne, Paramount Pictures, 1987.

Fowles, John. *The Collector*. Little, Brown and Company, 1963.

Friday the 13th. Directed by Sean S. Cunningham, Georgetown Productions Inc., 1980.

Hall, Alice. *Concept of Life Satisfaction*. Springer, 2017.

Halloween. Directed by John Carpenter, Compass International Pictures, 1978.

Kafka, Franz. "The Metamorphosis." 1912. *Modern World Literature: Compact Edition*, mlpp.pressbooks.pub/worldlitshort/chapter/the-metamorphosis-franz-kafka/. Accessed 21 Oct. 2023.

Leatherface. Directed by Julien Maury and Alexandre Bustillo, Millennium Media et al., 2017.

Madman. Directed by Joe Giannone, Jensen Farley Pictures, 1981.

Madsen, Michael. "A Namelessness Wheeling in the Night": Shapes of Evil in Cormac McCarthy's *Blood Meridian* and John Carpenter's *Halloween*. *Intertextual and Interdisciplinary Approaches to Cormac McCarthy: Borders and Crossings*, edited by Nicholas Monk, Routledge, 2011, pp. 100-11.

"Monster." *Oxford English Dictionary*, 2023, www.oed.com/dictionary/monster_n. Accessed 11 Oct. 2023.

My Bloody Valentine. Directed by George Mihalka, Paramount Pictures, 1981.

Nesseth, Nina. *Nightmare Fuel: The Science of Horror Films*. Tom Doherty Associates, 2022.

Newell, Chris. "Conservatism and Identity in *The Stepfather*." *Scriptophobic*, 3 Sept. 2018, scriptophobic.ca /2018/09/03/conservatism-and-identity-in-the-stepfather-1987/. Accessed 14 Oct. 2023.

The New York Ripper. Directed by Lucio Fulci, 77 Cinematografica, 1982.

Office for National Statistics. "Measuring National Wellbeing." *National Archives*, 30 May 2013, webarchive.nationalarchives.gov.uk/ukgwa/20160107113217/http:/www.ons.gov.uk/ons/rel/wellbeing/measuring-national-well-being/what-matters-most-to-personal-well-being-in-the-uk-/sty-personal-well-being.html. Accessed 12 Sept. 2023.

Pacific Heights. Directed by John Schlesinger, 20th Century Fox, 1990.

The Plumber. Directed by Peter Weir, South Australian Film Corporation, 1979.

Psycho. Directed by Alfred Hitchcock, Paramount Pictures, 1960.

"Referendum on an Aboriginal and Torres Strait Islander Voice." *National Indigenous Australians Act*, www.niaa.gov.au/indigenous-affairs/referendum-aboriginal-and-torres-strait-islander-voice. Accessed 16 Jan. 2024.

Scream. Directed by Wes Craven, Dimension Films, 1996.

The Silence of the Lambs. Directed by Jonathan Demme, Orion Pictures, 1991.

Silent Night, Deadly Night. Directed by Charles E. Sellier Jr., Tri-Star Pictures, 1984.

Single White Female. Directed by Barbet Schroeder, Columbia Pictures, 1992.

The Stepfather. Directed by Joseph Ruben, New Century Vista Film Company, 1987.

Stout, David. "John E. List, 82, Killer of 5 Family Members, Dies." *The New York Times*, 25 Mar. 2008, www.nytimes.com/2008/03/25/nyregion/25list1.html.

Terror Train. Directed by Roger Spottiswoode, 20th Century Fox, 1980.

Weir, Peter. "Quotes." *IMDB*, www.imdb.com/name/nm0001837/quotes/. Accessed 26 Oct. 2023.

Zahavi, Dan. *Self & Other: Exploring Subjectivity, Empathy, and Shame*. Oxford University Press, 2016.

Chapter 7

She Floated Away: Vampirism and Identity in *The Pallbearers Club*

Josh Hanson

Abstract

This chapter analyzes Paul Tremblay's novel *The Pallbearers Club* and attempts to place it within the larger tradition of vampire literature. Tremblay's use of tropes from *Dracula* and *Carmilla*, as well as real, historical New England vampire panics, are investigated to underline the way in which the novel is in constant meta-referential conversation with its predecessors. By studying the way Tremblay utilizes and subverts vampire tropes and character types, we can better understand the novel's unique position within the tradition, creating a startling psychological profile of a man who sees himself as cursed.

Keywords: vampires, *Dracula, Carmilla, The Pallbearers Club*

* * *

Paul Tremblay's 2022 *The Pallbearers Club* is a vampire novel that is not a vampire novel, though it is neither an allegory nor some naturalized version of the vampire legend. Rather, it employs the full gamut of vampire tropes, stacking them up and cataloging them as evidence of a supernatural cause for our narrator's perceived failures, ailments, and general dissatisfaction with life. Art Barbara, the novel's protagonist, sees himself as "cursed," and the source of that curse is his vampiric friend, Mercy Brown (Tremblay 48).

   The novel, like many of Tremblay's works, is deeply ambiguous, acting more as a psychological study than any kind of vampire adventure. However, this chapter examines how the novel's use of vampire tropes, both old and new, go beyond simple genre markers and instead become meaning-making tools, transforming the protagonist's experience and providing the only connection possible between him and Mercy.

Telegraphed Tropes: *Dracula*

Bram Stoker's *Dracula* is, without a doubt, the great vampire archetype (Leppälahti 191; Summers 173). It is here that an amorphous Eastern European legend is transformed into a creature that follows certain rules, most of which are so well-worn as to be part of the collective unconscious. These vampire tropes include the fear of garlic and religious symbols, the seductive power of the vampire, and the need to sleep in a coffin (Stoker 11, 141, 45, 59). While all of these tropes float through *The Pallbearer's Club* as the evidence Art collects, the way that they are employed is highly ironic.

The Pallbearer's Club is presented as a memoir by Art Barbara, detailing his life and its many intersections with his "friend" Mercy Brown. The narrative is broken up by Mercy's written feedback, in which she casts doubt on Art's memory and attempts to defend herself from the text's claim that Mercy Brown is a vampire who has, at various times, drained Art's life force and perhaps transformed him into a creature of the night, as well. This quasi-epistolary form is itself a little nod to the great-granddaddy of vampire fiction, *Dracula*.

It is clear throughout the novel that Art is using repeated nods to *Dracula's* tropes, as well as its characters, for the specific purpose of telegraphing the idea that this is a vampire story. Mercy's apparent agelessness is one such nod; in addition, at one point, Mercy Brown "haunts" Art from a basement chamber and—at least in Art's view—holds him in her otherworldly, seductive thrall (Tremblay 122).

But there is no one-to-one concordance between the ways in which *Dracula* and its myriad tropes operate in the novel. Art is not Jonathan Harker. He is not even Lucy. Art is more interested in casting himself as her Renfield. The purpose of the Renfield figure is to act as a harbinger of the vampire, a kind of dark John the Baptist, declaring the arrival of the master. In Stoker's novel, Renfield is Dracula's familiar who continuously proclaims the approaching arrival of his godlike "Master" to liberate him from his bondage. Renfield enacts a kind of parodic imitation of Dracula by collecting, breeding, and eating insects and small animals (Stoker 77).

Art's identification with Renfield seems to run deep. Most obvious is the fact that from the first moment he hears Mercy's voice, he is absolutely in her thrall. For all of the book's promise that there might be a blossoming romance there, Art's narrative refuses this interpretation. Critic Nina Auerbach claims that Dracula's power over others is less about seduction than ownership (71). Art is truly Mercy's slave, beholden to her for—it seems—his very life, as long as one considers broadening musical horizons and getting out of one's parents' house life-saving, and teenaged Art absolutely does. In his own words, he has transformed himself into his "story's secondary or supporting character" (Tremblay 136). But he is also her John the Baptist, her harbinger, and there is a sense that the entire book is Art's crying out in the wilderness, a desperate plea that someone recognizes Mercy's true nature.

To clarify, these are not fanciful connections but rather direct identifications Art makes throughout the novel. Art peppers the early chapters with these kinds of nods to *Dracula*, and in Mercy's written responses, she comments upon them. In Art's version, Mercy essentially bullies him into having fun, and there is even a recurring bit in which Mercy, a certified pothead, always "eats the roach" when they finish smoking (Tremblay 59). This is a rather obvious allusion to Renfield's bug-eating mania.

To solidify the connection, in Art's version of events, Mercy comments upon Art's increasingly emergent scoliosis, saying, "We need to get our Renfield straightened out," and then quickly correcting herself (Tremblay 54). She was thinking of Igor, the hunchback from Shelley's *Frankenstein*, of course. Mercy responds to this passage, calling it as fabrication. She knows her Universal Studios monster movies and would never make such a slip. But it's *not* a slip. It's all part of Art's careful reconstruction of his own story, giving it some understandable shape. That shape just happens to be a Gothic horror novel.

It goes on. The vampiric fear of mirrors is here transformed into pages upon pages of Art describing just how repulsive his teenage face and body are, compounded by a burgeoning—and very literal—hunchback due to his scoliosis. This illness, eventually treated with surgery and followed by a very painful recovery, introduces the second essential vampire trope. Vampirism may be about seduction or ownership, but it is, traditionally, also a metaphor for illness (Groom 9), and Art ascribes all of his physical woes—and later, his mother's—to vampirism (Tremblay 126).

Add in Renfield's final fate, a broken back, and the reader has almost complete identification. Art has both extreme scoliosis and a heart defect. He is, throughout his life, aware of his own life's tenuousness. In Stoker's novel, it is averred that Renfield somehow broke his own back and also that the primary means of killing a vampire is a stake through the heart, so the stage is set for Art as a doomed lackey (Stoker 193, 230).

This all seems very clever and a little arch, this continual allusion to vampire lore in relation to Art's life story, but this is less the author's move than it is Art's own. These hints and identifications all add up to a game Art is playing with his reader, the only reader who matters: Mercy. Mercy plays her part perfectly, reacting first with confusion and then with horror at the implications of this use of vampire tropes (Tremblay 48, 99).

Hidden Tropes: *Carmilla*

As the author, Tremblay has little use for the Dracula myth outside of Art's games. He instead has a much better source for both the tropes and the narrative shape: Joseph Sheridan Le Fanu's 1871 novel *Carmilla*.

Though the novel never directly cites *Carmilla* as it so often does *Dracula*, one might argue that the narrative itself owes its shape to Le Fanu's tale of a young woman who is visited by a strangely magnetic friend who drains her blood and almost her life. In both stories, the protagonists are noted for their solitary nature. *Carmilla*'s first-person narrator, Laura, describes her provincial existence, with "neighbors" some leagues off, but goes out of her way to assure the reader that her life was "rather a solitary one" (Le Fanu 5). That solitude is broken by the arrival of the beautiful and mysterious Carmilla, who transforms Laura's life into a romantic adventure even as a plague arrives in the surrounding villages (Le Fanu 45).

Similarly, Art Barbara's one defining feature is his detachment from others. His descriptions of his teenage self are unsparing. He is a skinny, overly tall young man who has scoliosis and raging acne (Tremblay 8-9). Art has no real connections beyond the members of his short-lived after-school program, The Pallbearers Club, itself a Hail Mary attempt to show some form of community service on his college applications. Even the scant members of the club are there for similar reasons, and one of them outright bullies Art and never returns.

This trope of the irresistible vampire, transformed into pure horror a quarter of a century later by Stoker, is framed as romantic seduction. In *Carmilla*, a life of isolation is simultaneously opened up and made smaller, with the vampire figure becoming the protagonist's object of obsession. In both *Carmilla* and *The Pallbearers Club*, that figure represents certain transgressions against everyday society. While Dracula is figured as a monster almost from the beginning, Carmilla is the epitome of the "vamp," using her sexual allure to draw in victims— in this case, a teenage girl. The desire between Laura and Carmilla is framed as monstrous in its homosexuality in that it "defies the traditional structure of kinship by which men regulate the exchange of women" (Signorotti 607). Similarly, teenage Art wonders very little as to why an older woman (of indeterminate age) would devote so much of her time to him; when looking back, he ascribes evil intent. This is itself an inversion of the typical predatory gender dynamic, underlining Mercy's supposed monstrousness.

Interestingly, it is the sexual element that is all but absent in the relationship between Art and Mercy. Instead, Mercy offers Art ways to break out of the dull round of his suburban existence through music and drugs. Music seems to be Art's savior, while drugs become his undoing. There is something to be said about the trope of vampirism as a metaphor for addiction, which is well-established in films such as Tony Scott's *The Hunger*. Throughout *The Pallbearers Club*, Mercy attempts to fill in the part of the narrative that Art pointedly leaves out: his own addiction to pain medication. This can be considered as a sub-species of the larger trope of vampirism as an illness.

Throughout its history, the vampire is associated with the trope of consumptive illness (Groom 10-11). In fact, in *Dracula*, it is Lucy Westerna's sudden illness that precipitates much of the novel's action. After her "infection," Lucy "was ghastly, chalky pale; the red seemed to have gone from her lips and gums, and the bones of her face stood out prominently; her breathing was painful to see or hear" (Stoker 130). All of this is lifted almost en masse from *Carmilla*, where several decades earlier, Le Fanu described not an isolated case of this wasting disease but a veritable plague. There, it begins not with those in a high society like Lucy but with the peasants; however, in *Carmilla*, the sickness is already mixed up with stories of nocturnal attacks, which Laura's father disregards out of hand as peasant superstition. But tuberculosis, just like vampirism, knows nothing of social class, and soon Laura herself falls ill. As the story progresses, it becomes clear that it is Laura's dearest friend who is responsible for her failing health.

Art diagnoses his own slow and painful recovery from his back surgery as a direct symptom of Mercy's proximity. When he learns later that she has spent some days lurking in his basement, he's both convinced and terrified. He believes that Mercy Brown is a vampire who is somehow draining his essence (Tremblay 124). When Art banishes her, his condition improves, though it is left to the reader to determine how much of this is the result of the natural healing process, how much is due to an increasing dependence on pain medication, and how much might be the sudden lack of Mercy's supernatural influence.

Either way, Art appears to believe not only in Mercy's vampire curse but that he now carries this curse like a contagious disease. It becomes not only the explanation for a lifetime of disappointment, but—more to the point—he holds himself responsible for his mother's later death, which follows Art's return home: "The infection killed her before the cancer could, and I know it's my fault" (Tremblay 213).

By this point, Art is filtering all of his pain and trauma through the wide lens of vampire tropes, using the folkloric and literary tradition to explain away his own failures, his probable addiction, and his mother's death. In fact, he's so immersed in this tradition that his plan for solving his problems could just as well have come directly from the mouth of Van Helsing: "I will find Mercy" (Tremblay 218).

It's not terribly clear what Art plans to do when he finds her, but vampire lore tells us that she should be very concerned. Both *Dracula* and *Carmilla* reference the method for dispatching the undead: decapitation (Stoker 400, Le Fanu 114). Rather than riding off into the Carpathian Mountains or venturing down into the tombs, Art attempts to draw Mercy to him, seemingly to test out just how his understanding of his life stacks up against her version. Like Hamlet, Art requires proof before he can finally act.

Historical Tropes: Mercy Brown

The main drive of the novel is taken up with a struggle of belief: Mercy Brown is accused of vampirism and somehow still acts as the voice of reason in the face of Art's Van Helsing-like mania. This is an odd twist on the formula, and it paints Art as a monster, victim, and, in his mind, tragic hero. To understand this odd shift, one must factor in the final ingredient in the novel's mélange of tropes: the historical Mercy Brown.

Early in the novel, Mercy helps Art complete a high school history project by introducing him to a New England legend (Tremblay 62). It's worth noting that the historical Mercy Brown is quite real. A teenage girl in Exeter, Rhode Island, in the 1890s, she had the misfortune to live through a TB outbreak. The two friends do some library research, and Art eventually turns in his history project: an "interview" with Mercy Brown, the New England Vampire, in which Mercy is played by none other than her namesake, the present-day Mercy Brown (Tremblay 64).

The reader might expect this shift away from classic tropes to dispel any talk of vampires, as both the research and the interview point to a scientific understanding of the phenomenon. Tuberculosis is a wasting disease that sometimes simply skips over certain people, and the historical Mercy Brown is simply a victim of a mob mentality that saw the survivors as somehow feeding off of their families, using them up until they finally wasted away (Tucker). In the same way, the Salem witch trials would seem to disprove the existence of witches, demonstrating a lesson in group psychology rather than an investigation into the supernatural, Art's research into the Mercy Brown legend should have been the end of any talk about vampires. Instead, it offers a beginning.

Like the residents of Exeter, Rhode Island, Art feels helpless at the whims of larger, unseen forces. He imagines himself unlovable, isolated, and cursed. And, like those New England villagers, he believes there must be some external force that is responsible. That force, of course, is Mercy herself, and the legend of Mercy Brown offers not only an answer to Art's despair but a solution. Through this historical event, which predates the release of *Dracula*, there are unique methods for both testing for and disposing of vampires.

In this tradition, which appears to have American roots going back at least into the early eighteenth century, bodies of suspected victims were dug up, and their hearts were removed. While practices seemed to vary widely, even in Exeter, burning the heart was a common practice (Tucker). In *The Pallbearers Club*, filtered through Mercy's telling, these practices are codified in the way they might be in a Hollywood movie. We can almost hear Mercy as Van Helsing delivering the essential exposition: to identify a vampire, you remove the heart; if there is still blood in it, that means it has been feeding; the heart must be burned, the ashes mixed with water or wine; this concoction is drunk by the suffering victim, breaking the vampire's curse (Tremblay 68).

Art, in his misery, convinces himself that not only is this true, but that Mercy—*his* Mercy—is the historical Mercy Brown, still living her undead curse and now feeding off of him. Worse, as years go by, Art believes that he is a vampire himself, draining the lives of those he loves. This is his explanation for his mother's cancer.

Art's supposed vampirism has none of the drama or marks of obvious mental illness that we find in George Romero's 1977 film *Martin*. There, viewers find a young man struggling with his insatiable blood-thirst. This common-enough trope is thoroughly naturalized, placed in modern Pennsylvania, and, despite all the blood, is really a psychological study. One could easily imagine *The Pallbearers Club* operating similarly, but it somehow does not. Vampirism here is not so much an affliction as it is an identity. Art uses a kind of inductive reasoning to search through the detritus of some pop-cultural unconscious, latching onto the legend of Mercy Brown, her affliction, and, finally, her end.

As with so much of vampire lore, it is the ending that seems most important. In order to stop spreading the pain of his cursed existence, he must find and dispose of his maker. This is a powerful idea for Art. He of a tortured body and a weak heart, and it doesn't take long before he becomes obsessed with curing himself by stopping Mercy.

In one of many such scenes, Art witnesses a creature of blue light crouching on his mother's chest while she sleeps, feeding on her. Compounding this moment of horror is Art's revelation:

> It has a head and a face. A face I've seen twice before, but also I've never seen it before, but also I see it every day. …I'm allowed to wonder, would mom or anyone else see it is so clearly my face, or made of the same clay as my face? Its lips move in synch with my thoughts, my worst thoughts. It turns away, and I still feel its lips moving and whispering my whispers. (Tremblay 207)

For all of the flip references to the all-familiar pop culture tropes of *Dracula* and all of the novel's borrowing of shape and theme from *Carmilla*, it is finally the legend of Mercy Brown that gives Art a set of tropes that allows him to understand his own life and its horrors. Once the moment of feeding is over, he is once again able to breathe, and he observes that "It doesn't feel like breathing. It feels like floating," which may well point to the prescription drug addiction that Mercy has alluded to throughout the book, adding another layer to Art's understanding of the vampire's role (Tremblay 207). What's important here is Art's continual insistence that he himself is a monster, created by Mercy, seemingly unable to resist his cravings—for life, for prescription painkillers, for connection.

This subtle twist on traditional tropes is part and parcel of the novel's methodology. In fact, the blob of blue light that bears Art's face is just one of several unique elements that make Art's vampirism wholly his own.

Unique Mythology: Identity Crises

Tremblay utilizes established vampire tropes in various ways: *Dracula* to telegraph the theme, *Carmilla* to give the novel its shape, and the story of Mercy Brown to give Art what he sees as a concrete, historical basis for his obsession. But no great vampire story fails to add its unique twists, additions, or revisions to the classic tropes, and *The Pallbearers Club* is no exception.

Considering Mercy Brown is a uniquely Gen X vampire, it is unsurprising that she represents something to do with the uncertainty of the self and the ambiguity of identity. At the beginning of the novel, Art sees himself as a cipher. He is apparently friendless, painfully uncool, and without interests of which he is not ashamed. The creation of The Pallbearers Club as an afterschool project is the most unique thing about him, and it appears almost completely arbitrary, not born out of any deep feeling. He just wants *something* on his college applications to make him stand out.

Arguably, it is the weirdness of this project that catches Mercy's attention, or maybe it's the hundreds of flyers Art has pasted up around town to advertise, all done up in Art's attempt at a font imitating his favorite heavy metal bands. Mercy isn't even a high school student, but she's apparently drawn to the oddness (and morbid nature) of the whole project. When she enters Art's life, she brings along with her a new set of tropes that, when coupled with the legend of Mercy Brown, transforms Art's understanding of not just Mercy but also of himself.

When Mercy arrives at the funeral home for The Pallbearers Club's first engagement, she presents herself as everything Art is not. She is markedly confident, brash in the face of death, dressed in what will come to be her trademark green fatigue jacket, and carrying a Polaroid camera (Tremblay 33-35). One of the first things she does is to photograph the corpse, introducing the first new trope to Art's understanding of the vampire world.

Mercy later explains that she is looking for proof of vampires, so she shows Art a photo from their recent funeral with a green blob hovering above the body (Tremblay 79). Art is almost sure that this is a joke, that she has pressed her thumb onto the developing film, but this new concept takes hold, and Art will organize much of his thinking around the concept that seeing blue light above a grave is a sign that a vampire is buried there, à la the historical Mercy Brown, waiting to rise and drain the life from those she loves. It is this light that is later transformed into Art himself, feeding on his mother's life force.

Art's response to this information is, "But it's green," an argument that stretches out over decades. This would seem a minor detail, except for how it plays off of another vampire trope unique to the novel: jackets. Not long after meeting Mercy, Art begins to change, and, as in any vampire story, this change appears to be for the better. He gains a certain degree of confidence. He has a friend. And, through music, he begins to form his identity. Though this is typical of teenage development, it is transformed into something supernatural in Art's hands. So much of teen vampire fiction presents this transformation as an allegory of teenage angst (Kellner 58), but here, its function is to highlight Art's supposed helplessness. It is the upside of some hellish deal that has been made without his consent. It is the damning evidence of his cursed nature. Finally, the lynchpin of this transformation is the purchase of a denim jacket that he carefully scuffs and decorates to announce his punk status (Tremblay 49). This denim jacket later gives way to Art's trademark leather jacket, which he carries through college and beyond as a sign of his transformation and identity.

There's much here that smacks of the natural mirroring that occurs in strong friendships as well as romantic relationships, and that mirroring fits neatly into a long literary tradition of identifying the self with the vampire. Auerbach argues that Jonathan Harker's escape from Castle Dracula by climbing down the wall is an explicit emulation of his captor. The identification with the vampire is itself the curse (Auerbach 89), and this seems especially true in Art's case.

The concept that this transformation is something bestowed upon Art by Mercy is made explicit in a conversation where Mercy describes her first Pallbearers Club meeting. Art says, "And you met me and wanted to turn me into a punk" (Tremblay 73). What's interesting is that this interjection comes because Mercy was saying nice things about the club and, by extension, about Art, and he was "afraid where this was going or not going" (74). Presumably, Art is concerned that the conversation is about to turn romantic (or not), and this seems to fill him with dread. Time and again, scenes that would lead to romantic interactions in another story are headed off or, more often, transformed into actual horror.

This is the case with both scenes in which Mercy and Art sleep in the same spaces overnight. The first time is in high school when the book's most unique and recurring trope announces itself. Art creeps into the room where Mercy is sleeping off a night of heavy smoking, and it has the distinct set-up of a teenage boy unable to resist the nearness of this object of desire, perhaps gone to make some bold declaration in the night. What we get instead—unsurprisingly, at this point—is a scene of horror: Art finds Mercy sleeping on the couch, her blanket bunched up and floating above her:

The blanket pulsed like exposed musculature made of a glistening, convoluted network of connective and vascular tissues. And it flexed and squeezed, fluid, readjusting its hold and position. [...] Swirled within the mass of this impossible external heart [...] was a human face. [...] Ageless and, somehow, clearly adult, its eyes had lids, and its eyes were eyes (iris, pupil, sclera), and it had defined cheeks and brows. And it looked at me with an expression so matter-of-face, so ho-hum in its indifference as to be the most malign, baleful look I'd ever received. (Tremblay 99-100)

This spectral being, which appears to be feeding off Mercy, is clearly connected to both the legend of the historical Mercy Brown and Mercy's spirit photographs, but the trope here is domesticated in a very odd way. The blanket turns out to be Mercy's green jacket, and the being both is and is not the jacket. When Art attempts to take a picture of the scene and breaks the spell, the jacket "stretched and taffied toward the floor," suddenly anthropomorphized into a hunting creature (Tremblay 102). Art runs, and the jacket pursues.

This image is absurd and almost comical but deadly serious in Art's telling, and it points to the novel's central understanding of the vampire. The jacket, which in Art's teenage cosmology represents the character's identity, is a parasite that feeds on its owner. Art's insistence that the blurs above the bodies in Mercy's photograph are green (and/or Mercy's insistence that they are not) connects directly to this understanding of how the vampire works. Mercy *is* the green shape that devours, but it is also a jacket, a symbol of her individuality and outsider status.

If this seems strange and just a little muddy, Mercy agrees. In her responses to this chapter, she attempts to work out the cosmology to make it fit into some kind of framework. But, in the same way that Van Helsing declares that vampires fear garlic, this is simply how the narrative works (Stoker 141).

And it happens again. Many years later, Mercy reappears, tracking Art down at one of his musical performances, where he plays under the name of The Pallbearers Club. After a night of catching up and drinking, Art stays over on the couch. Mercy sleeps just on the other side of a curtain, but Art appears completely uninterested in any kind of sexual scenario. Like Jonathan Harker before him, Art is driven by an almost manic curiosity, and a long night of fear and self-recrimination ends with a bizarre scene in which that same green jacket plays a starring role.

Art awakens during his second night at Mercy's basement apartment to find this subterranean castle gone mad. The dresser and coffee table rise off of the floor and float toward him, and he makes a dash for the front door, using Mercy's

Polaroid camera as an irregular light source. When he reaches the door, the coat rack tips and he is faced with that same demon from his teen years:

> There was that face again, the same from the sleepover, that face made of folds, buttons, and stitch lines, and it had a frozen, ambered look, and it blamed me, and it wanted something from me, and that naked-but-honest want was the most familiar and most horrible face one could ever see. (Tremblay 177)

Art grapples with this monster that is and is not Mercy, this thing that is either her true self or her curse, and escapes. Shortly after, he decides to leave town and gives away his trademark leather jacket, making a clean break from Mercy and his past.

What can the reader make of this obsession with, of all things, jackets? As far as horror tropes go, it's both absurd and decidedly un-frightening, though Tremblay's prose and the sheer uncanniness of the image go a long way. This odd choice of tropes casts the reader back to the originals, to *Dracula* and *Carmilla*, asking how those tropes came to be, what they represented, and what they told us about the vampire.

In traditional lore, the vampire's aversion to religious iconography tells us much about the character of the monster. Dracula is an unholy beast, and his character is tied up with his devilishness, right down to the way he enacts a kind of mockery of the Christian communion by giving off his blood to create more of his kind. Stoker's Dracula is inextricable from his Christian milieu and acts as both mockery and commentary upon it (Summers 107). Van Helsing's insistence on using garlic to ward off the vampire—a tactic with limited efficacy in the novel—points toward the of vampirism as a disease, with garlic acting as a primitive antibiotic, and readers have already seen the way that the vampire mythos is inextricable from fears of disease.

The tropes in each novel point to the fears and anxieties of their creators and their times. Together, Stoker's tropes create a figure who comes to represent the xenophobia of the Victorian fin de siècle, positing even hinterland royalty as godless and diseased (Carter 1). This interpretation is made most explicit in Murnau's 1922 film adaptation, *Nosferatu*, where xenophobia is given overtly antisemitic qualities (Harrabin 59). *Carmilla*, operating with almost all of the same tropes, adds in the element of the homoerotic, an element as essential to vampire lore as stakes and garlic, shining a light on yet another nineteenth-century fear of sexual "deviancy" and the corruptibility of the female sex (Signorotti 607). This is just as true of the spirit photographs and anthropomorphized jackets of *The Pallbearers Club*. What haunts Art Barbara is the question of identity Who is he? What does he represent? How do other people perceive him? These are classically adolescent anxieties, and, in the novel, Tremblay does what horror does: he extrapolates that anxiety outward and inward, transforming it into a source of genuine horror.

The *true* horror is Art's stagnation, his inability to change and grow, and his obsessive attitude toward the events detailed in the novel. His leather jacket, just like Mercy's green fatigue jacket, is a marker of identity, a way of asserting a self. What is elsewhere completely normal behavior—trying on different identities in order to zero in on one's "true self"—is transformed into a prison for Art. It is a curse. The transformation from sad loner to punk rocker is, in Art's understanding, as significant as the vampire's curse: permanent, debilitating, and inescapable.

After his second night at Mercy's apartment, after the jacket attack, Art tries to give his leather jacket away. He's moving on, leaving town, planning to finally break the curse. But when he once again tracks Mercy down later in life, she gives him a leather jacket that she says she purchased, but Art insists on the original, just as he insists that Mercy does not age. For Art, Mercy plays the role of Vampire Master: she controls him and is, by extension, responsible for how small and tragic he finds his life.

Mercy's spirit photography is obviously connected to these concerns. From their first meeting, Mercy continually snaps pictures of Art and then hides them away. It becomes a way between them. What is, in the beginning, a way for Art to feel finally seen slowly becomes a mystery to solve, as the concept of documenting the dead is conflated with Art's growing sense of helplessness in the face of the world. It helps him understand how his own body turns against him, acting as a metaphor for illness. It explains away his dissatisfaction and inability to connect to others, acting as a metaphor for depression. And, if Mercy's marginalia is to be believed, it all forms a kind of massive, nearly impenetrable wall between Art and the true source of his troubles: his addiction to pain medications.

What is important is *how* Tremblay employs these tropes, both new and long-established. At first, they are peppered throughout the novel in the usual way, playing upon the reader's cultural knowledge to build a vampire story. But, as the story continues, the tropes are transformed through a naturalizing, historical lens that both undercuts any supernatural element and also adds fuel to Art's fantasies. For Art, Mercy's guided immersion in New England's history of vampire-mania is less an education than it is a confession. When all of it is filtered through the lens of a disaffected teenager coming of age in the late 1980s, it takes on the talismanic power of childhood.

In the end, what matters is not whether Mercy is a vampire but that Art has, through his memoir, created a system of signs and symbols that allows him to communicate his fears. All his anxieties about health, sexuality, addiction, love, and music are bound up in a personal mythology that grows like a shoot-off the trunk of established vampire tropes, allowing for something like communication between Art and Mercy.

After Art decides to give in to his vampire nature to go and feed (his victim chosen based on childhood identities and class antagonism), he hides himself away under a carpet in the garage, where his heart finally gives out. Even Mercy can't work out the timeline for how he could have written the last pages of his memoir before recounting what he does in his last hours, but it's less about belief than it is about communication.

After Art's funeral, Mercy goes to his grave, digs up his corpse, burns his heart, and drinks the ashes. She also photographs the grave, insisting that there is a clearly defined blue orb floating above it. All of this is enacted (or at least recounted) in the spirit of concession, if not confession. Mercy's closing words are that she is finally willing to be the monster he needed her to be, and she enacts this change by carefully adhering to the language of tropes that she and Art have built throughout the novel. It is an act of love, this willingness to make herself monstrous so that she might be able to love and be loved by Art, who has, all along, thought himself a monster.

This is the emotional core of the novel, this gap that exists not just between Art and Mercy but Art and the world, and it is only through the novel's tropes that this emotional release can be achieved. There is no reason to believe that Mercy does any of the things she recounts at the end of the novel, but in writing them down, she has entered into the solemn agreement between reader and writer, accepting the terms of the novel's invented universe. For Art, that is freedom.

Works Cited

Auerbach, Nina. *Our Vampires, Ourselves*. University of Chicago Press, 1996.

Carter, Margaret L. "Xenophobia and Its Subversion in Darker Than You Think." *Journal of Dracula* Studies, vol. 4, no. 6, 2002, research.library.kutztown.edu/dracula-studies/vol4/iss1/6?utm_source=research.library.kutztown.edu%2Fdracula-studies%2Fvol4%2Fiss1%2F6&utm_medium=PDF&utm_campaign=PDFCoverPages.

Groom, Nick. "Viral Vampires." *Critical Quarterly*, vol. 62, no. 4, 2020, pp. 9-16, https://doi.org/10.1111/criq.12576.

Harrabin, Molly. *Representations of "Jewishness" in Weimar Cinema*. 2021. University of Warwick Master's thesis.

The Hunger. Directed by Tony Scott, MGM/UA Entertainment Co., 1983.

Kellner, Douglas. "Teens and Vampires: From Buffy the Vampire Slayer to Twilights Vampire Lovers." *Kinderculture: The Corporate Construction of Childhood*, edited by Shirley R. Steinberg, 3rd ed., Routledge, 2018, pp. 55-72.

Le Fanu, Joseph Sheridan. *Carmilla,* edited by Carmen Maria Machado, Lanternfish Press, 2019.

Leppälahti, Merja. "From Folklore to Fantasy: The Living Dead, Metamorphoses, and Other Strange Things." Translated by Clive Tolley. *Journal of the Fantastic in the Arts,* vol. 29, no. 2, 2018, pp. 179-200. *JSTOR,* www.jstor.org/stable/266 27620.

Martin. Directed by George A. Romero, Laurel Productions, 1977.

Nosferatu. Directed by F. W. Murnau, Film Arts Guild, 1922.

Shelley, Mary. *Frankenstein or the Modern Prometheus,* edited by Maurice Hindle. Revised ed., Penguin, 2006.

Signorotti, Elizabeth. "Repossessing the Body: Transgressive Desire in 'Carmilla' and 'Dracula.'" *Criticism,* vol. 38, no. 4, 1996, pp. 607-32. *JSTOR,* www.jstor.org/stable/23118160.

Stoker, Bram. *Dracula,* edited by Maurice Hindle, Penguin Classics, 2003.

Summers, Montague. *The Vampire: His Kith and Kin.* Trubner and Co. Ltd., 1928.

Tremblay, Paul. *The Pallbearers Club.* William Morrow, 2022.

Tucker, Abigail. "The Great New England Vampire Panic." *Smithsonian Magazine,* 1 Oct. 2012, www.smithsonianmag.com/history/the-great-new-england-va mpire-panic-36482878/.

Chapter 8

Blacks in Horror and Cultivated Bias

Lisa Wood

Abstract

In *The Birth of a Nation,* the seeds of what has become a deep-rooted bias toward Black people were planted. Black people were depicted as violent and lustful, ignorant and animalistic, all amid the film advancements that are credited with innovating the medium. Old wounds were reopened—the largely dormant KKK experienced a resurgence after the film's opening—and new wounds were created, some that would not bubble to the surface or be unpacked and examined for decades. Most importantly, Black people were effectively "othered." Society was indoctrinated with imagery and rhetoric that systematically compromised the cultural footprint of Black people, positioning them as outsiders, different, something to be feared because their true nature could never be understood. This chapter will conduct a deep dive into this misconception, reviewing how it is chronicled in horror over decades as well as how Black people began being portrayed in four predominant ways: in service of Whites, as monsters, as victims, or not at all—as though they didn't exist. An important review of history juxtaposed against the present day, this chapter will discuss the manner in which subconscious thought is cultivated, especially as it relates to people from the African diaspora.

Keywords: Black, stereotype, race, bias, "other"

* * *

Rarely is one able to pinpoint the beginning of a phenomenon, to accurately determine when something started, when it began to permeate the mindset of a culture. While the argument made here may be easier to timestamp, choosing one moment serves to minimize the pervasive nature of this reality. Slavery could be marked as the starting point of inherent bias toward Blacks, as could the moment that it was decided that Africa could be invaded and the people enslaved, a moment driven by the assumption of superiority that existed long before the execution of the plan to overtake Africans was completed. But those start dates are almost too easy to identify and set in stone. The knowledge of slavery, if not the practice and aftermath, is not the beginning of the inherent bias toward Black people and the subsequent minimizing of our contributions to society. While people have changed and societal norms have bent, twisted, and, in some instances, snapped apart to be reconstructed by something equally malleable and unstable, people are still people, social creatures swayed by popular opinion who are susceptible to groupthink. It is in this reality that the truth of the otherness that separates Blacks and Whites in America lives; it is here where bias forms opinion and voices it as truth. Therefore, the pivotal moment that solidified the perception of Blacks as inherently inferior to and different from White Americans was the release of D. W. Griffith's *The Birth of a Nation*. The longest, most technically advanced visual work of the time, the 1915 release of the film adaptation of Thomas Dixon Jr.'s novel *The Clansman* was met with overwhelming appreciation. It was the first movie to have a musical score and was thus treated as a stage play, replete with an intermission and souvenir booklet. *The Birth of a Nation* has the distinction of being the first movie to ever be screened at the White House and to have secured national distribution (Hobbs). It was widely viewed and wildly popular... and it was about the savage Black and the ways that the Ku Klux Klan (KKK) could protect White society from them.

In *The Birth of a Nation,* the seeds of what has become a deep-rooted bias toward Black people were planted. Black people were depicted as violent and lustful, ignorant and animalistic as they engaged with White characters, all amid the film advancements that are credited with innovating the medium. Old wounds were reopened—the largely dormant KKK experienced a resurgence after the film's opening—and new wounds were created, some that would not bubble to the surface or be unpacked and examined for decades (Pietrusza). Most importantly, Black people were effectively "othered." Society was indoctrinated with imagery and rhetoric that systematically compromised the cultural footprint of Black people, positioning them as outsiders, different, something to be feared because their true nature could never be understood.

This message did not only make its way into the natural call and response of emotions for White America; cultural biases perpetrated through media informed the impressions that Americans and people from other countries have about Blacks in America. Indeed, Black people have suffered challenges to their sense of self-based on the messages being pushed through entertainment and media. As a Black female creator, I have felt the weight of the "othering" that films like *The Birth of a Nation, Black Moon,* and others have brought. I have seen results of implanting the subliminal message of Black inferiority in the consciousness of people of all races reflected in the perception of differences White editors and readers have claimed when reading work written by Black authors. It is for this reason that I reviewed and deconstructed films of their ilk in this commentary.

The concept of Black people as expendable, invisible, or unimportant is ubiquitous. Robin Means Coleman, the author of *Horror Noire*, a study on Blacks in film, recounts that scholar Sterling Brown talked about Black character types in the 1930s, stating that Black characters in literature during the early twentieth century were predominately portrayed as the "content slave" or the "wretched freeman" (2). These categories were later expanded and reimagined. Black people began being portrayed in four predominant ways in both movies and literature, horror or otherwise: in service of Whites, as monsters, as victims, or not at all, as though they didn't exist. These categorizations can still be seen in media today.

Blacks in Service of Whites

When in service of White characters in horror movies and literature, Black characters provide comic relief as the sidekick or as a guiding light to people in need if they are embodying the magical/soothsaying/clairvoyant presence. They may sacrifice themselves to save a White protagonist or be the first to die, even as the murdering force has several characters of other races to choose from, thus allowing everyone else a chance to escape. Black characters may even literally be "the help," filling roles such as an enslaved person, maid, butler, field hand, chauffeur, and handyman.

These characters, often hyper-protective and fiercely dedicated to the White character to whom they are attached, can be seen in many horror films and books. The horror genre has made use of this characterization, notably in Stephen King's *The Green Mile* (both the book and the film) with John Coffey, a larger-than-life man portrayed as intellectually challenged who was incarcerated for a crime he did not commit. Coffey was caught in the act of trying to use his mystical healing powers on two dead little girls. This characterization was also on display in *The Shining*. While the movie and book differ in the handling of Dick Halloran, the benevolent chef who shared a supernatural connection with the antagonist's son, Danny, the character's "magical Negro" depiction is prevalent throughout both offerings.

Earlier cinematic entries used more direct imagery to illustrate the hierarchy. The 1934 release *Black Moon* depicted Blacks as primitive and brash. It also showed them seeming to worship the White family that returned to their island, the fictional Caribbean paradise of San Christopher, throwing flowers at their feet and fawning over them as they walked. In a scene where the Black boat-running transplant from Georgia, Lunch McClaren, is transporting Stephen Lane, a White male, to the island, he is found singing "Roll, Jordan, Roll," an enslaved person spiritual, as he works. Lunch invites Stephen Lane to sit with him. In conversation, Lunch describes the islanders, including his love interest—"natives" as he calls them—as "monkey chasers." Lunch then asks

Lane to help him for a moment by taking the wheel—in essence, asking him to drive the boat—because he's "got some business up there with these monkey chasers" (*Black Moon*). Lunch then proceeds to say something in French in a harsh tone, and heretofore unnoticed Black men scurry, jumping into action, some seeming to rise from repose. The term "monkey chaser" is problematic, to say the least, especially as uttered by the Black character in the scene. While the movie attempts to explain the comparison by likening the islanders' love of coconuts to that which monkeys also displayed, the remark pours salt into the wound that Jim Crow propaganda opened, and that was part of the fabric of America when the movie was released. For the line to be delivered by a Black character speaks volumes about the subliminal messaging capabilities in media. These kinds of disparaging remarks from a Black person about their own people create an emotional impact that challenges one's self-worth. These messages from Blacks to Blacks have recurred throughout history. Perhaps one of the most famous examples is the spectacle that occurred in the sports world when the promotion of a fight between Muhammad Ali and Joe Frazier became racially abusive; however, it has also happened in smaller, less publicized interactions. An "us" vs. "them" quality became an acceptable discussion in Black America on the heels of such behavior, further separating an already fractured community from mainstream acceptance.

There are other moments where the characterization of Blacks in service of Whites shows itself in the film *Black Moon*, but one of them bears relating here because of the subliminal seed-planting at play. In a scene where Lunch tenders Lane to shore, an unnamed Black male, shirtless and stoic, performs the effort of rowing four adult males alone. A phrase in French is virtually spat at the man by Lunch, to which he simply responds, "Oui," and continues to work (*Black Moon*). These images of subservience and laziness, as illustrated in the initial boat scene, abuse, and disrespect at the hands of a member of the same race are not showcased as part of the story or something to be paid attention to—indeed, in the tarry scene, two White male characters act outlines related to what they will find once they get ashore. The back-breaking work of rowing them to shore and the disdain etched on the enterprising Lunch go unnoticed by the two White characters—from their perspective, there is work to be done, and the Black characters are doing it… end of story. They could just as easily have been off-screen doing the same job entirely unseen. This imagery works to create subliminal triggers. These triggers form stereotypes—responses and expectations—that the viewer is unaware they are cultivating in their psyche, building the framework for what Blackness is and isn't and inexorably linking them to the persons connected.

Blacks as Monsters

While the characterization of Blacks having the sole mission of being in service of Whites is problematic, the notion of Blacks as monsters is perhaps more difficult to digest. H. P. Lovecraft, progenitor of the contemporary horror subgenre, cosmic horror, likened Black people to "a beast in semi-human form" in his 1912 poem "On the Creation of N—s." Before that, the concept of the Black male as a brute was popular in literature and film, with creators casting aside the worry of the "self-fulfilling prophecy" such propaganda might bring about (Pilgrim). Once slavery was over, there was no longer a need for Whites in power to paint Blacks as docile and childlike—the subliminal message for both races that had been borne out of necessity was no longer required. In the film, there are additional metaphorical references that inform the view of Black people as monsters, in effect, the monstrous other. Consider racialized monsters like Audrey II in *Little Shop of Horrors* in the inflection of speech, the titular character of *Predator* with its locked hair, and the connection linking King Kong, a primal and inarticulate beast, to Black people, falling back on a tradition of simianization and racial propaganda dating back to the early 1900s (Hund and Mills). Coleman says this of The Gill-man in *The Creature from the Black Lagoon*: "Bodily, the monster resembles a racist caricature—its lips are large and exaggerated. Its skin is dark" (98). Tananarive Due, author, educator, and filmmaker, suggests that "…the physicality of monsters like the titular creature could be compared to the way black facial features were misrepresented and caricatured back in the 40s" (Adjei-Kontoh). Coleman surmises, "The monster permits a counter-image to evolution, which is pictured as modern, intellectual, and civilized" (98).

Blacks as Victims

Blacks as victims is probably the most identifiable trope in horror movies. The Black character dying first has become par for the course in films in all genres, as first illustrated in 1967's *Spider Baby* and consistently perpetuated in films such as *Gremlins*, *Scream 2*, and *The Shining* over the decades. It is anticipated behavior, as expected as the fall a running character will take as they try to escape the antagonist and as commonplace as the high-pitched shriek moviegoers have come to expect from fearful female characters. When reviewing Black characters in 1980s horror films, Coleman notes, "Not only were the vast majority of Black characters killed off during this period, but they were often the first to die" (xii-xiv). These deaths were frequently used to establish the strength of the antagonist; the characters were usually nameless or undeveloped—forgettable aside from the fact that their deaths gave the White protagonists time to escape while simultaneously allowing the audience to witness a brutal, bloody, dominant display.

While sacrifice is the most prominent example of Black character death in all genres of movies, as Miles Dyson in *Terminator 2: Judgment Day*, Captain Miller in *Event Horizon*, and Stacker in *Pacific Rim*, it is heavily replicated in horror. There is, however, another example of Black character death that has a deeper, more poignant psychological impact. George Romero's 1968 film, *Night of the Living Dead*, was a groundbreaking effort for both its coverage of the American zombie and for casting an unknown Black actor, Duane Jones, as the film's hero, Ben. Not only was this Jones's first on-screen role, but it was the first time that a Black person had ever been cast as the hero of a horror movie (firehouse 44). Ben's character continues to be discussed by Black Americans decades after the film's release with a range of reactions: exultation that a Black man was shown as having the intellect to devise a plan to stay alive and lead the others throughout the ordeal even though he was challenged by the other occupants of the house—all White, two male—to surprise, which was quickly replaced by awe when Ben slapped a White woman on camera in the racially precarious 1960s, and finally to frustration that, in the end, the Black man was not allowed to live. After brazenly taking control of the situation, offering plans, fortifying their hideout, and engaging in battle to protect himself and the people in hiding with him, Ben was "put in his place" in the end.

The Invisible Black

Even more shocking than the buffoonish comic relief characters that Blacks have played in film and literature, more jarring than the assimilated sidekick, and, indeed, what has impacted Black and White Americans' views of each other the most is the marked absence of Black people on the screen and the page. Coleman explains how horror often "mark[s] Black people and culture as 'other'—apart from the dominant (White) population and cultures in the US," and one of the ways to accomplish that is to make them seem different enough that they don't fit into the narrative, at least not meaningfully (7). Whether that relates to the places that they go, where they live, the kinds of cars they drive, the jobs they hold, the music they listen to, or the things that bring them joy, great lengths are taken to show how different those choices are from what White society may deem suitable. As Kinitra Brooks states so succinctly in her exploration of the Black feminine contribution to contemporary horror, *Searching for Sycorax*, "…we black girls were absent—we were never there!" (x). She continues, further pondering the lack of representation, "[Why] were there never any black women in the group of survivors? …There weren't even any women of color—no Puerto Ricans, no Koreans, no Chicanas, no Pakistanis—none of the many different shades and incarnations of womanhood I encountered on a daily basis" (Brooks xi). The omission is glaring.

Black omission or othering is not always obvious. Sometimes, there is one Black character—usually the aforementioned sidekick—present. As in films like *I Still Know What You Did Last Summer* and *The Skeleton Key,* this character is visible, shallow as they may be, designed to ingratiate themselves with audiences, to dissuade them from thinking that there is any bias at all… designed to persuade them into thinking that the movie is reflective of life. This singular Black character is assimilated into the fabric of the story but in a cursory way. There is little to no backstory for these characters, and none of the major plot beats involve them; audiences have a hard time relating to or caring about what happens to those characters, which makes them expendable. They are, however, integral to the success of the White character's goals. The language used about and around them is often surface and noncommittal unless a direct attack or negative interaction serves the White character's story arc, allowing them to emerge as the hero. Instead, words like "exotic" and "ethnic" have been batted about to describe the Black character, comical in a way that makes the White character feel safe or as if they belong. While those are not inherently descriptions intent on creating a racial divide, they allow for the delta between the Black and White communities to remain. Readers and viewers can sometimes miss the moment when they deem the character different than other Blacks either based on demeanor, intellect, or interests because the othering is so insidious, so covert.

The separation of communities adds to the concept of difference. Robin DiAngelo, academic and author of *White Fragility: Why It's So Hard for White People to Talk About Racism,* notes that "Virtually any representation of human is based on white people's norms and images" (57). This reinforces the perpetually ingrained notion that White people—how they look, what they do—are the norm and erases Black people and their contribution to society. This dynamic extends to Black characters in horror: protagonists, antagonists, and supporting roles. Bram Stoker nominated author and academic Rhonda Jackson Joseph, whose scholarship focuses on the visibility and perception of Black women in horror fiction, posits that, "The absence of black female vampires in the horror genre creates a disservice for fans and black females by denying them the opportunity to experience vampires and monstrosity through a lens of black femininity: to encounter a vampire forged by the fires of black womanhood." That erasure contributes to the overall sense of distance, of alienness, of unfamiliarity. As humans, we are the products of our environment. If the environment we live in is not diverse, if the media we consume does not introduce us to other people and cultures, there is no opportunity for growth and acceptance.

This lack of accurate representation in horror media impacts the way that Black people are perceived creating repercussions that go beyond genre. This dynamic applies both inside and outside of the United States. Homogenous societies have no true understanding of other cultures because they have no exposure to them. While the U.S. is a larger structure that is often described as a melting pot of ethnicities and cultures, it is, in many ways, still separated by race and, further, by gender. This means that if a Black person is seen in handcuffs on the nightly news often enough, people from other cultures who do not have access to imagery that shows them otherwise will have no other reference to determine what Blackness is and may ascribe that negativity to the people as a whole. Coleman posits that "Perhaps the most damaging aspect to the limited spectrum of roles portrayed by Black actors in early horror films is that there were no contrasting positive images for a sense of balance" (xii). The absence of Black people in horror movies that reflect normal daily life imparts the same message and, in turn, garners the same response. The same can be said of Black representation in literature. This lack of visibility serves to perpetuate the idea structure of Black people being inferior to White people. These mindsets are easily reinforced by the human propensity to believe what is shown or told to them without critical assessment and/or research on their part to corroborate the sentiment as fact.

Movies in the Black Horror genre made in the late twentieth century were set in urban centers with communities that lacked diversity. Mainstream horror movies and literature omitted the presence of Blacks in their created neighborhoods. Black people didn't see themselves reflected on screen or in books, which forced them to consume whatever media existed if they wanted entertainment. At the same time, White people did not encounter Black people in movies or books, further perpetuating the concept of Black people as different from them, as "other." Blacks and Whites didn't occupy the same spaces, live in the same towns, work the same types of jobs, or have the same interests, or so the majority of movies and books would have people believe. This deepened dissonance and fed the undercurrent of racial discord. In more deliberate circumstances, the divide allowed for the proliferation of bias in the form of race talk, which is the deliberate insertion of "racial signs and symbols that have no meaning other than positioning African Americans into the lowest level of the racial hierarchy" (DiAngelo 45). DiAngelo surmises that "Casual race talk is a key component of white racial framing because it accomplishes the interconnected goals of elevating whites while demeaning people of color; race talk always implies a racial 'us' and 'them'" (45). For example, horror movie classics such as *Halloween, Friday the 13th*, and *A Nightmare on Elm Street* are designed to reflect any town U.S.A.; however, there are no Black characters present. This separation is a form of segregation, one that continues to pervade the media and mindsets of Americans without pause because it is not blatant or overt. It is ingrained in the fabric of our socialization. It is so camouflaged that many people don't understand the impact or implications that come with it. Many, in fact, are wholly unaware that anything unusual is at play at all. DiAngelo submits that White people "are taught that we lose nothing of value through racial segregation' (68). Therefore, any omission or erasure barely registers, if at all.

While film and literature are meant to be forms of entertainment, they are also part of pop culture, of what is trendy, of the collective consciousness. The images that we see in media today—ones that reflect what is considered beautiful or metropolitan, ones that define which brands should be used and which shouldn't—inform our mindsets toward people, places, and things. While it may seem that we are more susceptible to suggestions of this nature in modern times, society's proclivity for trend following is related to access rather than changing interests or redefined quests for social acceptance. There are more ways to gain access to materials that shape impressions than before, but the human psyche has always been open to groupthink and the comfort to be found therein. Examples of this can be found in the history of lynching in the U.S., where these brutal slayings were often turned into events where people would gather, enjoy food and socialize. Ferris State University's Jim Crow Museum offers newspaper clippings and accounts of such events for review in their archive, citing that attendees, in the midst of and with full understanding of what kind of gathering they were attending, "made merry as the blood from multiple wounds dripped from the suspended body of the victim" at these so-called lynching picnics (Hughes).

The characterizations of Blacks and the resulting depictions of them in horror film and literature dehumanize Black people. Indeed, they summarily dismiss Black people's importance altogether. Waytz et al. discuss how "a subtler form of dehumanization of blacks persists [that] increases endorsement of police brutality against blacks ... and reduces altruism toward blacks" (1). This finding is directly related to these culled impressions, the mindsets that snowball as they permeate communities, becoming a part of the patina, so intrinsically linked to Blackness that they are ingrained as legitimate descriptors of Black people. These descriptors work in concert with other symbols and messages that pummel society from all angles to include standards of beauty, education, health, and wealth, coming together to create an "other," an entity that is wholly different from White society and, therefore, something to be held at arm's length, regarded with cautious curiosity, novelized, and feared in differing measures. Foor punctuates this reality by restating Eugene Horowitz's belief that "Attitudes toward Negroes are now chiefly determined not by contacts with Negroes, but by contact with the prevalent attitude toward Negroes."

Black people have been significantly minimized culturally. That perceived lower status has created an automatic bias and skepticism when that bias is challenged. Coleman notices that "Blacks have been rendered deficient—

childlike, carrying taint, lower in socioeconomic standing, a metaphor and catalyst for evil and demonized, even though not always cast, physically, in the role of demon" (9). That Black people will not be able to do something, whether that is comprehending a task or thinking deeply about an issue, has become expected. Black creators were effectively put in a box—allowed to produce, but the resulting work was shunned, criticized, or outright ignored. Accomplishments such as being one of the best-known poets in the nineteenth century worldwide, even though she spent nearly all of her life enslaved in the case of Phyllis Wheatley (Lubering), or being the first Black person to win a starring role in a motion picture in the case of Clarence Muse (Warner), go unheralded in history, not unlike the scientific, medical, and aeronautical contributions of Black people that are routinely muted.

So Black people created their own.

Reclaiming Agency in Literature and Film

An argument could be made that the earliest submissions of Black writing captured in the U.S. were part of the horror genre. Some of the first entries into literature penned by Black authors were slave narratives. These important works recounted the author's experiences in bondage and represent some of the most authentic accounts of life in America in the eighteenth and nineteenth centuries. While *The Interesting Narrative of the Life of Olaudah Equiano, Or Gustavus Vassa, The African* by Olaudah Equiano out of London was the first international bestseller, notable entries from the U.S. include works by Harriet Ann Jacobs, Frederick Douglass, Sojourner Truth, Phyllis Wheatley, and Booker T. Washington, each of whom told stories about life on plantations and the brutality and abuses they experienced (Andrews).

There was a breakthrough in prose in the 1940s, one that represented the turning of a corner, brought on by one tale that dared to be something different. Researcher and author Jess Nevins reasserts the notion that "at least through the 1960s, the preponderance of black literature might be considered a 'literature of terror,' with slavery, of course standing in as the 'original sin' which provided the artistic matrix for subsequent black authors." But Ann Petry's novel *The Street* stood apart from that tradition at a time when further distinctions on Black literature had been assumed, marking "African American literature [as] tacitly understood to be African American male literature, and women's literature was coded as white women's literature," author Ann Petry wrote a thriller that included hoodoo, murder, and economic tension nestled in a reflection of the American tenets of hard work yielding results (Vinopal and Jones). Novelist and professor Tayari Jones recount, "For Petry, 116th Street is the gritty antagonist, representing the intersection of racism, sexism, poverty and human frailty." Nevins goes on to list the qualities that *The Street* has in common with a Gothic novel, including "catatonia, paroxysmal, blood-curdling violence; confinement and entombment; psychosexual neuroses; villainous and shape-shifting characters who worry and dislocate the line separating 'good' and 'evil'; and an omnipresent and palpable specter of impending death." One of the early entries in crime novels and a literary powerhouse, *The Street,* was the first novel by a Black woman to sell over a million copies (Vinopal and Jones).

Black horror fiction found its way to the market slowly but surely. Joseph Nazel released the novel *The Black Exorcist* in 1974, which has been described as a blaxploitation version of Blatty's *The Exorcist,* and it is just one of the crop of pulp novels that hit the market in the 1960s and 1970s. *The Black Exorcist* uses familiar blaxploitation tropes, from a Satanic cult that was a front for the Mafia to the protagonist, a former pimp who found God. It also offers a surprising dose of realism. Nevins explains, "Nazel was an African-American man deeply tied to his community, and so *The Black Exorcist* has a real feel for L.A. street life. However, *The Black Exorcist* did not spawn imitators or create a wave of African American authors writing commercial horror novels." It wouldn't be until after Toni Morrison's *Beloved* that a movement toward publishing Black voices with diverse and, indeed, genre focuses would gain ground. At the same time, embracing the distinction of horror author within the African American community remains rare. African American and African authors alike tend to dabble in the genre, creating a varied body of work rather than focusing primarily on horror. For example, Octavia E. Butler, who is known for her work in the science fiction genre, also penned paranormal fiction such as *Wild Seed,* where shapeshifters are the main characters, and *Fledgling,* which has a vampire protagonist. Likewise, Alain Mabanckou, who wrote *African Psycho* (a nod to Ellis's *American Psycho*), the story of a man who consults a deceased serial killer in preparation for committing his own crimes, is known predominantly as a comedy and nonfiction author. Other writers who contribute to the horror canon but do not claim the genre include Nalo Hopkinson ("Nalo Hopkinson: Author, Creator") and Nnedi Okorafor (@Nnedi). Still, some African American practitioners claim the horror genre, including Linda Addison, Wrath James White, Tananarive Due, Paula Ashe, and myself, L. Marie Wood. These authors are award-winners in the field, claiming the genre's top honors, including the Bram Stoker Award, the Golden Stake Award, the Shirley Jackson Award, and the Ignyte Award.

Black practitioners have utilized film since the early days of the medium. *Son of Ingagi* is the first horror film to feature an all-black cast. Released in 1940, the monster is a creature brought back from one of the doctor's excursions abroad. The creature is kept in the basement of the house and, upon drinking a potion found there, turns murderous and slays her. An unwitting couple inherits the home and later discovers the creature in residence. This film was written by

Spencer Williams, a pioneer in the Black producer and director spaces, as well as an accomplished actor in his own right. This film, as well as the work of Oscar Micheaux, who is regarded as "the most successful African American filmmaker of the first half of the 20th century," are part of a genre of movies called race films (Moos 53).

Race films are movies that are produced with Black audiences as the intended market. They often were comprised of all or predominantly Black casts and had a Black crew, producers, writers, and directors attached. Race films, as explained by writer and producer Paul D. Miller, showcased Black people in a variety of roles, unlike early film submissions produced by Whites that routinely cast Black actors as "singers or dancers, or as maids, butlers, porters, and other servants." Miller notes that race films "featured actors who were of African heritage, and the films were significant for showcasing how talented actors could do more than play the stereotyped roles offered to them in major studio releases. And they were produced by independent production companies and focused on the everyday life of what it meant to be Black in America." These films countered traditional depictions of Blackness onscreen, dispelling the stereotypical and disparaging precedents set in movies where White actors appeared in blackface, where Black people were quietly tending to the duties of servitude in the background, or where they were omitted from society altogether. Race films "gave African American audiences and actors a forum to articulate their own identity outside of the studio system, which rarely bothered with the full spectrum of that identity" (Miller). The need for race films speaks of the response to the oppressive machine that relegated Black imagery to lesser or "other" status. While race movies were "a product and mirror of segregation," they stoked a desire to produce images depicting Blacks as real people rather than as caricatures of themselves, in equal part subservient, buffoonish, and villainous, and to have some control over the messages being propagated, consumed, and internalized by other races, as well as their own (Miller).

The 1970s brought in what were termed blaxploitation films, a genre named as such by NAACP Chapter president Junius Griffin (Mittan). While the number of films under this umbrella varies, it is estimated that "nearly 300 films in the genre were released" by the midway point of the 1970s in many genres, including action, westerns, comedy, drama, and horror, all of which featured stereotype-busting characters that were self-motivated and driven (Spigner). There were many horror gems produced during that era, such as *Ganja and Hess*, *Blackenstein*, and the movie that started it all in 1971, *Blacula*. While these films were polarizing during the 1970s and are still controversial today, when looked at through a modern lens, there are some important considerations to be taken into account about that style of movie as a whole. It should be noted that "[f]rom Hollywood's beginnings, Black people were mostly given roles as subservient maids, butlers, slaves and sharecroppers" (Manasan and O'Connell). While blaxploitation movies are largely considered to work in the extremes, films like *Dr. Black, Mr. Hyde* had Black characters who were doctors, scientists, detectives, pimps, prostitutes, business owners, and average Joes. This kind of variegated approach to moviemaking presented a kaleidoscope of the human experience through a Black lens.

In the end, however, these efforts in both literature and film may have served to polarize audiences rather than act as vehicles to showcase the kinship between the racial groups. Several questions arise from the racialization of writing, nearly all of them from within the Black community. White Americans rarely seek out Black literature. Books sales for what were once called "issue books" and have now donned the more contemporary term "anti-racist books" often rise when something happens in the world: a murder at the hands of a police officer, a demonstration of racism caught on film, news coverage about a racial slight. A month after George Floyd was killed by police in Minnesota, seven out of the ten books that topped the *New York Times* Best Seller list were related to race ("Combined Print and E-book Nonfiction"). White readers flock to bookselling venues all over the country to buy the latest collection of essays from Ta-Nehisi Coates or Jabari Asim when racial conflict occurs, presumably trying to educate themselves about the plight of Black people in the country they share. However, the author of *Homegoing*, Yaa Gyasi, challenges that motivation:

> So many of the writers of color that I know have had white people treat their work as though it were a kind of medicine. Something they have to swallow in order to improve their condition, but they don't really want it, they don't really enjoy it, and if they're being totally honest, they don't actually even take the medicine half the time. They just buy it and leave it on the shelf.

This suggests that much of the work by Anna J. Cooper, Ralph Ellison, and James Cone read primarily by Black people, which equates to espousing a message that is already being contemplated by the audience—in effect, preaching to the choir. Therefore, if White Americans are not reading Black authors consistently, is the message to be understood that Black readers only want to read books that relate to the race narrative or trauma? A bigger question for genre writers emerged through that apparent truth. Can Black writers find success if they do not write within the confines of race narrative, which effectively guides story creation to a specific end goal rather than allowing authors the latitude to develop them organically? This represents a lack of agency that many Black authors write in the horror genre and, by extension, under the speculative fiction umbrella experience.

The question of the human experience is at play when considering a point of view: what it can be defined as and how it can be displayed on the page and screen. Should the human experience be defined from a socioeconomic perspective, which would include variables such as the type of job one has, how much one earns, and what kind of living conditions one experiences; a racial perspective, which would bring with it advantages and disadvantages gleaned from societal norms; or, an educational perspective, which would speak to exposure and hierarchy? Or should there be a shared experience in which all humans interact, a common understanding that exists regardless of the aforementioned status, race, and education distinctions... indeed, an experience that exists in spite of them?

Black filmmakers have experienced similar categorization to Black authors as they create and release the films that interest them. In 2001, the Hughes brothers, biracial twins who had previously released films like *Menace II Society* and *Dead Presidents*, found their movie *From Hell* under scrutiny because it departed from a genre called "hood dramas," or "...movies that amplified the troubled and dysfunctional lives that many young black men in the U.S were going through" (Collymore). Researcher Deron Overpeck states,

> In *From Hell* (2001)—based on the graphic novel of the same name—the brothers attempt to examine the Jack the Ripper murders within a similar framework, but also with the goal of maki[ng something] different from their "black movies." Unfortunately, in doing so, they lost the social critique of both the source material and their previous films. The brothers' ideas about black movies and about themselves as filmmakers and the critical response to *From Hell* illustrate how black movies continue to exist in a cinematic ghetto.

A curious situation unfolds as we review the history of Black film. The race films of the early twentieth century did not change the mindset of society about Blacks and our contribution to entertainment. The blaxploitation films produced prolifically in the middle of the twentieth century have problematic undertones that impede the genre's legitimacy in scholarly study. Indeed, Brooks called the genre's seminal work, *Blacula*, "superfluous and culturally problematic" (55). The effectual role reversal that the exaggerated masculinity, bravado, and inherently "hip" demeanor that many of the actors portrayed in blaxploitation films didn't help matters. It had an opposite effect, one that perpetuated the concept of a marked difference between communities, encouraging the idea that there is little to no common ground between Blacks and Whites. The focus on showcasing these differences and celebrating them in a manner that appeared antagonistic, critical, and disparagingly humorous further cemented the notion that there is an "other." Coleman suggests that movies of this ilk often contain "a self-consciousness in the narrative that makes it plain to audiences that the disruption and reversal of type is purposeful-part retribution, part forced atonement" (12). This practice alienated White viewers, having a polarizing effect as opposed to a unifying one. What was discovered was that characters created to embody the stereotypical characteristics that society has been groomed to recognize as Black perpetuates the same problem that the concept of tokenism does: they create a false reality of acceptable Blackness and paint a whole subset of people with the same brush. This practice results in an effectual segregation of Blacks and Whites inasmuch as separate products for separate audiences do.

As the 1980s dawned, Black filmmakers searched for new ways to showcase Black people and Black life. The newest foray into this effort, from a speculative fiction standpoint, is Black Horror. Black Horror is the natural extension of race films and blaxploitation movies in the contemporary market. With a cast and crew that is predominantly Black, this genre boasts movies like *Def by Temptation*, the *Tales from the Crypt* film *Demon Knight, Eve's Bayou, Tales from the Hood,* and *Bones.* Films in the Black Horror genre in the 1980s and 1990s took a page from the blaxploitation era, producing films that served as racial delineators, adding fodder to the argument of segregation—or separation. At the same time, some concepts made it out into the world that inadvertently perpetuated stereotypes set in place by White filmmakers years before.

The 1992 release of the movie *Candyman* did a lot of things at one time: it cemented a Black character as a terrifying antagonist who is as formidable as his press suggests; it features a Black character with staying power considering how few minutes he appears onscreen; and it secures an irrational fear in the back of every viewer's mind, regardless of age, race, or creed—one that makes them remember what happens if the warning not to summon him is ignored. It also reveals some of the racial biases that exist within the Black community, putting them on display and creating a canvas about which we are unsure how to feel.

One might assume that the lynching of the character Daniel Robitaille, or perhaps even the twin communities of Cabrini Green, where the Black people reside, and the upscale apartment complex where the lead character, Helen Lyles, lives—the two dwellings separated primarily by socioeconomic status— and the resulting consternation, is what is being dissected, but there is a more insidious point to be made with this film. The glimpse into the brutality of racism is artfully displayed in this film, forcing moviegoers to reckon, in some way, with what has occurred in order to experience the story they paid to see. Then, a muted form of racism comes to the foreground. A microaggression within the Black community is displayed in startling clarity, one that sows the seeds of the kind of racial honesty that films like Jordan Peele's *Get Out* and *Us* harvested, when Bernadette, the doomed Black sidekick of Helen Lyles, is lumped into the collective "White folks" bucket by Anne-Marie, the mother of the child who is later kidnapped by Candyman. Even though she is Black, Bernadette is not seen as such because of the nature of her presence in Cabrini Green—her appearance and reason for being there are at the forefront, even before her shared racial makeup. Coleman notices that "The two women are Whitened through class positioning and education level by Anne-Marie, who views such status as the root of Black exploitation" (189).

Familiar landscapes are shown in the film: an inner city and a tenement slum that put viewers, both Black and White, at ease because these locales have become associated with movies cast with predominantly Black actors. Of enduring confusion, though, is why Candyman's wrath is mostly wrought on the Black community of which he is a part—except when in service of his White love interest. Indeed, it is Helen Lyles who summons him, committing the act that results in death for everyone else who has done so, but not her. That the film endures as a shining moment for Black Horror, being viewed simply as horror for the masses, is both encouraging and problematic.

The 2000s represented a new, more outspoken version of Black Horror and Black characters in horror. *Scream 3's* Tyson Fox character, who was an actor cast in *Stab 3*—the movie within the movie—had interactions with his White counterparts that did not portray him as subservient or "other." Black filmmakers continued to create their own movies and submitted entries that garnered mainstream audiences, including the *Scary Movie* franchise created by the Wayans brothers that successfully linked horror and humor. Black actors found more work that did not force them to perpetuate the stereotypical behavior to which their counterparts in the early 1900s were relegated. Black stories were being told in a more mainstream and consumable way, but there was still a chasm between the understanding of experiences that a diverse lens could provide to mainstream viewers. The 2017 release of Jordan Peele's *Get Out* changed the vantage point of Black Horror and its underpinnings rooted in racism, discrimination, and classism. It gave life to the idea of elevated horror. *Culture* journalist David Jesudason posits, "Jordan Peele's 2017 directorial debut masterfully skewered racism in US society by satirizing the prejudice a young black man faces in modern America, among white people of all political persuasions – but it was also a watershed moment for horror." This groundbreaking film also reinforced the concept of disparate fear in a meaningful way.

What people consider scary relies on several factors, including history and environment among them. Black people in the U.S. have different triggers that incite fear in them, ones that may be different from people from other racial backgrounds, even if they are close in age, even if they are members of the same community. Scenarios such as being followed in stores, not being believed by those in positions of authority, and not being allowed to be a child—such as in the 1955 case of Emmett Till, who was brutally murdered after being accused of menacing a White woman, an accusation that was recanted decades after his death ("The Murder of Emmett Till"), and in the 2014 case of Tamir Rice, who was killed while playing with a toy gun ("Say Their Names: Tamir Rice")—spark terror in the minds of Black people, ordering their steps in a manner that precludes carefree living. This is markedly different than the traditional offering of ghosts, goblins, and supernatural beings that make up the mainstream horror genre. While those characters present opportunities for escapism in the form of entertainment for many Black people, they do not represent true fear that is visceral, or that has a lingering impact. Dr. Chesya Burke, the author of *Let's Play White*, offers this explanation: "When you look at Black Horror versus other types of horror, you will see people not fearing the supernatural or not fearing the horrific elements as much as they would white supremacy because white supremacy [is] an actual real reality in their life" (Copeland). The creator of *Nightlight* podcast, a venue that showcases short stories written by members of the Black diaspora, Tonia Ransom, goes further to define Black Horror by stating, "A lot of Black horror really centers around the fact that there are people out there who want to hurt you and kill you for something that you can't control. And that's super frightening" (Copeland).

The aforementioned breakout movie, *Get Out*, a movie rife with *Invasion of the Body Snatchers* vibes, crafts a tale of shattered illusions and the body coveted that manages to bring to life the very real fear that Black Americans experience at some point in their lives: the worry that something isn't as it seems. Audiences came together to watch the horror film as they did in the 1980s; they were able to scream directions to the screen, talk with the people around them about what was happening in the story, and react out loud as a result of this shared experience (Wilkinson). The difference this time was that both Black and White audiences could see themselves on screen, see the truths and exaggerations for what they were, and take away messages that were fodder for open discourse once the lights came on.

Black Horror films continue to gain their footing in this new space created by Peele's thought-provoking movie. Some entries continue the work, bringing imagery to the screen that reflects realistic Black characters. An example of this includes Osei-Kuffour Jr.'s 2020 science fiction horror release, *Black Box*, about a man who struggles to put fragments of his memory together after a tragic accident. Others have gone further, focusing on "more" rather than "what." Jesudason, brings up a new pattern, citing "…the new wave of black representation in horror – the way the historical plight of black Americans has sometimes been played upon by directors for scares in a way that turns real suffering into 'trauma porn.'" Releases such as *Antebellum* in 2020 and Amazon's limited series *Them* in 2021 represent examples where the continued aggression toward the Black characters overrides the horror elements. Jesudason credits Dan Hassler-Forest, a popular cultural theorist, as saying that the new outcropping of Black Horror films "are kind of exploitative and are shoving the indignities and the physical suffering of slavery and anti-black racism in our face over and over again." This sentiment, of course, does not encompass all of the recent submissions.

Black Horror and its very definition are changing as movies are released and old ideas are revisited. The 2019 movie *Ma*, about a Black woman who was humiliated as a teenager, sets an elaborate trap for the children of those who harmed her, subverts the trope of the Black character dying first, instead taking a page out of *Candyman*'s book and casting the Black character as the antagonist. There are also inroads being made in cable/streaming television with the 2020 release of *Lovecraft Country*, which was developed by Misha Green, a Black woman. There is something to be said about the influx of images that portray Black characters doing the same things that White characters do, and the movies coming out reflect that shared existence. It is empowering, regardless of how controversial the execution may be. Tananarive Due corroborates this assertion on the current state of film, "There is a lot of racial PTSD in the US…[a]nd horror is uniquely suited to give people, who have survived trauma or people who fear trauma, an outlet" (Jesudason).

Life does not imitate art, as the old adage indicates. Instead, a symbiotic relationship exists between the two, each assuming qualities of the other, reflecting truths and repelling them, moving as water does. They coexist, contribute, and detract from each other; they are in constant states of reconstruction, of rebirth. Without a marked vicissitude of both states, neither art nor life can change.

Works Cited

Adjei-Kontoh, Hubert. "From *Blacula* to *Get Out*: The Documentary Examining Black Horror." *The Guardian*, 7 Feb. 2019, www.theguardian.com/film/20 19/feb/07/horror-noire-documentary-black-horror.

Andrews, William L. "Slave Narratives." *Encyclopedia Britannica*, www.britanni ca.com/art/slave-narrative.

Antebellum. Directed by Gerard Bush and Christopher Renz, Lionsgate, 2020.

The Birth of a Nation. Directed by D. W. Griffith, Epoch Producing Co., 1915.

Black Box. Directed by Emmanuel Osei-Kuffour Jr., Amazon Studios, 2020.

Blackenstein. Directed by William A. Levey, Frisco Productions Limited, 1973.

Black Moon. Directed by Louis Malle. Cinema International Corporation and Filmverlag der Autoren, 1975.

Blacula. Directed by William Crain, American International Pictures, 1972.

Blatty, William Peter. *The Exorcist*. Harper & Row, 1971.

Bones. Directed by Ernest Dickerson, New Line Cinema, 2001.

Brooks, Kinitra D. *Searching for Sycorax, Black Women's Hauntings of Contemporary Horror*. Rutgers University Press, 2018.

Butler, Octavia E. *Fledgling.* Jane Langton, 2005.

Butler, Octavia E. *Wild Seed.* Doubleday Books, 1980.

Candyman. Directed by Bernard Rose, TriStar Pictures, 1992.

Coleman, Robin Means. *Horror Noire, Blacks in American Horror Films from the 1890s to Present*. Routledge, 2011.

Collymore, John-Mark. "Hood Dramas: Celebrating the Genre Plagued with Criticism." *Mixtape Madness*, 24 Sept. 2022, www.mixtapemadness.com/blog/exclusives/hood-dramas-celebrating-the-genre-plagued-with-criticism.

"Combined Print and E-book Nonfiction." *The New York Times*, 21 June 2020, www.nytimes.com/books/best-sellers/2020/06/21/combined-print-and-e-book-nonfiction/.

Copeland, Carolyn. "As Black Horror Rises in Popularity, Horror Writers Discuss Its Evolution." *Prism*, 26 Oct. 2020, prismreports.org/2020/10/26/as-black-horror-rises-in-popularity-horror-writers-discuss-its-evolution/.

Dead Presidents. Directed by Albert Hughes and Allan Hughes, Buena Vista Pictures Distribution, 1995.

Def by Temptation. Directed by James Bond III, Troma Entertainment, 1990.

Demon Knight. Directed by Ernest Dickerson, Universal Pictures, 1995.

DiAngelo, Robin. *White Fragility: Why It's So Hard for White People to Talk About Racism*. Beacon Press, 2018.

Dixon, Thomas, Jr. *The Clansman: A Historical Romance of the Ku Klux Klan*. Doubleday, Page & Co., 1905.

Dr. Black, Mr. Hyde. Directed by William Crain, Dimension Pictures, 1976.

Ellis, Bret Easton. *American Psycho*. Picador, 2022.

Event Horizon. Directed by Paul W. S. Anderson, Paramount Pictures, 1997.

Eve's Bayou. Directed by Kasi Lemmons, Trimark Pictures, 1997.

firehouse44. "Duane Jones Biography." *IMDB*, www.imdb.com/name/nm0427977/bio.

Foor, Sheila Marie. *Depiction of Blacks in the Works of Ernest Hemmingway*. 1978. Eastern Illinois University, Master's thesis, thekeep.eiu.edu/cgi/viewcontent.cgi?article=4221&context=theses.

Friday the 13th. Directed by Sean S. Cunningham, Georgetown Productions Inc., 1980.

From Hell. Directed by Albert Hughes and Allan Hughes, 20th Century Fox, 2001.

Ganja and Hess. Directed by Bill Gunn, Kelly-Jordan Enterprises, 1973.

Get Out. Directed by Jordan Peele, Universal Pictures, 2017.

The Green Mile. Directed by Frank Darabont, Warner Bros., 1999.

Green, Misha, creator. *Lovecraft Country*. Warner Bros. Television Studios et al., 2020.

Gremlins. Directed by Joe Dante, Warner Bros., 1984.

Gyasi, Yaa. "White People, Black Authors Are not Your Medicine." *The Guardian*, 20 Mar. 2021, www.theguardian.com/books/2021/mar/20/white-people-black-authors-are-not-your-medicine.

Halloween. Directed by John Carpenter, Compass International Pictures, 1978.

Hobbs, Allyson. "A Hundred Years Later, *The Birth of a Nation* Hasn't Gone Away." *The New Yorker,* 13 Dec. 2015, www.newyorker.com/culture/culture-desk/hundred-years-later-birth-nation-hasnt-gone-away.

Hopkinson, Nalo. "Nalo Hopkinson: Author, Creator." *Nalohopkinson.com,* www.nalohopkinson.com/skin-folk.

Hughes, Franklin. "Lynching Picnic." *Jim Crow Museum,* 2021, www.ferris.edu/HTMLS/news/jimcrow/question/2021/july.htm.

Hund, Wolfe D., and Charles W. Mills. "Comparing Black People to Monkeys Has a Long, Dark Simian History. *The Conversation,* 28 Feb. 2016, theconversation.com/comparing-black-people-to-monkeys-has-a-long-dark-simian-history-55102.

Invasion of the Body Snatchers. Directed by Don Siegel, Allied Artists Pictures, 1956.

I Still Know What You Did Last Summer. Directed by Danny Cannon, Sony Pictures, 1998.

Jesudason, David. "*Candyman* and Horror's Dubious Reckoning with Racism." *BBC.com,* 1 Sept. 2021, www.bbc.com/culture/article/20210901-candyman-and-horrors-dubious-reckoning-with-racism.

Joseph, Rhonda Jackson. "Where My Girls At? The Absence of Black Femininity in Vampire Culture." *Speculative Fiction Academy,* 30 Oct. 2021, www.speculativefictionacademy.com/course/how-to-academic.

King, Stephen. *The Green Mile.* Signet Books, 1996.

——. *The Shining.* Doubleday, 1977.

Lovecraft, H.P. "On the Creation of N—s." 1912. *Brown University Library,* repository.library.brown.edu/studio/item/bdr:425397/.

Lubering, J. E. "Phillis Wheatley." *Encyclopedia Britannica,* www.britannica.com/biography/Phillis-Wheatley.

Ma. Directed by Tate Taylor, Universal Pictures, 2019.

Mabanckou, Alain. *African Psycho.* Soft Skull, 2007.

Manasan, Althea, and Mary O'Connell. "From Servants to Outlaws: 100 Years of Black Representation in Hollywood Films." *CBC Radio,* 18 Mar. 2021, www.cbc.ca/radio/ideas/from-servants-to-outlaws-100-years-of-black-representation-in-hollywood-films-1.5953758.

Marvin, Little, creator. *Them.* Amazon Studios et al., 2021.

Menace II Society. Directed by Albert Hughes and Allan Hughes, New Line Cinema, 1993.

Miller, Paul D. "'Race Films': The Black Film Industry that Told Black Stories in Cinema's Earliest Days." *Rotten Tomatoes,* 31 Jan. 2021, editorial.rottentomatoes.com/article/race-movies/.

Mittan, Kyle. "UArizona Researcher Investigates Untold Stories of Blaxploitation Film." *The University of Arizona News,* 27 Jan. 2021, news.arizona.edu/story/uarizona-researcher-investigates-untold-stories-blaxploitation-film.

Moos, Dan. *Outside America: Race, Ethnicity, and the Role of the American West in National Belonging.* University Press of New England, 2005.

Morrison, Toni. *Beloved.* Alfred A. Knopf Inc., 1987.

"The Murder of Emmett Till." *Library of Congress*, www.loc.gov/collections/civil-rights-history-project/articles-and-essays/murder-of-emmett-till/.

Nazel, Joseph. *The Black Exorcist*. Holloway House Publishing Company, 1974.

Nevins, Jess. "A Short History of 20th Century African-American Horror Literature." *Jess Nevins.com*, 18 Feb. 2019, jessnevins.com/blog/?p=842.

@Nnedi. "My story is called [']Dark Home['], and it's the 2nd horror story I've ever written (I love reading horror, but writing it is … My 1st horror story was "On the Road" (later adapted into the graphic novel AFTER THE RAIN). "Dark Home" was inspired by this creepy (3AM) moment: …" *X*, 12 July 2023, 1:07 p.m., twitter.com/Nnedi/status/1679175662249312257.

A Nightmare on Elm Street. Directed by Wes Craven, New Line Cinema, 1984.

Night of the Living Dead. Directed by George Romero, Image Ten, 1968.

Overpeck, Deron. "From Hell." *Film Quarterly*, vol. 55, no. 4, 2002, pp. 41-45, https://doi.org/10.1525/fq.2002.55.4.41.

Pacific Rim. Directed by Guillermo del Toro, Warner Bros., 2013.

Pietrusza, David. "The Ku Klux Klan in the 1920s." *Bill of Rights Institute*, billofrightsinstitute.org/essays/the-ku-klux-klan-in-the-1920s.

Pilgrim, David. "The Brute Caricature." *Jim Crow Museum*, Nov. 2000, www.ferris.edu/HTMLS/news/jimcrow/brute/homepage.htm.

"Say Their Names: Tamir Rice." *Stanford University Green Library Exhibit*, exhibits.stanford.edu/saytheirnames/feature/tamir-rice.

Scary Movie. Directed by Keenen Ivory Wayans, Dimension Films, 2000.

Scream 2. Directed by Wes Craven, Dimension Films, 1997.

Scream 3. Directed by Wes Craven, Dimension Films, 2000.

The Shining. Directed by Stanley Kubrick. Warner Bros., 1980.

The Skeleton Key. Directed by Iain Softley, Universal Pictures, 2005.

Son of Ingagi. Directed by Richard C. Kahn, Hollywood Productions, 1940.

Spider Baby. Directed by Jack Hill, American General Pictures, 1967.

Spigner, Clarence. "Blaxploitation Reexamined: One Critic's Reinterpretation." *BlackPast*, 25 Feb. 2022, www.blackpast.org/african-american-history/perspectives-african-american-history/blaxploitation-reexamined-one-critics-reinterpretation/#:~:text=The%20numbers%20and%20dates%20of,in%20the%20genre%20were%20released.

Tales from the Hood. Directed by Rusty Cundieff, Savoy Pictures, 1995.

Terminator 2: Judgment Day. Directed by James Cameron, Tri-Star Pictures, 1991.

Us. Directed by Jordan Peele, Universal Pictures, 2019.

Vinopal, Courtney, and Tayari Jones. "5 Book Covers that Show How Ann Petry's *The Street* Was Depicted over Time." *PBS*, 1 June 2020, www.pbs.org/newshour/arts/5-covers-that-show-how-ann-petrys-the-street-was-depicted-over-time.

Warner, Tom. "Black History Month Spotlight on Clarence Muse." *Pratt Chat: The Blog of the Enoch Pratt Free Library*, blog.prattlibrary.org/2021/02/26/black-history-month-spotlight-on-clarence-muse/.

Waytz, Adam, et al. "A Superhumanization Bias in Whites' Perceptions of Blacks." *Social Psychological and Personality Science*, 2014, pp. 1-8, https://doi.org/10.1177/1948550614553642.

Wilkinson, Alissa. "Get Out Is a Horror Film about Benevolent Racism. It's Spine-Chilling." *Vox*, 25 Feb. 2017, www.vox.com/culture/2017/2/24/1469 8632/get-out-review-jordan-peele.

Chapter 9

Why Are Female Protagonists Not Believed in Horror Fiction?

Cass Heid

Abstract

In horror novels, there is a specific trope where women are not believed by the surrounding characters. Their level of believability, whether it is directly or indirectly influenced by general misogyny, is a separate entity from the primary conflict that the female central character must confront. This chapter tackles the many ways in which misogyny is prevalent in contrast with elements that contribute to the systemic biases that affect the credibility of fictional women, such as power dynamics, age, temporal setting, and societal setting. When the story revolves around a female protagonist, there are certain techniques used by horror authors in order to subdue them.

Keywords: women, credibility, female protagonist, misogyny

* * *

Introduction

When it comes to the horror genre, one might notice that protagonists face their own share of obstacles. These may include the supernatural, like Jeremy Thorn in David Seltzer's *The Omen*; the law, like Cal Hooper in Tana French's *The Searcher*; or even mental decline, like Jack Torrance in Stephen King's *The Shining*. While many of these protagonists come with baggage, such as a tragic past or the burden of a shameful mistake, these backstories are merely devices used to explain why the protagonists are the way they are and thus have little effect on their credibility as witnesses.

When a protagonist is male, he may be considered, at most, a bit eccentric, and if his past is known, others may not necessarily embrace it. However, the shame he may carry from his previous actions is typically something that he needs to fight from within if the need arises to confront it at all. Cal Hooper, for example, moves to Ireland to distance himself from the shame he harbors from his divorce (French 27), pressure from his job (59), and the mounting derailment of his personal moral code (299).

Jack Torrance also has reasons to escape. Formerly a high school teacher, Jack moves his young family from Stovington, Vermont, to Sidewinder, Colorado and accepts a job as the caretaker for the Overlook Hotel (King 17). Like Cal, his reason for doing so is to separate himself from a lapse in character, which King reveals to be the physical assault of a student (19). Regardless of the conflict at hand, both Cal's and Jack's torments are mostly internal.

Such protagonists may be perceived as a bit paranoid, but when we consider their female counterparts, that façade begins to fall away. The men's delusions, which are typically about how others may perceive them if their secret comes out, do not so much reflect the support they may already have: Cal is quickly accepted by most of the residents of Ardnakelty, Ireland (French 35), and Wendy Torrance is still devoted to Jack, despite her brewing resentment towards him (King 24). While both Cal and Jack are correct about something being amiss, it takes more external factors for them to catch on. It is not until page 78 of *The Searcher* that Cal is first made aware of Brendan Reddy's disappearance by his younger sister, Trey, but he does not begin to suspect the possibility of foul play until being subtly warned by his neighbor, Mart, much later in the book (212-13). Meanwhile, of the Torrances, Wendy's suspicions are aroused much earlier than Jack's: "The tears which had threatened all day now came in a cloudburst, and she leaned into the fragrant, curling steam of the tea and wept. In grief and loss for the past, and terror of the future" (21). Her intuition is keen on Jack, the central figure, while he turns so inward that he descends into madness.

When the story involves a heroine, though, these delusions are not so much her own but are projected by the characters around her. This is especially prevalent when the primary conflict involves a supernatural force, as the reason for the protagonist's hunch is not so much accepted as the result of substance abuse or a traumatic past but further stigmatized because of it. While both male and female central characters may deal with such situations, the decline of male characters is more often met with a different respect. They can be shown justification from society, such as Cal's former career with the Chicago police force (French 3), or sympathy, such as how Wendy enables Jack (King 21). Meanwhile, female characters are often met with scrutiny for the same flaws and presented as outcasts, unbelieved and unsupported by the supporting characters.

Power Dynamics

Authors depict female central figures in certain ways in order to discredit them. One way this is done is by crafting a power imbalance into the primary conflict. Mallory Quinn in Jason Rekulak's *Hidden Pictures* is a 21-year-old former athlete recovering from a narcotics addiction which she endured as a result of a car accident that killed her younger sister. Through her recovery program, she is granted a sponsor, adopts a distance-running regimen, and surrenders her life to Jesus Christ. Mallory's sponsor sets her up to work as a nanny for Ted and Caroline Maxwell, an educated, successful couple who have a young son. In contrast to Mallory's newfound dedication to her religion, the Maxwells are staunch atheists. Caroline shows Mallory a list of house rules forbidding behaviors such as drugs and partying The last of these rules prohibits any mentions of religion or superstition: "My husband insisted on number 10 ... He's an engineer. He works in technology. So science is very important to our family. We don't say prayers, and we don't celebrate Christmas. If a person sneezes, we won't even say God Bless You" (Rekulak 16).

To Mallory, everything seems perfect. The Maxwells live in the affluent Philadelphia suburb of Spring Brook, New Jersey, where the streets are paved smooth and the sidewalks are immaculate. They live right around the corner from a shopping plaza and have a large swimming pool in their backyard. Mallory is given a cottage on their property as well as the freedom to use the pool for her workouts and go on daily distance runs on her own time. Caroline also goes out of her way to make Mallory feel welcome, and they quickly develop a bond where Mallory feels like her mother is watching over her again (Rekulak 41). According to reviewer Tammy Sparks, the Maxwells seem almost "too perfect." Between their claims to have moved from Barcelona, their long list of house rules, and Ted's inappropriate behavior towards Mallory, Sparks suggests that the "weirdness" of the Maxwells may have been intentionally created to "add[] to the unsettling feeling of the story."

Rekulak depicts multiple power imbalances. First, the age difference between Mallory and the story's antagonist, Caroline, leaves her more vulnerable to deception than Jack and Cal, who are middle-aged. One could also account for the obvious religious differences between Mallory and the Maxwells, which Caroline is often seen scrutinizing whenever Mallory challenges her: "Caroline glances at the cross hanging from my neck, like somehow that's the problem" (Rekulak 117). Coinciding with the age difference, Caroline is also a doctor at the VA Hospital, which gives her the authority to refute Mallory's supernatural claims when it comes to her young son, Teddy (108). Meanwhile, Mitzi, Maxwell's eccentric next-door neighbor, is known for practicing séances and giving tarot readings to clientele from her home. The Maxwells are so put off by her superstitious practices that they assume Mitzi is a drug user and thus forbid Mallory to speak with her (108).

However, the key difference in Mallory's treatment (as opposed to Cal's and Jack's) lies in her recovery. At the beginning of the story, she is eighteen months clean, and Caroline, due to her medical background, takes a particular interest in Mallory, while Ted appears apprehensive, saying, "You seem like a nice person. I wish you all the best, I really do. But I want a nanny who doesn't have to pee in a cup every week. You can understand that, right?" (Rekulak 32). Later, it is revealed that Ted did this to protect Mallory, as Caroline specifically sought her out because, from what she knew, a recovering addict would not typically suspect the Maxwells' secret. It is also important to note that Ted's concern for Mallory is motivated by lustful reasons, and he makes numerous sexual advances towards her throughout the book, such as when he not-so-subtly points out a tattoo on the base of Mallory's thigh after she finishes working out in the pool (77).

Overall, Mallory's treatment by the supporting characters is, in terms of power dynamics, influenced by her womanhood. First, this is shown in the effort Caroline makes to establish herself as a mother figure to Mallory by buying her new clothes, showing her physical affection, and gifting her a taser to protect herself when she runs (Rekulak 41). Next, Ted's unwarranted lust towards Mallory plays a key role in the plot. While he first comes across as intimidating and uncompromising (32), his effort to protect Mallory is refuted by his behavior. After rescuing Mallory (340), he begs her to run off and start a new life with him, but she soon learns through Caroline that Ted "had his eye on her since she first got there" (340); in fact, he had installed a webcam in her cottage. Although Ted claims to have only hired Mallory because he was persuaded into doing so, it could be inferred that his attraction towards her played a role in that persuasion.

Meanwhile, the support Mallory receives from Mitzi and Adrian has a similar connotation. When Mitzi is first introduced, she is shown walking across the backyard to give Mallory "a bit of friendly advice" in telling her not to "sit out by the pool with everything on display" (Rekulak 60). Adrian, the college-aged landscaper who befriends Mallory and tries to help her solve her mystery, quickly becomes a love interest, so regardless of the innocence behind his intentions, they are still influenced by Mallory's womanhood.

Age

Another way authors control the way characters are perceived is by introducing younger protagonists. In "Where Are You Going, Where Have You Been?" by Joyce Carol Oates, Connie is a 15-year-old girl with a conventional appearance and a zest for life. At home, her mother scolds her for how often she looks in the mirror, but, according to Connie, this is because her mother no longer has a reason to look at her own face (Oates 25). Connie's older sister, June, is 24, still lives at home, and works as a secretary at the high school. Described as plain, chunky, and steady, she receives a lot of praise because she saves money, helps clean the house, and cooks while Connie sits around with her mind full of trashy daydreams (26). Fortunately, June has friends of her own and goes out with them several times a week. June's responsibility is what ultimately earns Connie her own small sense of freedom, as she is only allowed to do as June does (26).

As Oates's story takes place in the 1960s, the expectations placed on women are different from today. Connie's vanity earns her the place as the "black sheep" in her family, and it is that particular power imbalance that renders her a target to the story's antagonist, Arnold Friend. Oates uses foreshadowing to address the role Connie plays in this situation in the following lines:

> Everything about her had two sides to it, one for home and one for anywhere that wasn't home: her walk, which could be childlike and bobbing, or languid enough to make anyone think she was hearing music in her head; her mouth, which was pale and smirking most of the time, but bright and pink on these evenings out; her laugh, which was cynical and drawling at home - "Ha ha, very funny" - but high-pitched and nervous anywhere else, like the jingling of the charms on her bracelet. (27)

This draws an interesting parallel between Connie and Arnold, whom she meets a few paragraphs later. Despite the effort Connie puts into her appearance, her intentions are innocent. She enjoys the attention of some boys and the satisfaction of being able to ignore the ones she doesn't like (27), and these experiences directly contrast with her life at home, where her mother's approval doesn't come so easily. The suggestion of jealousy being at play between mother and daughter further brings out the theme of age as a power imbalance, and both this theme, along with the efforts Arnold takes to deceive Connie, work well in a horror setting despite the genre of this short story.

There are several references to music playing that show Connie's innocence and remind the reader of her age. No matter how familiar she is with the scene—the shopping plaza, movie theater, and drive-in restaurant across the highway where the older kids hang out—Oates makes no mention of Connie crossing any boundary with the boys she meets. She simply enjoys the attention they give her, spends her days daydreaming about it, and gets in her mother's way (29).

It is only when Connie is immersed in a familiar, friendly scene, with music playing around her, and she has the attention of Eddie, a boy she likes, that she first meets Arnold. In a passing glance, she falls for his guise as a teenager, even though he is, in fact, much older. When Arnold shows up at her house the next day unexpectedly, she is unable to recognize him from the drive-in. Oates's use of irony in Arnold's methods provides another interesting dynamic when it comes to the difference in age.

When he first drives up, Connie is listening to a radio program called XYZ Sunday Jamboree, and he greets her with a radio playing the same program when she comes to the door on the following page. These effects—the familiarity of the drive-in, the many references to music either playing in actuality or Connie's head, Arnold's overhanded yet failing attempts to continue fooling Connie after she quickly realizes his age, and the overall way Connie ends up in an unsafe situation when she is least expecting it—are all elements that add to the unsettling nature of this piece, alluding to how easily danger can hide in plain sight when one's guard is down.

As Connie gets a better read on Arnold and begins to understand his true intentions, Arnold leans into the musical references. When he tries to coax her into his vehicle, Oates writes, "He spoke in a simple, lilting voice, exactly as if he were reciting the words to a song" (35). Similar to the dynamic between Caroline and Mallory, Arnold seeks out Connie due to her vulnerability and uses his resources to deceive her. He reveals information about Connie by naming her friends and stating that he knows the exact whereabouts of Connie's family. As the protagonist, removed from the stimulation of the drive-in restaurant, quickly catches on to the real ages of Arnold and his accomplice, Ellie, the afternoon takes on a more sinister turn. Arnold instills fear by threatening Connie's family while also reminding Connie of her place in her family's dynamic: "Now, come out through to the kitchen to me, honey, and let's see a smile, try it, you're a brave, sweet little girl, and now they're eating corn and hot dogs to bursting over an outdoor fire, and they don't know one thing about you and never did and honey, you're better than them because not a one of them would have done this for you" (47).

Arnold's method for seducing Connie is, ironically enough, shown through his commitment to appearing young. Connie's youthful traits, such as "her high, breathless voice" (26), are used to discredit her, but despite his claims to know all her friends, it is obvious to Connie that Arnold is not who he says he is. Oates writes, "His whole face was a mask, she thought wildly, tanned down to his throat but then running out as if he had plastered makeup on his face but had forgotten about his throat" (41). There are also several references to Arnold appearing to stuff his boots in order to seem taller, and he is shown running through all the youthful sayings he'd learned, unsure of which ones were in style. Unfortunately for Connie, her intuition is not enough to save her. The unexpected nature of the antagonist appearing in the environments where Connie feels safest and Connie's helplessness are additional elements that work well in horror.

Temporal Setting

The element of setting also plays a crucial role in the believability of a female central character, especially when that setting pertains to a different time period. On the surface, it does not seem that Rosemary Woodhouse from Ira Levin's *Rosemary's Baby* is much affected by this. At the opening of her story, she is 24 years old, living in New York City, and newly married to Guy Woodhouse, an up-and-coming actor. She is excited to be married and wants to begin family planning as soon as possible, but first, the couple must settle into their new apartment and wait for Guy's acting career to take off.

Because this story takes place in the 1960s and she is a woman, Rosemary is not left with many options outside of her prospects as a wife and homemaker. Regardless, she is eager to assume these roles. When she meets her new neighbors, Roman and Minnie Castevet, they appear to be a nice, hospitable older couple, but Rosemary isn't quite as fond of them as Guy is. Their behavior seems odd to Rosemary—they can be heard shouting at each other through the paper-thin walls of their adjoining apartment (Levin 36-37). Still, this can be chalked up to nothing more than those of a well-meaning older couple who have poor boundaries. The way the Castevets portray themselves causes Rosemary to go against her intuition and let her guard down, especially upon seeing how quickly Guy warms up to them (87).

The most chilling facet of this novel is the depth of the mask worn by the many antagonists: Guy as a supportive, hardworking husband; the Castevets as friendly, well-intentioned neighbors; members of their coven as a community for Rosemary to turn to; and Dr. Sapirstein as a professional experienced in his field.

As a product of her time, Rosemary is repeatedly shown second-guessing her intuition. When she first becomes pregnant, she immediately brushes off the circumstances in which it happened as a bad dream, and she later dismisses her odd symptoms since she believes Dr. Sapirstein would have told her if something was wrong (Levin 147). Similar themes continue to present themselves throughout Rosemary's pregnancy: Minnie and Roman specifically recommend Dr. Sapirstein, who is later revealed to be part of their scheme and urge Rosemary to see him over her obstetrician, Dr. Hill. During her visits, Dr. Sapirstein tells Rosemary never to confide in other women regarding her symptoms (under the guise of preventing false hysteria) and grows impatient when she does. Guy plays a part in this, too: he throws away books Rosemary brings home and loses his temper at Rosemary's friends when they express concern for her symptoms, begging her to find another doctor. As she is estranged from her family, and in a time period where women have few options outside of the homemaker role, Rosemary tries to advocate for herself as best as she can, yet she is steamrolled by the other characters and regarded as a hypochondriac.

Levin continues to weave a network of webs throughout the intentions of the characters and the measures they are willing to take to keep Rosemary in the dark about their Satanic practices. When Rosemary becomes pregnant, Minnie falls into a maternal role, coming over at the same time every day to give Rosemary a special drink full of "vitamins" to help nurture the fetus through its development (148). She and Roman do a fantastic job at keeping their scheme from Rosemary: their coven meetings, their accomplices, and the final leg in their plan, a going away party for the Castevets, complete with a tearful goodbye from

Roman, who pretends to be terminally ill (235-36). Despite Rosemary's rather sharp instincts, the other characters are able to use many elements from the respective time period and the roles women played to their advantage, presenting Rosemary as a hysterical young woman.

Societal Setting

Finally, societal pressures become more impactful on the perception of female protagonists the further back in time their stories take place. While societies at any different time are distinct from one another, Jane from Charlotte Brontë's *Jane Eyre* hails from an era far enough removed to place her in a different society altogether. To accommodate this distinction, this section is dedicated to addressing the impact of the vastly differing traditional norms, opinions, and beliefs at play.

One distinctive factor between Jane's time and the other periods mentioned is the way she and everyone around her are shaped by tradition. Mallory is from a secular time where her religious beliefs are weaponized against her; no one in Connie's family "bothers with church" on Sundays (Oates 30). Meanwhile, Rosemary becomes estranged from her Catholic family for marrying Guy, an atheist, and is also mocked by other supporting characters for sticking to certain principles, such as admitting she still respects the pope (Levin 77). However, Jane does *not* question her faith. Her society is entirely governed by religion, and she studies the Bible without hesitation because she is expected to do so. She admits to enjoying these studies and lists the books of which she is she is fond, although she does not like the book of Psalms (Brontë 32).

Due to the effect tradition had on society during Jane's time, she is much more likely to be punished for failing to adhere to the rules. Jane is proportionately more restricted by Victorian standards. She is not discerned by her actions but by her *re*actions to the way she is treated since she was born into homelessness prior to being taken in by the Reed family. Jane has many notable skills: playing the piano, drawing, teaching, and speaking French (Brontë 96). Unfortunately, these traits are overlooked by her lack of relations, plain appearance, and unwillingness to adhere to the staunch values of her time by remaining passive to disrespect.

Like Oates, Brontë's work contains elements that apply to horror. One example is the recurring theme of hopelessness. From the start of the novel, Jane is written off by everyone around her. As both a child and a young adult, she is scrutinized for her appearance. Young Jane, in contrast to the other children in the Reed family, is not an attractive child. This, along with her status as the late Mr. Reed's orphaned niece, renders her an outcast within the family.

As a result, hopelessness is a major theme in this work. A key example of this is shown in Jane's friendship with Helen Burns, whose characterization opposes that of Jane. Unlike Jane, Helen is shown taking her mistreatment in stride, for she believes it is her responsibility to bear it. Helen, much like Jane, had little support of her own: both characters are orphaned, and neither have been given enough emotional support in their upbringings, yet this manifests in opposite ways. While Jane speaks out against her abuse and suggests that Helen should do the same, Helen does not see the point in doing so, for she believes herself to be fundamentally flawed and, therefore, deserving of frequent punishment.

Helen accepts the hand she is dealt, for she believes it is her duty to endure her pain rather than feel sorry for herself (53). Like many devout Christians of this time, Helen sees the world as much larger than herself and uses her faith in God to detach from the pain of the cruelty she is repeatedly shown. She tells Jane that she will understand her purpose when she is older and suggests that Jane's thirst for vengeance is for "heathens and savages" as well as a product of her younger age (55). This radical acceptance of Helen's fate ends up being her downfall.

When many girls at Lowood School contract typhus, Helen becomes one of the many casualties, and it is before her death that she states that she is okay with dying young, for she was too flawed to make it in this world (77). While Jane is repeatedly chastised for her belligerent nature, it is Helen's endurance that ultimately kills her, for it can be inferred that the physical abuse Helen was dealt at Lowood contributed to her contracting typhus.

That being said, a comparison can be made between the untimely demise of Helen and that of Connie from "Where Are You Going, Where Have You Been?" Although the characterizations of both contrast each other, it is the element of obedience that leads to their respective fates. Both characters are villainized for having flaws that, if it weren't for the product of misogyny prevalent in the periods, should be seen as human traits. Helen endures corporal punishment whenever her mind wanders during class, and Connie is the subject of her mother's disapproval for showing an interest in her appearance. The difference between the two characters is that while Connie actively rebels against what is expected of her, Helen is willing to accept any punishment that comes her way. But, it is ultimately Connie's obedience (doing as Arnold tells her) and Helen's acceptance (allowing harsh treatment) that lead to their deaths.

Both characters see themselves as fundamentally flawed, but they deal with it in different ways. Connie deals with her perceived flaws by enjoying her life regardless of what others think, as she does not believe she will ever win her mother's approval like her sister. Helen, on the other hand, sees her frequent chastisement as something she needs to endure due to her flaws. In that regard, one could argue that both characters have given up on any form of hope for themselves as products of their respective periods.

Without any legitimate families and thus wards of the state, Jane and Helen are already under examination. Helen is repeatedly lashed and made to stand on a stool in front of her classmates simply for turning her feet the wrong way, averting her eyes, or losing focus during lectures (Brontë 51-52). One could infer that these behaviors are not a byproduct of any type of character flaw but a result of her trauma, as dissociation is a trauma response. Neither Helen, Jane, nor any other girl at Lowood school are even allowed to indulge in the simple pleasure of braiding their hair or any other form of vanity (61). Meanwhile, Georgiana, the youngest daughter of the Reed family, is adored for her features, regardless of how ill-mannered she presents herself (14).

Conclusion

A common thread amongst these protagonists is that they are ultimately driven to hopelessness due to an imbalance of power in age, contributing to their stigmatization or setting. This can be looked at as a continuum; the further back in time that the setting of the story takes place, the more scrutiny the female protagonist and/or supporting characters will face. Conversely, the more current the story's setting, the more tragedy must strike the central character to hinder her perceived capabilities. Jane and Helen are products of a time when women were held to strict standards when it came to their respective roles, but these rules typically seem to apply most to those from lower incomes.

From these accounts, one can conclude that the believability of women in horror comes down to three points. First is the power dynamics: while the protagonists mentioned in this chapter are mostly female, the (binary) gender of the antagonists does not discriminate, nor do the roles they play. Caroline Maxwell, Minnie Castevet, and Mrs. Reed are just as overhanded as Arnold Friend and Guy Woodhouse. They are just as able to conceal their motives by income status (Mrs. Reed), social power (Caroline Maxwell), and an innocent, friendly disposition (Minnie Castevet); this does not thwart, but, in fact, is *enhanced* by their respective time periods.

Next, one can conclude that, regardless of the time period or one's social power, authors discredit female protagonists by crafting their stories to the experience of younger characters with less life experience where they can be more easily swayed. Mallory is 21, while Ted and Caroline are 55 and 40. Connie is 15, and Arnold is in his 30s. Rosemary is 24, while Guy is 33, and the Castevets are in their 70s. Jane is 10 at the introduction of her story, while Mrs. Reed is in her 40s. Meanwhile, Cal and Jack are middle-aged, while the other parties in their respective conflicts are of equal or younger ages. It does *not* add up. While there are also power dynamics at play in the above examples (excluding Cal and Jack, whose plots were shaped from the other side of that dynamic), the imbalances run concurrent with age, whether by life-experience (Minnie Castevet), expertise

(Caroline Maxwell), guardianship (Mrs. Reed), or by being the target of a predator (Arnold Friend).

Finally, whether the time comes with respective gender roles or is of the current era where there is a need to prove oneself, the social obligations that come with both leave these characters at a disadvantage in terms of plausibility.

While these works do not individually transcend any specific horror tropes, there is not enough dialogue on the credibility of female protagonists (or lack thereof). Furthermore, analyzing the preceding works together, along with dissecting the factors that contribute to the use of this trope, may ignite more discussions that will lead to its transcendence in the future.

Works Cited

Brontë, Charlotte. *Jane Eyre*. 3rd ed., Dover Publications, 2002.

French, Tana. *The Searcher.* Viking Press, 2020.

King, Stephen. *The Shining* Doubleday Publishing, 1977.

Levin, Ira. *Rosemary's Baby*. Penguin Random House, 1967.

Oates, Joyce Carol. "Where Are You Going, Where Have You Been?" *Women Writers: Texts and Contexts*, edited by Elaine Showalter, Rutgers University Press, 1994, pp. 25-48.

Rekulak, Jason. *Hidden Pictures*. Flatiron Books, 2022.

Seltzer, David. *The Omen.* Futura Publishing, 1976.

Sparks, Tammy. "*Hidden Pictures* by Jason Rekulak - Review." *Books, Bones & Buffy*, 17 May 2022, booksbonesbuffy.com/2022/05/17/hidden-pictures-by-jason-rekulak-review/.

Chapter 10

Schlock and Awe: Transgression and Trash Aesthetics in Nick Zedd's *They Eat Scum*

Stephan Zguta

Abstract

This chapter examines Nick Zedd's 1979 film *They Eat Scum*, which carries in its celluloid a transgressive ideology and challenges the status quo of popular culture. The film passes the limit of taboo, not just for the acknowledgment of such but to expose its mutability. With this stylistic choice, Zedd creates a dual reaction in the viewer: humor and disgust. The film leans into tropes like cannibalism, bestiality, and trash aesthetics, highlighting and transcending them. Horror presents the abject for the audience to turn away from it, but in *They Eat Scum*, Zedd entices us to look on. This exposure to the abject creates a moment of reflection around the limits of taboos and social structures, bringing the viewer closer to the edge of continuity.

Keywords: transgression, taboo, subversion, *They Eat Scum*, abject

* * *

Introduction

The underground auteur Nick Zedd screened his first film, *They Eat Scum*, in 1979 at a small standing-room-only theater in New York City. During the late 1970s and early '80s, a generation of underground filmmakers had emerged, branded "No-Wave," including Lydia Lunch, Amos Poe, Beth B, and Jim Jarmusch. But Zedd, despite the relative success of his contemporaries, saw his film relegated to the gutter due to its unique and unapologetic use of taboo subject matter. On its surface, *They Eat Scum* deals in shock value and the grotesque à la John Waters's early films, presenting the audience with images of what Amos Vogel calls "disruptive elements," those which "society requires the excommunication of": the abject, the taboo, the dangerous (263). But there is something else beyond the screen's surface—beyond the camp aesthetic and gratuitous shock and awe—deep in its celluloid, there is intentionality.

Upon its release, *They Eat Scum* became the seminal film of the Cinema of Transgression, a movement coined by Zedd (under the pseudonym Orion Jeriko)

in a 1985 issue of *The Underground Film Bulletin.* The Cinema of Transgression called for a rejection of both the art and commercial spheres of film in favor of a more subversive and original work coalescing around transgressive and abject imagery to confront the audience on a more physical and visceral level (Jeriko, "Manifesto"). The No-Wave filmmakers of the art scene took influence from the French new wave genre and made what Zedd called "imitation '60s underground films that were pretty bad" (*Deathtripping* 60). Zedd was more influenced by the over-the-top camp found in the films of Jack Smith (*Flaming Creatures,* 1963) and Herschell Gordon Lewis (*Blood Feast,* 1963), which were films that leaned into the use of excess.

Although *They Eat Scum* was released before the conception of The Cinema of Transgression, Zedd's film exemplifies the movement's ideology and allows the analysis to be informed by the movement retroactively, from a teleological standpoint, giving weight and purpose to his low-brow and subversive film. A mostly unknown film, *They Eat Scum* has had a great influence on the genre and helped to usher in a wave of low-budget and underground gore and black comedy flicks that appeared throughout the 1980s and '90s. In an article for *Vice* magazine, Avi Davis speaks with the filmmaker Richard Kern, who states that Zedd's film was an "incredible movie for Super 8," confessing it made him realize "you can actually make a movie for nothing."

The film is extremely low-budget, depraved, disgusting, corny, and, despite it all—or because of it—a real gem of trash cinema. The narrative focuses on the protagonist, Suzi Putrid, as she escapes her repressive middle-class home life and becomes a celebrity in the "death rock" music scene. She turns her fanbase into a cannibalistic cult of punks who run through the streets of New York chewing on the passerby. Their mayhem eventually leads to a meltdown at a nuclear power plant, which ushers in a postapocalyptic society under the rule of Suzi; however, the population of mutants then stages a rebellion and brings Suzi face-to-face with her death at the hands of a giant cockroach.

The graphic imagery and violence of the film lean into certain clichés and tropes of horror and exploitation—cannibalism, drug use, bestiality, and bodily disfiguration—but, in the choice to present the grotesque with a camp sensibility, the film does not deify these features, instead rendering them laughable through an absurd and unbelievable presentation. With this stylistic choice, the film provides a new perspective toward the taboo, transcending boundaries and convention, allowing *They Eat Scum* to manifest Zedd's ideological purpose— the rejection of tradition—confusing the "normal" reaction to the tropes of horror and exploitation films and urging the viewer to question why it is we react that way in the first place.

The Human Abject

Julia Kristeva's work, *Powers of Horror*, situates the abject as an ambiguity, something "ejected beyond the scope of the possible, the tolerable, the thinkable," yet it is something that evokes deep feeling—the impulse to turn away at the sight of an open wound, the disgust felt in the presence of human excrement and bodily fluids (2). This reaction to the abject seems instinctual, natural even. The blood coursing throughout us becomes abject when, outside the barrier of the skin, a corpse that was once living threatens us with our own inevitable demise. So, we turn from the abject and we reject it. This reaction to, and rejection of, the abject then becomes a path toward forming an identity—on a personal, organizational, and cultural level—we are *this* because we reject *that*.

The use of the abject, especially in works of horror, is meant to exploit these reactive impulses. The viewer, confronted by the abject, turns away, cover their eyes, and squirm in their seat, waiting for the scene to end. George Romero's 1968 film *Night of the Living Dead* features corpses that rise from the dead, become animate, and blur the line between dead and living. There is a sense of horror evoked by something that won't adhere to our shared worldview—something that crosses a line, sets a boundary, and becomes a marker of an agreed limitation, or, as Kristeva states, the "primers of culture" (4).

They Eat Scum brings the viewer to this same limitation but then pushes it further, crossing beyond the boundary again and again. However, the film defies the viewer's expectations and pairs the abject imagery with a camp sensibility, making the violence and depravity unbelievable and ironic. This mismatch of elements elicits a confused response, one of disgust and simultaneous laughter, and this laughter, as Kristeva states, is "a way of placing or displacing abjection," demonstrating borders as mutable, constructed, and laughable (8).

The film itself is abject in its entirety, not only because of its subject matter but because of its incredibly low production value. However, this lack of production creates a buffer between the viewer and the depraved acts of the film, as every element is "in quotation marks," exaggerated to absurdity, a self-parody, representing what Susan Sontag calls, "Being-as-Playing-a-Role" ("Notes on 'Camp'" 280). Suzi Putrid is not just a punk but a crazed psychopath who engages in cannibalism. Her brother, Jimmy, is not just a cross-dresser but a zoophile. These excessive qualities become unbelievable and even laughable in their presentation, mocking themselves as they appear on the screen, bringing the viewer closer to the abject rather than turning them away, and allowing an engagement with the film and all its possible implications. These exaggerated representations of "low brow" humor bring the film into the realm of trash cinema, a certain type of cinema that "reject[s] not only Hollywood conventions but also the visual pleasure or intellectual demands of art cinema and the avant-garde" (Barefoot 48). Through its trash aesthetics, *They Eat Scum* rejects the mainstream representations of what a film can and should be while also going "beyond the narrow concerns of film theory" (Jeriko, "Cinema of Transgression").

The opening scene focuses on a seemingly mentally deficient figure, convulsively waving their arms and strapped to a chair, being force-fed a dripping green "scum" while a record of Mr. Rogers's "You Are Special" skips along. The scum becomes a stand-in for our ready-made culture, dictated and handpicked by an off-screen motherly entity who spoons it into the mouth of the chair-bound figure as the camera zooms in and out of focus on the dripping scum. The taste becomes irrelevant when strapped to a chair. All one can do is swallow it or regurgitate, spit it back up, and abject it. Possibly this opening scene is meant to taunt the viewer who, about to be subjected to the 73 minutes of the underground schlock that is *They Eat Scum*, is the chairbound figure themselves. The scene becomes ironic and playful in its ambiguity, simultaneously existing in the realm of trash cinema with its low quality and unpolished techniques and reducing popular and mainstream culture to trash or "scum" itself.

After the opening shot, not even ten minutes elapse before Suzi's brother, Jimmy, fellates his miniature poodle, Polio. The scene starts with the family sitting around the table in a middle-class home. A figure of Jesus, backlit for emphasis, sits on the table while the father, Mr. Stank, announces, "A day doesn't go by that I don't pray for you" to his children. The family dynamic is set up in this shot: a devoutly religious father trying, by any means but failing, to keep his children within the restrictive tenets of Christianity. He goes on to tell Suzi, who is slathered in her punk makeup, about a date he has set up for her with a "mechanical scientist" named Herman Barbell. Meanwhile, Mr. Stank has seemingly given up on his cross-dressing son and frequently locks him away in the bathroom.

Once the family dynamic is set, the film quickly moves into more transgressive territory. We cut to Jimmy alone in his room, wearing a white dress and blonde wig, talking to his dog, Polio, in a seductive and "feminine" voice. Jimmy then sings "Getting to Know You" from *The King and I* before lifting the dog to his face. After some gagging and heavy breathing, he puts the dog down and opens his mouth to reveal voluminous ejaculation that he spits out into a tissue. By spitting out the dog's sperm, Jimmy casts all social norms away from his identity with the Kristevian notion, "I expel myself, I spit myself out, I abject myself within the same motion through which 'I' claim to establish myself" (3). Instead of reinforcing boundaries (such as Christianity, family values, and/or sexuality) through the exploitation of the abject, here, Zedd's film positions Jimmy as outside the bounds of morality. The dog, Polio, is not just man's best friend but man's sexual desire, and the relationship between Jimmy and Polio is portrayed throughout the film as a romantic love story rather than animal abuse.

The scene inspires disgust; however, just as Susan Sontag suggests that a work of camp entails "something *démesuré* in the quality of the ambition," the film renders the act unconvincing and semi-humorous in its presentation, leaving the viewer with an ambivalent reaction to the obscene ("Notes on 'Camp'" 440). It is immediately apparent that the act on the screen is fake, and the disgust felt for any abuse or sexual relations with an animal becomes momentarily eclipsed by the absurdity of artifice. This dual reaction of disgust and humor creates a moment that breaches into the repressed unconscious and results in what James Cody Walker calls "difficult laughter" (2). This "difficult laughter" is the inevitable failure of modern culture's aims to repress sex and violence, and, in this failure, bits and pieces slip past the repression, causing a reaction "in an immediate [and] visceral way," which "contains both a laugh and a gasp," pulling the viewer "in two different directions" (Walker 32). Laughter then becomes an unconscious moment of reflection, an internal questioning of our own preconceived notions. In these moments of difficult laughter, Zedd's film asks where the boundaries are while pushing past them.

Sexual depravity is not the only aspect that confronts the audience with the abject in *They Eat Scum*, as cannibalism is also informed by Kristeva's theory, playing on the idea that the corpse is the "utmost of abjection," something occupying a liminal space at the borders of life and death (4). Cannibalism has seemingly always existed as a basic taboo of humanity, and the reaction to the corpse, on a cultural level, is a "respect for the body of the other" (Kristeva 79). *They Eat Scum* then portrays the breakdown of a fundamental barrier crossed by Suzi and her followers who regularly engage in cannibalistic behavior; unthreatened by the taboo of the corpse, Suzi and her followers embrace their abject status and renounce their humanity. Without any self-identification with the corpse, the respect for the other is eliminated, and the taboo is ignored.

However, the use of cannibalism in the film also highlights that the abject is not absent from humanity. Halfway through the film, Suzi and her gang of "death rockers" kidnap a young woman outside Studio 54. They then tear at her clothes and—with the help of a buzz saw—dismember the body and devour it. This young woman quite literally becomes the "scum" that "they" eat, representative of the gang's rejection of social constructs or culture. Through the act of slicing the body apart, Suzi reveals the hidden abject within the woman, the everyday violence of our society that is rationalized and accepted. The kidnapped woman's mutilated corpse can be seen as a stand-in for Mr. Stank's patriarchal parenting. As a morally upright citizen, Mr. Stank operates with his piousness as a façade for violence. He abuses his son, locks him in the bathroom for a week, and leaves him to die for the sin of being a "smut peddler." The exposed violence underneath the surface of humanity becomes the abject; just like the mutilated body of the kidnapped woman, it becomes the "death infecting life" (Kristeva 4). Through the violence and bodily harm of cannibalism, the body becomes disassembled, displayed, transformed into grotesque, and rearranged from the human subject to the human abject.

Even though this entire scene is gruesome, its execution lacks realistic representation and comes off as humorous. The props used for the corpse, including rubber breasts and a skeleton hand (as if the cannibals were able to lick her clean), almost poke fun at the excessive violence that it represents through their lack of realism. The violence of cannibalism and dismemberment becomes a trope used in the horror genre, but here, it doesn't quite mesh with the tone and production quality of the film. The scene creates an incongruity, a necessary detachment that juxtaposes the subject matter with trash aesthetics— laughing at it—and separates the viewer from any normative or learned responses to the violence, allowing a difference of perspective.

Zedd continues with the notion that humanity is itself abject in a sequence toward the end of the film. Suzi and her followers cause a meltdown at a nuclear power plant, leaving New York City and its entire population to die. While the rest of the film is saturated with abject imagery, this sequence—the deserted streets of a post-apocalyptic New York—shows images of beauty and polish through Zedd's camera. A montage begins with a pan shot from a television screen to a family sprawled out dead on their sofa. Zedd then cuts to an empty New York City, mid-day, and pans up to the high-rise buildings, catching glares from their reflective surfaces, accentuating the alienating aspects of the architecture with the movements of his camera. Futuristic synthesizer music accompanies the montage, imparting a sense of the sublime as if looking upon a science-fictional setting rather than the streets of New York.

The quality of the camera work, the focus on the landscape, and the change of tone in the lush synthesizer music (as opposed to punk rock music) juxtapose this scene with the entirety of the film. The human subject is nowhere in this scene, and in its absence, the depravity and abject disappear. This abandoned city montage, the most palatable scene of the movie, demonstrates the film's notion that humanity is a disease or that humanity is abject, as the human subject is absent, and the beauty of absence takes its place. With no lines to speak—as language is a referent of meaning—and no actors to direct—as "good" and "bad" acting is subjective—the shot becomes pure as opposed to the "scum" that occupies the rest of the film.

The Transcendence of Trash

Zedd's aim as an underground filmmaker was to transgress as much as possible; through themes such as a rejection of religion, family values, and sexual norms as well as flagrant acts of bestiality, incest, and cannibalism, *They Eat Scum* was a successful first attempt. No taboo in the film goes unnoticed as the transgressions are thrust upon the viewer, shown "with a sense of gleeful outrage and exaggerated punk aggression" (Sargeant 29). There is no shame, and that was the point of Zedd's work, to "shock in as direct a manner as possible"; however, it was not just a cheap tactic to gain notoriety through infringing social mores but instead intentionality in its celluloid: not *only* to shock but to "shock and make people think" (Jeriko, "Cinema of Transgression").

By the time *They Eat Scum* premiered in 1979, censorship in cinema had already waned. The taboo images, excluded from studio films of the previous four decades under the Production Code, were increasingly included after the rating system came into being in 1968—for example, the violence and gore portrayed in *The Texas Chainsaw Massacre* (1974) and *Rabid* (1977) was something previously unseen in movies with a wide release (Culture Shock). This increase of visual taboo in the horror genre was shepherded in by the 1973 release of *The Exorcist*, which John McCarty states in his book, *Splatter Movies: Breaking the Last Taboo of the Screen*, "succeeded in charting a new course for filmmakers," bringing horror with excessive gore "out of the cultural sub-basement and … into the limelight as an established and extremely vital form of filmmaking" (105).

Claire Cronin jests in *Blue Light of the Screen* that "*The Exorcist* did more to bring people back to the Church than any efforts of the Vatican" (83). The use of transgression in *The Exorcist* works to situate the taboo as marginalized, supernatural, or outside of the human experience. The shot of a young girl aggressively masturbating with a crucifix shocked audiences everywhere, but, at the same time, it contextualized the scene through a lens of Christian magic and demonic possession. As Amos Vogel writes in *Film as a Subversive Art*, "commercial film" uses transgression as a tool to reaffirm the taboo, becoming "an important purveyor of Establishment values" (263). The same can be said of most works in the genre of horror, which include acts of transgression, but only within certain boundaries that reinforce a status quo, deifying taboo as something separate—the other. *They Eat Scum* works to dethrone the taboo, remove the implied dichotomy of "good" and "evil" or "right" or "wrong" and question the sacred status of all taboos.

Suzi transgresses family values, turning to punk, drugs, and cannibalism, while her Christian father, faced with her rebelliousness, commits his own act of transgression in the form of filicide. Jimmy, emotionally abused by the family, sexually abuses their dog. No character remains untouched. At the end of the film, Suzi, who starts a fascist monarchy in a post-apocalyptic New York, becomes the dominant power structure, the administrator of prohibitions, and is thus killed off by a group of rebelling mutants. The film demonstrates an inherent feature of the system of taboo: when transgressed, a new definition of taboo is defined; a new limit is established. The process of transgression then becomes continual, and in his effort to "break all the taboos of our age," Zedd pushes the limits again and again throughout the film, showing the mutability of taboos that are taken as universal and natural ("Manifesto").

Aiming for transgression itself is not such a remarkable quality in a film since transgressions often only reinforce an existing taboo. According to Georges Bataille, the system of taboo "is made up of the profane and the sacred … two complementary forms," one dependent on prohibitions and the other on transgressions (*Eroticism* 67). The taboo works to regulate these separate spheres, to dictate what acts are punishable and which are deemed permissible. The allowed transgressions limit excess and dictate rules around how transgressions can occur: murder is punishable by law, but war is normal foreign policy; prescription drugs are okay, but addiction is frowned upon (Bataille, *The Tears of Eros* 39). Acts in excess of these "limited … transgression," therefore lacking in purpose or utility, are bound to the world of punishment, restriction, and, for Zedd, underground film (Bataille, *Eroticism* 68).

But *They Eat Scum* ignores the prescribed purpose of the visual taboo, and the transgressive acts of the film work to disrupt meanings (limitations) that any purpose would usually ascribe. The unlicensed use of "Good Vibrations" by The Beach Boys plays as two men are jumped and eaten by a group of cannibals, making the scene discordant. The song, an anthem of the nonviolent flower power movement of the late 1960s and early 1970s, is set against acts of cannibalism, mutating the film's tone through the disregard of learned associations of violence. The oppositional aspects are situated within a singular scene—the violence of the image and the nonviolence of the audio—and neither one defines the other through a correlated association; but, by existing in tandem, they create a sense of unease through a lack of definition.

The violence, if accompanied by traditional elements such as suspense and tension, would conform to our expectations for horror. But, in *They Eat Scum*, the images are turned on their head, allowing an ambiguous response. Toward the beginning of the movie, during a date with the "mechanical scientist" set up by her father, Suzi sits at the edge of the shot with a large swastika painted on her face. The visual of the swastika is peripheral and pointless in its inclusion; however, the swastika's dissociation from any contextual meaning confuses the viewer's immediate and visceral reaction to the symbol. The swastika's refusal to adhere to its assigned cultural definition disrupts its own meaning and association. Through this type of disruption, *They Eat Scum* does not dismiss the taboo as abnormal or outside the human experience (as in *The Exorcist*) but allows it to exist in the film without dramatization. By refusing to marginalize the taboo imagery within the film, the boundary is confused, and the process of assigning meaning is disrupted, even if momentarily. Up is down, down is up, and, just as Zedd wrote in his 1984 manifesto, "Nothing is sacred." The taboo is stripped of its power and utility and is shoved onto the screen to confront the viewer with the absurdity of their prefabricated reactions.

When it comes to the taboos surrounding sex, the horror genre often creates the usual trope that insinuates engaging in sexual activity brings about death. Again, we see a limit here, aligning sexual pleasure with death, something to avoid, a boundary that is to not be crossed. Zedd skews this, as well, not only subverting the taboo by incorporating sexual depravity in his film but also through the complete denial of sex from Suzi and her cult of death rockers. In *The Tears of Eros*, Bataille discusses the dissolution of the boundaries surrounding a taboo through an image depicting Lingchi, or death by a thousand cuts, a method of torture practiced in China through the early twentieth century. Bataille's interest was not in the practice of torture itself but in the boundary between pain and pleasure and the "ecstatic appearance of the victim's expression" (*The Tears of Eros* 205). There is a similar demonstration of the physical manifestation of this dissolution of boundaries in *They Eat Scum* in a scene where Suzi calls for her fanbase to remove their genitals. During her band's performance at the CBGB's nightclub, Suzi screams from the stage, "There will be no sex!" and "If you can't control yourself, cut off your cock, or sew up your c—!" She continues: "Where's my first sacrifice?" and proceeds to bend over a volunteer's body, cut off his appendage, and throw it to the floor; all the while, the victim wears a smile on his face as the fake blood stains the white sheets covering his body.

At this point, you can hear (presumably) Zedd from behind the camera, laughing as the prop dildo bounces around on the ground in spurts of fake blood. The victim's smile in reaction to the genital mutilation in *They Eat Scum*, as well as the laughter imprinted on the film by Zedd's style, is similar to the expression on the face of Bataille's Ling Chi victim. Both represent a momentary transcendence of taboo and confuse the separation of life and death, pain and pleasure, the profane and sacred. The abandonment of sexual organs by Suzi's cult—or the abandonment of their utility—becomes an abandonment of life; the act abolishes the taboo, if only for a moment when the pleasure and pain of transgression meet.

The film's aim to transgress leads to a type of transcendence itself, which Zedd achieves in allowing the audience to experience taboo differently, drawing them in with the trash aesthetics to laugh—even if it is Walker's "difficult laughter"—instead of recoil. Just as Zedd laughs from behind the camera when the prop dildo bounces on the floor, the viewer finds humor in the taboo and, by doing so, participates in the transgression as a voyeur—from a distance.

This distance is what allows *They Eat Scum* to enact transgression successfully and subvert the typical presentation of and reaction to the typical tropes of horror and exploitation films. The low production value, the fumbling lines, and the over-the-top violence and gore that eschew believability all contribute to the trash aesthetics that maintain this distance. In his article "'Trashing' the Academy," Jeffrey Sconce argues that the "potential" of trash aesthetics is found in movies that are "so histrionic, anachronistic and excessive that it compels even the most casual viewer to engage it ironically," allowing "the cultural, historical and aesthetic politics" to break through the excessive qualities (393). This ironic engagement with film breeds an authenticity, not located in its reflection of reality but in the film's effort to imprint upon its audience; in the case of *They Eat Scum*, in its unabashed intent to transgress.

Although the production and technical ability of Zedd's film do not match up with many of the films of its time (and especially not to those of our current time), this lack of ability matched the transgressive nature of his film and worked to further his anti-status quo agenda. Amy Taubin, in a review of *They Eat Scum*, notes how the scenes "are uniformly revolting, but they are conceived and performed with an innocence … preferable to the calculated slickness of someone like John Waters." Lacking this slickness or polish, *They Eat Scum*, with its focus on gore and the perverse, could mistakenly be labeled a splatter film— a genre of film that operates with the medium as the message, shock for shock's sake, and everything else, originality and intentionality, irrelevant next to the draw of sensationalism (McCarty 106). But an increase in violence and depravity does not inherently make a work transgressive. In the article, "Nothing's Shocking: What Does It Mean for a Film to Be Transgressive," cultural critic Calum Marsh discusses this at length, referencing the films *Saw* (2004) and *Hostel* (2005) to highlight the tendency of modern horror to rely on shock value that, shortly after its release, will no longer shock our values at all. "[T]he obsolescence…is built into the material," Marsh states, and "it can never qualify as effectively transgressive in the way something more purposeful can."

With each new release of the *Saw* franchise, the level of gore increases and tries to push past some boundaries for the sake of *only* pushing past them. In the first of the franchise, the killer abducts people who, according to him, do not appreciate life. He then gives them a choice: fight for their lives in his game that involves some sort of torture and violence and come out with a new appreciation for their life, or simply give up and die. The film's title is taken from one of the most promising scenes when Dr. Lawrence Gordon (played by Cary Elwes) shows his dedication to survival by using a saw to cut off his leg. But nothing in this film moves toward transgression. That is to say, nothing about this film assaults the viewer on a deeper level. The gore is excessive, but it is fleeting. Watch that movie today, and it seems tame in comparison to films that came out only a few years later (for example, Spasojević's *A Serbian Film* released in 2010). The *Saw* franchise, in actuality, upholds certain boundaries and taboos: the body's refusal of self-harm, the fear of the corpse, murder, etc.

With truly transgressive works, including *They Eat Scum*, the point is to "pass beyond and go over boundaries," to call attention to their arbitrary forms, and, in a sense, to alienate the audience (Jeriko, "Manifesto"). The substance of the work is so outside of a normative sense of morality and limitations that it transcends their understanding. The tropes of horror are tropes for a reason: working on a superficial level. The haunted doll is a convenient host for an unknown spirit; characters split up to allow for more kill scenes, and the jump scare is always a guarantee. But even by subverting tropes, it becomes an acknowledgment of the dichotomous relationship they set up; tropes "subordinate the subject to a determination, a fixation, of attributes" (Weiss 62).

Does this mean for a film to be transgressive that tropes must be thrown out? No, as *They Eat Scum* harbors tropes as well: the deeply religious father, cannibals, nuclear mutants, humans as the true evil, etc. Instead, tropes should be used to challenge the audience and their sensibilities. The entirety of *They Eat Scum* brings the viewer closer to an unknown, the unknown of the other, of the marginalized or the queer. The ways in which the religious father, Mr. Stank, reacts and ostracizes his punk daughter and cross-dressing son poke fun at society's fear of the unknown. But the elements of *They Eat Scum* that inspire disgust (bestiality, genital mutilation, and cannibalism) and the unorthodox way they are represented (undramatized, jovial, and sarcastic) are what bring the viewer closer to a fear of the unknown—not the fear found in jump scares and ghosts, but by a deep mental scar, something that truly cannot be unseen.

Conclusion

The distinguishing factor that separates Zedd's work from the throngs of schlock horror films measured by their body counts is the underlying seriousness the film carries while still embracing the aesthetics of trash and humor. The transgression of Zedd's film is further understood through the similarities it shares with Antonin Artaud's theater of cruelty; both operate from a need to break the "long habit of seeking diversion" and to reinstate the "spiritual therapeutics" that come with engaging with art (84).

The purpose of transgressive work such as *They Eat Scum* is to break down this cycle. However, this purpose is not found in perverse and violent acts, and any interpretation will never be able to find a moral high ground or some liberal ideal at the film's center. Jimmy violates his dog, Suzi is a murderous cult leader, and the punks are cannibals. Maybe, as in splatter films, the medium truly is the message; but, unlike *The Exorcist* or *Saw*, films that exploit and, in effect, manufacture our predetermined reactions of shock and awe, the violence in Zedd's film is not only on the screen but violence on our sensibilities. It is not the blood and gore of the film that make it hard to watch but the feeling of unease while watching a naked man rub up against a German Shepherd. It is the close-up shot of a sewn-up vagina and the willingness to self-mutilation.

This idea of instability or a lack of definition is the horror of the film—the horror of uncertainty. This feeling of ambiguity toward your reaction is what affects and challenges you. As Cronin states, "We carry conscious, partly conscious, and seemingly concealed beliefs to the screen with us, and they put a frame around our sight" (203). But any art—whether film, literature, or anything else—also helps to define that frame; it becomes a cyclical loop of the interpretation of a text and the text's force of will and influence upon the viewer.

In the afterword to *Haunted: Tales of the Grotesque*, Joyce Carol Oates writes, "The art of the grotesque and horror renders us children again, evoking something primal in the soul" (307). And, like children, when faced with the "blunt physicality" of the grotesque, the viewer is impressionable (Oates 304). It is not often that a work of horror provides any thoughtful introspection or true transgression, and this fact makes the intent one of the essential factors of whether a work transcends or plays into the tropes of the horror genre. Recent big-budget horror films such as Jordan Peele's *Get Out* (2017) and Ti West's *X* (2022) could be considered subversive but do not transcend any real boundaries; they still acknowledge a binary, which, instead of dismantling, only reinforce the status quo. There is a crucial moment when an audience can look toward the abject instead of turning away from it. That moment becomes an area to exploit and to engage with the audience; it should not be wasted but used in new ways and with new ideas to pass beyond the boundaries, define the shape, and add resilience to the genre. Nick Zedd's *They Eat Scum* uses shock, but not just for the sake of shock; through the use of grotesque imagery paired with discordant associations, the film's underlying purpose instills a skepticism, one toward the constructions of tradition, tropes, and identities that dominate the horror genre, mainstream film, and culture at large.

Works Cited

Artaud, Antonin. *The Theater and its Double*. Grove Press, Inc., 1958.

Barefoot, Guy. "Trash Aesthetics." *Trash Cinema: The Lure of the Low*, Columbia University Press, 2017, pp. 48–69. *JSTOR*, www.jstor.org/stable/10.7312/bar e18037.6.

Bataille, Georges. *Eroticism*. Penguin Classics, 2012.

——. *The Tears of Eros*. City Lights Books, 1989.

Blood Feast. Directed by Herschell Gordon Lewis, Box Office Spectaculars, 1963.

Cronin, Claire. *Blue Light of the Screen*. Repeater, 2020.

Culture Shock. "Hollywood Censored: The Production Code." *PBS*, www.pbs.o rg/wgbh/cultureshock/beyond/hollywood.html. Accessed 12 Jan. 2024.

Davis, Avi. "Why Cinema of Transgression Director Nick Zedd Stayed Underground." *Vice*, 6 June 2014, www.vice.com/en/article/dpwd7v/a-new-bre ed-of-asshole-0000327-v21n5. Accessed 12 Jan. 2024.

The Exorcist. Directed by William Friedkin, Warner Bros. Pictures, 1973.

Flaming Creatures. Directed by Jack Smith, The Film-Makers' Cooperative, 1963.

Get Out. Directed by Jordan Peele, Universal Pictures, 2017.

Hostel. Directed by Eli Roth, Lionsgate Films, 2005.

Jeriko, Orion. "Long Live the Cinema of Transgression." *The Underground Film Bulletin*, no. 3, 1985.

Jeriko, Orion. "The Cinema of Transgression Manifesto." *The Underground Film Bulletin*, no. 4, 1985.

Kristeva, Julia. *Powers of Horror: An Essay on Abjection*. Columbia University Press, 1982.

Marsh, Calum. "Nothing's Shocking: What Does it Mean for a Film to Be Transgressive Today?" *The Village Voice*, 9 July 2013, www.villagevoice.com/20 13/07/09/nothings-shocking-what-does-it-mean-for-a-film-to-be-transgres sive-today/. Accessed 15 Sept. 2022.

McCarty, John. *Splatter Movies: Breaking the Last Taboo of the Screen*. St. Martin's Press, 1984.

Night of the Living Dead. Directed by George Romero, Image Ten, 1968.

Oates, Joyce Carol. "Afterword: Reflections on the Grotesque." *Haunted: Tales of the Grotesque*, Plume, 1995, pp. 303–07.

Rabid. Directed by David Cronenberg, Cinepix, 1977.

Sargeant, Jack. "Spitting with a Mouth Full of Black Stones." *You Killed Me First: The Cinema of Transgression*, edited by Susanne Pfeffer, Koenig Books, 2012, pp. 27-33.

Saw. Directed by James Wan, Lionsgate, 2004.

Sconce, Jeffrey. "'Trashing' the Academy." *Screen*, vol. 36, no. 4, winter 1995, pp. 371-93.

A Serbian Film. Directed by Srđan Spasojević, Unearthed Films, 2010.

Sontag, Susan. "Notes on 'Camp.'" *Against Interpretation and Other Essays*, Farrar, Staus & Giroux, 1966, pp. 275-292.

Taubin, Amy. "The Other Cinema." *Soho Weekly News*, vol. 7, no. 1, 1979.

The Texas Chainsaw Massacre. Directed by Tobe Hooper, Vortex Inc., 1974.

They Eat Scum. Directed by Nick Zedd, Penetration Films, 1979.

Vogel, Amos. *Film as a Subversive Art*. Film Desk Books, 2021.

Walker, James Cody. *O Ho Alas Alas: Poetry and Difficult Laughter*. University of Washington, 2004.

Weiss, Allen S. *The Aesthetics of Excess*. SUNY Press, 1989.

X. Directed by Ti West, Little Lamb and Mad Sola Productions, 2022.

Zedd, Nick. Interview with Jack Sargeant. *Deathtripping: The Cinema of Transgression*. 2nd ed., Creation Books, 1999, pp. 56–77.

Zedd, Nick. *Totem of the Depraved*. 2nd ed., Pig Roast Publishing, 2022.

Chapter 11

The Monstrous Human: Exploring the Agency of Fear in Stephen King's *Misery*

Priyanka Bharali

Abstract

There has recently been an outburst of a tremendous transition in horror fiction where generic tropes have been replaced by upgraded ones, uplifting the genre into something that's quite multidisciplinary in its approach. Ghosts, supernatural forces, spectral presences, and other classical archetypes have been duly reformed, and now horror seems to be harboring alongside reality itself. Modern horror fiction has incorporated ways to indulge the growing mental and psychological traumas and anxieties of our day-to-day lives. As such, they have brought humans to the forefront to represent the inherent fear and terror in its most explicit form. This chapter aims to study this very representation in *Misery*, written by Stephen King, one of the most prolific and renowned horror writers of our generation. The novel blurs the periphery between fiction and reality while exhibiting a form of fear that is sadomasochistic and psychologically bewildering. The characters Annie Wilkes and Paul Sheldon are depicted in a provocative state as they transcend the margins of commonplace horror, elevating the genre into a more complex and intimidating position.

Keywords: fear, monstrosity, psychological, narrativity

* * *

The common values and traditions of the horror genre often rest in a somewhat simplified manner, where the subject matter limits itself to provoking the readers through obvious tropes of the supernatural, the spectral, the unseen, and the unknown. However, with the advent of new strategies and styles incorporated by different writers over time, horror fiction has emerged as an entity in itself that not only sticks to obvious motifs but also significantly demarcates from the normality of representing traditional tropes to including unconventional and neoteric trends. Stephen King's *Misery* is one such text where the aforementioned statement vividly finds a space to flourish, as readers see this particular body of work deviating from the commonly accepted goals of horror literature where jump scares, spectral and otherworldly occurrences, mystery, murder, and magic prevail.

Misery, the 1987 American thriller novel, stands upright in the face of the transition of the tropes used in the horror genre with its absolutely terrifying representation of gruesome human experience and action. The narrative technique of the fiction is quite intricate as one can witness the narrator blurring the bridge between imagination and reality, often overlapping and breaking the fourth wall by directly addressing the readers. Misery herself isn't real but is a central fictional character in a series of romance novels written by protagonist Paul Sheldon, and she is devoutly hero-worshipped by antagonist Annie Wilkes. King puts up an array of multiplicity of meanings and juxtaposition of two worlds, the world of Misery Chastain and the world of Paul Sheldon, where the latter is fighting tooth and nail to survive in the home of Annie Wilkes, one of his deranged fans. The plot of the narrative revolves around Sheldon's entrapment in Annie's house, as she holds him hostage until he revives her favorite character, Misery, after he kills her in the fourth book of *Misery's Child*. Readers of King's work must constantly jump back and forth between the two narrative worlds, one by the omniscient narrator following Paul's experience and one where Paul himself describes the fictional world of the heroine, Misery Chastain. K. Menaha says that the novel *Misery* strongly emphasizes King's three great strengths of "compelling storytelling, including horror and suspense; unique and emotionally effective characterization; and insight into both human nature and the mystery of creative writing" (58). The text embraces the genre of a metanarrative, interplaying fiction with fiction and demonstrating how such a technique intensifies the uncanny horror posited by a character like Annie Wilkes. King has vividly portrayed the dangers of hero-worshipping and extreme fanaticism through the character of Annie; as such, she becomes the archetypal monstrous human at the center of the novel. The novel begins with Paul drifting away to faraway memories of his childhood. One could later identify this as his last memory that he was ruminating over before his unfortunate car accident. He wakes up in a terrible moment as Annie gives him CPR, beginning the association of the writer and his psychotic fan with Paul's words, "I know. You're my number-one fan" (King 6).

King characterizes Annie Wilkes as someone who is completely detestable and repellant. She is initially described as someone whose mouth stinks and whose CPR has been described as "being raped back into life by the woman's stinking breath" (King 7). Her monstrosity is fueled through explicit descriptions of the narrator comparing her to "graven images worshipped by superstitious African tribes in the novels of H. Rider Haggard" and how she gave Paul an unwelcoming vibe and aura of deepening unease (King 8).

Following the accident, when one day Paul wakes up miraculously in Annie Wilkes's house, he realizes that she has been taking care of him. However, Paul's dependence on Annie is shown to be somewhat absolutely clinical, as she is on the hold of Novril, a codeine-based painkiller. She frequently comes in and out of his room to provide him with medical needs, which she uses to control him and his emotional outbursts of being trapped in her home involuntarily. The isolated atmosphere and space of Annie's surroundings in Sidewinder, Colorado, adds extra layers of thrill and suspense as this sadomasochistic woman carries on with her constant physical torture of her favorite author-cum-prisoner, Paul Sheldon.

Though Annie is not in love with Paul, she's in love with his creativity, mind, and ideal image of him as the author of her favorite book series, *Misery*. The series seems to be set in Victorian England, where a love triangle between the three characters Misery, Ian, and Geoffrey ensues, and Annie is preoccupied with her extreme cultish devotion towards these romance novels. Hence, on finding out that Misery Chastain dies in *Misery's Child*, Annie becomes violent and descends into a sort of madness, issuing threats to Paul to bring back Misery from the dead, just like Lazarus. Readers observe the monstrous human in Annie here, with her worst tantrums, fits, and psychological relapses, where she becomes the harbinger of pain and terror for Paul, with only one exception: he works fast on the typewriter she brings to complete *Misery's Return*. She changes her horrific demeanor when he willingly submits to her demand of writing a revival fiction of her favorite character, Misery, and even allows him a limited dose of Novril for which he keeps desperately asking.

In *Tradition of American Gothic in the Works of Stephen King*, Lenka Deverová discusses the peculiarity of King's protagonists as they are always seen undergoing a significant change throughout the story. They often summon their inner power or strength to endure the fear and terror they encounter, eventually emerging as independent survivors. In *Misery*, the text is radically set in terms of a binary: between a crazy lunatic and an educated urban writer, between irrational fantasies and rational intellectualism, between inhuman abuse and clever escapism, between fiction and reality, between fanatic love and wisdom, between a sadistic woman and an upright man and such, further intensifying the plot in all its extremity.

The violent imageries of torture imposed upon Paul are so explicit that one can sympathize almost immediately with his character; for instance, readers come across a part where Paul realizes that Annie has splinted his legs:

> The lower parts of both legs were circled with slim steel rods that looked like the hacksawed remains of aluminum crutches. [...] The legs themselves meandered strangely up to his knees, turning outward

here, jagging inward there. His left knee- a throbbing focus of pain- no longer seemed to exist at all. [...] He had thought his lower legs might be shattered. [...] They had been pulverized. (King 43)

The clinical undertones of the novel are readily apparent; one can analyze the narrative from the perspective of a flawless rendition and recreation of the horror genre in terms of how characters are capable of inflicting inhuman torture and pain upon others. Simultaneously, the narrative also throws light on the aspect of medical or clinical abuse through characters like Annie Wilkes, as readers see her illegally smuggling narcotics from hospitals and misusing them to gaslight and manipulate her captive for personal gain. Alongside the gore and graphical extremity of situations, this novel vividly brings forth an unmasking of humans in their nakedness of comprehending their moral behavioral actions. *Misery* becomes a test for Paul to come to terms with his conscience in the face of a psychotic, monstrous woman who is willing to do anything for the sake of her beloved fictional character.

The gaps between reality and fiction are often deducted by Paul himself as he takes the readers to different versions of the truth, including his memories from childhood, his fictional realm of Misery Chastain, and his current situation at his crazy fan Annie Wilkes's house. Somehow, he amalgamates all three worlds to give the reader a better understanding of his real world, one where he is an author who writes two kinds of books: the good ones and the best-sellers. The intertextuality is at play as readers can identify the narrator hopping across reigns where he offers us first-hand reports of Paul's and Annie's associations while simultaneously voicing out Paul's inner thoughts, thus externalizing his internal fears and traumas. From the opening chapters, the element of fear is heightened as Paul mysteriously gets caught up in an accident, which leads him to the isolated house of his borderline psychotic fan. The eerie atmosphere, the absence of a neighborhood, Paul's experience waking up in a stranger's home with a wrecked physical form, and Annie's constant administering to Paul of capsules, pills, and syringes are signs that undoubtedly foreshadow the horrifying events that are yet to come. The narrative builds up an aura of suspense and terror, slowly unfolding Paul's unfortunate landing in Annie's house, which is followed by macabre and somber activities.

In most cases, traditional horror fiction develops the idea of horror through frightening characters and events as well as a foreboding setting. Here, although *Misery*'s setting does not directly allude to the classic medieval haunted castles or mansions, the very isolation and solitary nature of Annie's house captivates horror addicts. The click-clack of the keys, the triple locks, the unkempt and disorderly parlor, the traditional kitchen, the cold dark cellar infested with rats, the barn where the pig named Misery dwells, and Paul's prison—i.e., the guest room where the Royal typewriter often glares at him mockingly—altogether posit a sinister demeanor for the readers who are aware of the pitfalls and the lurking danger among all these images with Annie at the center.

One can study the text from a psychological viewpoint, where the character of Annie Wilkes is a rigid representation of a mentally unstable woman lacking human feelings or emotions. This firm and radical understanding is one of the many reasons why the element of fear is at the center of the text from beginning to end, as readers can identify Annie Wilkes as a person who is capable of great horror and is a danger to society. In "An Analysis of Psychopathic Traits Towards Annie Wilkes in *Misery* Novel by Stephen King," Sri Yadriha and Ana Mariana make a clear-cut analysis of the character of Annie as a perfect embodiment of an egotistical psychopath, lacking in empathy, impulsive, and emotionally shallow; Annie has poor behavioral control, a need to maintain the outward appearance and a history of cruel social relationships with others. The narrator of *Misery* directly discusses the dehumanization of Paul Sheldon into "a pain-racked animal with no moral options at all" (King 98). Such explicit expressions of the narrator come off as appalling and ghastly for the readers, which sets up a perfect atmosphere of monstrosity and the macabre. Moreover, Annie's abode is presented as an odious and claustrophobic space: "The place smelled musty, unaired, obscurely tired. …the room seemed too dark- because its colors were too dark, he thought. Dark red predominated, as if someone had spilled a great deal of venous blood in here" (King 99). This description evokes a picture as dark as those Gothic medieval castles with its own secrets and foreboding stories, also vividly foreshadowing future blood spill. The grim and spine-chilling activities not only limit themselves to Paul's present conditions; readers also delve deep into the sickening and dreadful events associated with Paul's fictional world of Misery. After Annie rejects the first draft of *Misery's Return* for its lack of authenticity and originality, the second draft comes out as a charmer for her with its intense and exciting actions of Misery coming back to life most unexpectedly and uncannily. Here, Paul applies the "buried alive" strategy to resurrect Misery from the grave, which again is a very prominent horror trope mostly seen in American Gothic writings. The eeriness and abhorrent energy surrounding Misery's burial and how Geoffrey and Mrs. Ramage went out on this expedition in the dead of night sensitizes readers and takes them to a different fictional realm within the reality of Paul Sheldon's life. The narrative offers an opportunity for both the readers and Annie to relive those horrific moments of Misery's world, where characters are buried alive, involved in murder and mystery, and engaged in romantic love triangles. This fragmentation of the narrative is highly significant as readers are doubly terrorized, once by the electrifying world of Misery and again by the soul-stirring movements of Paul's and Annie's disorderly worlds. The reader is constantly reminded of how Paul is being tortured to death; King provides frequent and detailed descriptions of Annie injecting Paul with unprescribed medicines and syringes—thus making him addicted to pills like Novril in the long run—and making him drink from a floor-bucket out of pain.

Misery also seems to be an elaborate meta-commentary on writing and a writer with all the possible pitfalls lurking around the relationship between the two. Alongside graphic body horror and bloodshed, the narrative showcases how Paul's very identity as a writer comes under threat as Annie burns to ashes his work *Fast Cars*, which he believes will bring him literary respectability. She thinks it unworthy and profane of his career, preferring his *Misery* series. Paul, in the very beginning, was already rethinking his decision to move over to a new chapter of his life by initiating a divergent body of work. He seems to dread and despise his most successful creation, wanting to hop off that commercial hit in order to start afresh. In the review "Stephen King's *Misery* and the Uses of Horror," Akshay Ahuja states that the book's psychology is effective and convincing, especially the push and pull of power between Paul and Annie, which is aptly and ingeniously handled. He says that the novel is as good as a modern Gothic novel, evoking suspense, fear, unpredictability of events, and terror through the association of two genders.

From both a physiological and psychological perspective, the narrator captures the character of Annie Wilkes as an absolute creation of hatred and disgust. Annie has been presented in the absolute worst way possible time and again: her appearance, her fits and descent into madness, and her becoming the "crevasse," which acts as a tool to evoke a complete feeling of horror and anxiety. For instance, readers are made aware of Paul's perspective of Annie's appearance in the following way when she appears to him holding a dead rat in a rat-trap that she put in the basement:

> The flesh of her face… now hung like lifeless dough. Her eyes were blanks. […] There were more weals on her flesh, more food splattered on her clothes. When she moved, they exhaled too many different aromas for Paul to count. Nearly one whole arm of her cardigan sweater was soaked with a half-dried substance that smelled like gravy. (King 187)

If this was not enough to heighten up a grotesque interpretation of Annie, the narrator fuels her peculiarity through the scene of her absentmindedly sucking the blood of the dead rat. Suspense and mystery revolve around Annie's whole personality, as, at one point in the narrative, she abruptly leaves her house to go to her "laughing place" in the upcountry, as she calls it (King 299). Annie seems to harbor a kind of duality in her personality as readers observe her moving to and fro between gentle behavior and unexplainable neurotic actions. The possibility of the resurrection of her favorite character, Misery, through *Misery's Return* is the only thing that safeguards her self-control to keep Paul alive. Her final unmasking comes towards the latter part of the novel, where Paul finds her scrapbook "Memory Lane" in the parlor. Nevertheless, readers find the hair-raising records of Annie's life and the deaths associated with her since her childhood. The clippings from different journals and newspapers vividly expose Annie's homicidal history and demonstrate how crafty she has always been to get away with those violent crimes. The headlines list one horrific event after another: "FIVE DIE IN APARTMENT HOUSE FIRE"; "BAKERSFIELD ACCOUNTANT DIES IN FREAK FALL" (referring to Annie's father); "USC STUDENT DIES IN FREAK FALL" (King 202-04). Additional newspaper clippings allude to evidence, including Annie poisoning a cat, killing patients and infants in different hospitals where she was the maternity ward nurse, and briefly marrying someone. Finally, the latest clip from a newspaper is the reported missing case of Paul himself. For the readers, this comes as a final blow; this horrifying exposure of her crimes establishes Annie Wilkes as an entity of fear, unease, disgust, contemplation, terror, suspense, and mystery, which becomes the crux of the novel. Through her eccentric and neurotic nature, she emerges as a powerful, foreboding image who overshadows Paul. Stephen King has brought forth a very vivid expression of sliding into the world of an ambiguous persona like Annie Wilkes with her unreachable and incorrigible self, but, at the same time, leaving traces for the reader to help unravel her innermost thought processes. The duality of Annie Wilkes is striking; her nature is questionable most of the time with all the inhumane torture she inflicts upon Paul, but she also becomes understandable at times as readers see her rationalizing with him regarding her likes and dislikes, thus complicating her character. In his review, Ahuja further explains as such:

> To some extent, this obsession with psychopaths reflects a natural interest both in the macabre and the extremes of human experience. People have always wanted to hear about murderers. There's a difference today, though. Our fictional killers, like Annie, are less and less driven to crime by money or passion or revenge and more often are actually wired wrong. They kill and torture simply out of some error of the brain.

In his chapter "*Misery's* Gothic Tropes," in his larger work on King, John Sears focuses on King's ability to personify even the most non-living objects of Annie's house as some spectral brooding monsters lurking in corners or looking at Paul in ghastly awe. The narrator describes and personifies the typewriter, the basement, the kitchen, the parlor, and the showpieces as manifestations of Annie's evilness, further enhancing the fear quotient. Sears calls the novel a text full of an authorial horror which is haunting, where King not only rests upon the physical part of it but also divulges into the horror and fear imbibed into a potential disaster of authorship, the endless mechanical activity of writing, which can be a frightening thing for a writer, and the closure of creativity that Paul faces apart from his horrific encounter with the potential serial killer Annie Wilkes. Annie has maintained the agency of fear and horror throughout the narrative as a singular individual capable of terror, with Paul as her prisoner and victim. She provides him with clothes, bedding, and food but at the expense of her rage when her unstable mind assumes that Paul has somehow cheated her. Readers witness the ghastly image of Annie chopping off Paul's leg and then searing it: "The axe came whistling down and buried itself in Paul Sheldon's left leg just above the ankle… Dark-red blood splattered across her face… He heard the blade squeal against bone as she wrenched it free. He looked unbelievingly down at himself. The sheet was turning red" (King 246).

Annie appears as a full-fledged monster in disguise as a human; the narrator continues to present and describe her being merciless and unforgiving with each passing day. Towards the end of the novel, the gruesome murder of the young state trooper who came to enquire about the missing Paul Sheldon allows Paul to explicitly witness the grotesqueness and the abnormality of Annie's nature, as he had only previously observed her bloody past through the scrapbook clippings. She took a wooden cross as a spear and drove it into the trooper's back, buttocks, upper thigh, neck, and even crotch in the most violent way possible. After her victim somehow gained consciousness, Annie throttled the lawnmower and drove it over his head. Paul witnessed: "The Lawnboy's engine suddenly lugged down, and there was a series of fast, strangely liquid thudding sounds. Paul vomited beside the chair with his eyes closed" (King 289).

The trauma left by Annie becomes so deep for Paul that, even when she finally dies after the grim rift between the two, Paul sees her in the form of shadows everywhere, including her kitchen, behind her overstuffed sofa, in the barn, in the parlor, and in her medicine-stacked bathroom, and he could hear creaking floorboards. The fear was so deeply ingrained into Paul psychologically that, towards the end of the novel, months after his captivity ended, he even hallucinated her in the darkness with a bloody axe in her hands.

Misery has transcended the traditional utilization of horror tropes; here, one can witness only humans in their worst, most frightening demeanor. The lack of any sense of supernatural, phantasmagorical, or fantastical elements is not felt at all; terrifying human events and actions have replaced or substituted such aspects or tropes in the most fear-mongering way. *Misery* profoundly expresses the transition of Gothic and horror literature in terms of its use of those native tropes since its initiation. Stephen King acutely demonstrates how fear is multifaceted and can exist in different planes and forms and how it is very much identifiable within close realms of where people live and go. The trope of monstrosity through the figure of a human is omnipresent and based in reality; thus, it gives the readers a chance to purview situations and actions in terms of their actual existing nature rather than letting them dwell in the imaginary and irrational sensationalism of previously written or expressed horror. King has taken horror literature further into the realm of the actual and the realistic, something for which the genre has often been criticized for lacking, instead giving too much stress upon sensationalism.

Through the psychotic character of Annie Wilkes, who imprisons Paul Sheldon and inflicts physical torture upon him, *Misery* has all the fearful and frightening qualities of a horror narrative. The use of body horror and gore amplifies the text, further creating chaos and disorder. Another noteworthy facet is the merging of reality and fiction as readers travel between the worlds of Paul Sheldon and his creation, Misery Chastain. Further, King has elevated horror to showcase a writer's struggle and dilemma in maintaining or balancing his credibility. The narrator offers a clear insight into Paul going through turbulent moments where he becomes indecisive regarding the one craft for which he's famous. Stephen King's *Misery* can be read as a literary creation blatantly vocal about the horrors that humans are capable of thwarting and the fear they harbor, simultaneously taking horror fiction one step ahead in reaching new heights in terms of understanding human actions and behavior.

Works Cited

Ahuja, Akshay. "Stephen King's *Misery* and the Uses of Horror." *The Occasional Review*, 4 Aug. 2010, occasionalreview.blogspot.com/2010/08/stephen-king s-misery-and-uses-of-horror.html?m=1. Accessed 20 Oct. 2023.

Deverová, Lenka. *The Tradition of American Gothic in the Works of Stephen King*. 2021. University of South Bohemia in České Budějovice, Bachelor's thesis.

King, Stephen. *Misery*. Hodder & Stoughton, 2021.

Menaha. K. "Psychopath of Annie in *Misery* by Stephen King." *International Journal of Research and Analytical Reviews*, vol. 6, no. 2, 2019, pp. 58-59, www.ijrar.org/papers/IJRAR1ALP028.pdf.

Sears, John. *Stephen King's Gothic*. 1st ed., University of Wales Press, 2011.

Yadriha, Sri, and Ana Mariana. "An Analysis of Psychopathic Traits Towards Annie Wilkes in *Misery* Novel by Stephen King." *British: Jurnal Bahasa Dan Sastra Inggris*, vol. 8, no.1, 2019, pp. 55-68. *UMGO*, lppm.umgo.ac.id/ph p_assets/uploads/2021/03/Publik asi_Jurnal-Ana-mariana.pdf. Accessed 20 Oct. 2023.

Chapter 12

Archiving Horror: *Archive 81* and the Haunting of Analogue Media

Maria Juko

Abstract

Netflix's *Archive 81*, based loosely on the podcast of the same name, puts center stage the horror of facing the past—only for the past to haunt the present. Through found footage and archive material, parallel stories become increasingly intertwined; Melody Pendras's research on the fictional Visser building in New York in 1994 and Dan Turner's restoration of her videotapes in the present transcend space and time. This chapter argues that *Archive 81* confronts the viewer and its protagonists with the haunted-ness of relics of a bygone era. Re-viewing Melody's recordings and memories set in motion an echo of the past. This resurrection breaks quite literally out of the screen at which Dan is looking, allowing for the evil that Melody tried to control to break free.

Keywords: analog media, *Archive 81*, found footage, hauntology, horror podcast

* * *

Introduction

At a time when most people are glued to their phones and moving in digital clouds, Netflix's *Archive 81* (2022) dissects the haunted-ness of an analog past: memories that were worthy of recording but that have now come back to torment us. Through found-footage material, parallel stories become increasingly intertwined: Melody Pendras's research on the (fictional) Visser building in New York in 1994 and Dan Turner's present-day restoration of her videotapes, which were saved from the fire that destroyed the building and killed all inhabitants, collapse boundaries of time and space. With this, the ghostly apparitions and uncanny sounds that Melody recorded in the 1990s reach Dan in the present. Notably, and similar to horror podcasts such as *Archive 81* (on which the show is loosely based) or *The Magnus Archives*, analog media contain the secrets of the past but also evils that only wait to escape their confines. *Archive 81* confronts both viewers and protagonists with the haunted-ness of relics of a bygone era: Dan's digitization of Melody's found-footage material bridges the past and present, highlighting the deterioration of memories that become ghosts in their own right. Dan's resurrection of the past breaks quite literally out of the screen, allowing for the evil that Melody tried to control to be revived.

Netflix's *Archive 81* features a convoluted plot that heightens the complexity of the intertwined storylines. Dan is being commissioned to restore video tapes for the enigmatic Virgil Davenport at a secluded allotment in the woods. Doing so, he learns about Melody's research project at the Visser, where she is looking for her estranged mother. Dan enlists his friend Marc to help him figure out the mystery despite Davenport's explicit instruction to have no outside contact. Slowly, the truth emerges: Davenport is looking for his brother, Alexander Davenport, who is introduced on Melody's tapes as Samuel Spare. Samuel/Alexander is leading a renewed cult of worshippers of the demon god Kaelego, a cult that had already been in action when the Vos family owned the building in the early twentieth century. Melody's tapes reveal the house's uncannier features, such as creepy sounds, secret society meetings, and mold spreading all around the house. Watching the tapes, Dan and Melody are able to communicate. Melody, it is finally revealed, is trapped in Kaelego's world, but Dan's attempt to rescue her is thwarted by Samuel. Ultimately, Melody and Samuel seem to travel to the present while Dan is transported back to the '90s. The series stops here and remains open-ended; the show was canceled after the first season.

Ghosts and the horror genre have been linked for the longest time, evolving out of the Gothic tale. Similarly, *Archive 81* features variations of the figure of the ghost in their plot. At the center of the story lies the insertion of Kaelego, "both god and demon," into our world ("Through the Looking Glass"). What started with the original owners of the building, the Vos family, continues as the inhabitants of the Visser worship Kaelego as the savior of humankind. In their endeavors to revive this demon, the inhabitants of the Visser building echo the "[n]ineteenth-century Spiritualism on both sides of the Atlantic [that] was premised on the possibility of establishing communication with the dead that would usher in a new age of progress" (Weinstock 213). The ghost story has its roots in eighteenth- and nineteenth-century Gothic and horror fiction, with apparitions and unholy spirits tormenting innocent visitors of ruins and, most prominently, old houses (Kosofsky Sedgwick 9-10). Since then, it has been a fundamental element of the horror genre. On the evolution of the genre, Henry Bartholomew observes that "[u]nlike nineteenth-century Gothic fiction, which tends to fixate on the past, the haunted, and the ghostly, [twentieth-century] early weird fiction probes the very boundaries of reality—the laws and limits of time, space, and matter" (9). *Archive 81* reflects a twenty-first-century understanding of the ghost story as combining elements of these different periods. The Visser's ghost is a malignant intruder that Dan sets free when he rewinds the digital tape to watch the footage created by Melody, bringing the past into the present/future. At the same time, Melody and Dan also become ghostlike as they start to move across time and space.

An adaptation of the *Archive 81* podcast (2016-2019) on which a character releases tapes of his lost friend to garner help from the audience, the Netflix adaptation also relies on found footage to attain its horror effect. As such, the show joins works that base their storylines on found footage, and purportedly authentic recordings and makes use of the genre conventions. Most prominently, *The Blair Witch Project* (1999), a low-budget movie that styled itself as a recording of students foraying into the woods before supposedly getting murdered by the local witch, changed the horror movie landscape. Earlier examples, such as Shirley Clarke's *The Connection* (1961) and Ruggero Deodato's *Cannibal Holocaust* (1980), exist, but they neither veer into the supernatural horror nor have been as financially successful as the 1999 movie. Propelled by its success, numerous works followed *The Blair Witch Project*'s premise of incorporating found-footage material, such as *Paranormal Activity* (2007) and subsequent iterations or the TV show *Lost Tapes* (2008-2010). Take also Gore Verbinski's *The Ring* (2002), the American remake of Japanese Hideo Nakata's 1998 *Ring*, in which a VHS cassette tape curses its viewers and must be passed on to the next victim in time for the cursed person to survive. *Paranormal Activity: The Ghost Dimension* (2015) connects past and present through found footage, but only late in the story do characters of the present actually enter the past. Concerning the subgenre's emphasis on authenticity, Cecilia Sayad argues in *The Ghost in the Image: Technology and Reality in the Horror Genre* that "[t]he premise of all found-footage horror films is that they represent real events documented by the characters we are about to engage with" (69). *Archive 81* follows these earlier examples but also contrasts with the overarching premise. Although her recordings present a first-person perspective, Melody is most often seen in the process of filming, switching thus to a third-person perspective (the camera operator rather than part of the diegetic world). *No More Haunted Dolls: Horror Fiction that Transcends the Tropes* asks how popular tropes are used and perhaps revisioned in modern horror stories. My chapter suggests that *Archive 81* rethinks the found-footage trope as a gateway, connecting multiple storylines in which both past and present/future influence one another throughout the story.

Finding the right balance between authentic and theatrical is what makes the found-footage horror genre so complex. Take Christina Wilkins's review of *Archive 81*, in which she suggests that the show's labeling as found-footage horror might be misleading

> [A]lthough the series is described as such (and the podcast as a "found-footage horror podcast"), the transgression of boundaries pushes too far over the limits of the frame. We see this in the startling shift from the

> grainy footage of Melody in the nineties to a sudden clarity of image as
> the frame of the camera disappears. This is the clearest signal the series
> is not to be read solely as found footage, and perhaps the point at which
> we realize there is no threat of reality "spilling over," as we are far beyond
> it. ... [W]e do not get the sustained opportunity to believe in the lie of
> the footage. The series falters at this point; the moment the frame of the
> camera is removed, the subsequent use of it feels a bit like a contrived
> plot device. (461)

Adding to this observation, Dan's storyline in the present is never seen from a
first-person perspective; instead, the viewer takes Dan's place when watching
Melody's tapes (Wilkins 461). The tapes are at the center of the story; the demon
is activated by playing them, thus almost constituting a relic, which is a clear
contrast with the crisp image of the present and digital era. This way, the show
relies on the found-footage trope to emphasize the contrast between past and
present, with Melody's found footage becoming a gateway to the past and for
the action to take place. This connects to Jacques Derrida's observations on
hauntology. In *Spectres of Marx: The State of The Debt, The Work of Mourning
and The New International,* Derrida refers to Hamlet for an opening quote:
"The time is out of joint." This passage takes place after Hamlet sees the ghost
of his father for the first time, following the knowledge of who murdered him.
Derrida argues, "The haunt does not mean to be present, and it is necessary to
introduce haunting into the very construction of a concept. Of every concept,
beginning with the concepts of being and time, that is what we would be calling
here a hauntology" (202). To Derrida, haunting is always connected to a past
that comes back in the future; in *Archive 81,* this past connection is established
by the VHS tapes that Dan is restoring. Through the act of digitization, time
becomes "out of joint," and even Dan himself seems to be no longer tethered
to a certain time period.

   Further playing with the concepts of time and being, *Archive 81* perpetuates
suspense by switching to the first-person perspective, echoing the trajectories
of the found-footage mode. Sayad notes on the genre:

> It is usually through the abrupt intrusion of figures from off-screen or
> the appearance of threatening elements on the corner of the image that
> horror films aim to startle and disturb the audience. The sense of lurking
> danger is enhanced as much by our fear of seeing things as by our anxiety
> about what we do not see, and the generation of this uncertainty about
> whether or not we will see anything involves choices in framing. (74)

Tellingly, *Archive 81* relies on found footage for its more horrific moments but
switches to a third-person perspective for most of the show. Echoing Roger

Clarke's observation that "[s]o much of the ghost story is the anticipation," the show ties the viewer's anticipation to the found-footage mode, which is mirrored by protagonist Dan's reactions (5). As Dan's friend Mark says, "[p]eople used to believe that film could capture all kinds of shit that the human eye couldn't see. You know, ghosts, spirits, fairies, demons" ("The Ferryman"). Indeed, Dan becomes the camera(man) as he inserts himself in the past by rewatching and digitizing the tapes (Wilkins 461-62).

Two major elements in *Archive 81* form the core of this chapter: 1) the Visser building becomes a modern haunted house through the found-footage material, and 2) analog media serves as a method to make connections across time and space. Found footage bridges the differences between the dimensions. Together, these themes emphasize *Archive 81*'s adaptation of the podcast for streaming audiences, confronting the viewer with outdated technology that stores evil but also exposing the dangers of modern technology and its power to unleash memories.

The Visser Building: A Modern Haunted House

The Visser, the object(ive) of Melody Pendras's tapes, is a historical building in New York. In 1994, Melody set out to research what living in the Visser building looks and feels like for her Ph.D. thesis. The Visser becomes a haunted house through Dan's digitization of Melody's tapes and is imbued with a sense of foreboding. As early as Horace Walpole's 1764 *The Castle of Ontario*, Elisabeth Wilson notes, "…fear has a location, and, in a newly urban society, fear migrated to the built environment" (113). She argues, "The haunted house, then, is one particular manifestation of [an] irrational power of inanimate terror, and the idea that a house can have a malignant effect – can even harbor evil feelings or intent – is a powerful one" (Wilson 114). Externally, the Visser, couched between different buildings in New York, looks like any other apartment complex. But true horror lies inside: mold grows in the walls, spreads through the building, and takes over humans. A junkie describes the mold—which is used to produce the drug Stardust—as "running through this building like deep, dark veins" ("Through the Looking Glass"). It is also stored on the videotapes as residue that spreads into the machines Dan uses to restore the material. On building the uncanny atmosphere of the genre, Fred Botting notes that "Gothic fictions are traversed by darkly material disturbances, traces of unformed things operating beyond the reach of reason, rule and sense. Going bump in the night, making skin crawl or hairs stand on end, these things undo the laws of the known world, out of place, out of time and out of nature" (240). One such disturbance influences Jess a young girl born in the building. Her epilepsy-like shocks in the past, probably caused by her lifelong absorption of spores, are mirrored by Dan's hallucinations in the present in which he communicates with

Melody. Whereas Jess works as a vessel and is unwilling to sacrifice to the demon Kaelego, Dan is doing his employer Virgil Davenport's bidding. Similarly, Melody's roommate Anabelle, an artist who joins Melody at the Visser, becomes a victim to the building and particularly her neighbor Cassandra, suggesting that "[she] feel[s] connected to something there" ("Through the Looking Glass"). As she draws a face that she claims to see, the paint she uses is infused with mold, infecting her mind and driving her to a psychiatric facility due to sudden outbursts of violence.

The Visser's ulterior motive of reviving supernatural beings and other dimensional realms manifests itself as a disease in its most innocent inhabitants. Indeed, mold, itself a toxic material as a product of past negligence, works as the evil's gateway. By infecting the cassettes that Dan is restoring, the mold—and through it, Kaelego—infects the technology Dan uses to access Melody's videos. This way, the analog contaminates modern digital technology, echoing also Derrida's concept of hauntology as the past coming back to haunt the present. Mold, often found in a haunted house as a sign of waste and desertion spreads through spores that can be inhaled but also germinate objects. The found footage that Dan handles, its material, is infected by these spores and thus links analogue and digital media, in effect infecting him.

Playing with the found-footage trope, the Visser becomes a modern haunted house through the act of digitization. The Visser no longer exists in the present/future, as it has burnt down in a fire in which all inhabitants—including, allegedly, Melody—died in 1994. But, as it turns out, remnants of the building still exist, and Dan roams these remaining parts of the house and basement in the present. Dan's cabin is thus a relic like the cassette tapes that were saved from the fire. Built on the ruins of the Vos mansion, which was destroyed in a fire as well, the basement was the place for both the Vos and Visser society's ritual to revive the demon Kaelego. Once more, pieces of the past intertwine with the present: Dan is specifically asked to restore the videos at the secluded building, enforcing the effects of the mold's spores stored on the tapes and the walls of the building on Dan's psyche. Nick Freeman discusses the haunted house:

> Ghost stories are, in essence, fictions of historical collapse, in which distinctions between past and present are questioned, violated, or erased. The house, or similar "bad place," […] supplies continuity in that it exists in the present as both a historical artifact and a contemporary residence, aging and changing as the years pass. […] The house is a legitimate relic, the ghost is not. (328)

Mold is a clear sign of this "historical collapse" (Freeman 328), but *Archive 81* also controverts this notion. The combination of tapes and building, both infested with the spores, accelerates the process of haunting. The Visser building, though it does not exist in its old form, is saved on Melody's tapes, which create entry points to the original building through the process of (re)watching. The inhabitants, purportedly killed in the fatal fire, suddenly interact with Dan and even have the power to reach through the screen. Via the found footage, the house is (re)located on Dan's screen. Tellingly, Freeman further argues that "[h]aunted houses are the traditional setting for this intersection of the past with the present (or perhaps, the meeting between the ghost and the future it cannot participate in except through the re-enactment of what it has done before)" (329). The found-footage material—the infected tapes—allows for people, ghosts of the past, to interact with the future. Virgil Davenport tellingly argues in the show that the camera gives a moment "an eternity it was never meant to have" ("What Lies Beneath"). Furthermore, as Melody's mother clarifies, rewatching the tapes "unravels the spell that holds the door [between the worlds] shut" ("What Lies Beneath"). Like the past rituals at the Vos and Visser building, the tapes run in circles, with each rewind bringing Melody and Dan closer to the truth. At the same time as the infected video tapes become a conduit for Dan to enter the haunted Visser building, they also become a way for Kaelego to enter the human realm. The Visser thus presents a modern, digital haunted house accessible via the digitization of analog media.

Found Footage and Digitization

Archive 81 puts the revival of analog media on center stage. Through the process of digitization, Dan is reviving the demon. Equal to the act of (re)experiencing events as the progress directly leads to insertion into the past, Dan becomes an apparition, a ghost himself.

A particular aspect of the Netflix show is the way that the viewer (via Dan) is soaked into the events of the 1990s through watching the tapes. The technological mechanism functions as an entry point to directly participate in the events of the past and, at the same time, allows the past into the present/future. Sayad notes a similar storyline in *Paranormal Activity: The Ghost Dimension*:

> The found VHS footage [...] breaks away from the spatial and temporal boundaries that constitute it as a record of the past, for the past is not fixed on tape but, instead interacts with its viewing in the present time ... [which] puts the filmed image and the surrounding reality in direct communication. corroborating the idea that technology can invite the

supernatural into the natural world and also expanding the frame to incorporate the space inhabited by spectators. (86)

Dan's insertion into events of the past contrasts with these earlier found-footage examples; Dan becomes a ghost of the future reaching out to the past—as Melody becomes a ghost from the past reaching out to the future—through the process of modernizing analog media.

Embedding archive material to complement the show's intricate narrative, *Archive 81* heightens the connection between analog and digital, past and present. Archival material is used at the beginning of most episodes and often provides their titles, foreshadowing the storyline. This importance that the show attaches to the archival material connects to Derrida and Prenowitz's notion of "archive fever," as they argue that "if there is no archive without consignation in an *external place* which assures the possibility of memorization, of repetition, of reproduction, or reimpression, then we must also remember that repetition itself, the logic of repetition, indeed the repetition compulsion, remains, according to Freud, indissociable from the death drive. And thus from destruction" (14). Without external institutions to hold archives, there is no guarantee that memories will be stored or restored. Dan's job as an archivist is thus the nurturing of memories of restoring the past; he has the power to unlock those memories, whether positive or painful. Tellingly, the first episode, "Mystery Signals" (named after Dan's friend's podcast), after showing a yet-unnamed Melody pleading for help, starts with the word "tapes" as a vendor tries to sell an assortment of uncatalogued video memories scattered around in boxes. While restoring these VHS tapes is Dan's hobby, his job at the Museum of the Moving Image (and then for Davenport) is to retrieve memories. For Dan, the *material* matters; for his employers, what is important is the content of the tapes. As Dan watches the tapes, the viewer takes on his role, immersing themselves into the diegetic world presented on the small screen, echoing Sayad's observation on the genre that "the found-footage horror cycle create[s] all-absorbing narratives that invariably engulf those elements referring to a world existing outside of the fictional universe, locking them in" (73). After starting the process of digitizing, Dan increasingly connects with Melody but also begins seeing characters from his past, most prominently his late father. His reality merges with the Visser building and Melody's tapes, induced by the remains of mold to which Dan is exposed, and each becomes aware of the other's presence. Dan's rewatch allows him to participate in the events as he becomes a ghost haunting the past. Mirrored by the viewer, the show seeks to immerse the audience in the mystery through the found-footage material.

Emphasizing his enthusiasm for recovering the past, the opening sequence of the show demonstrates Dan's careful and gentle practice of curating video tapes

(Wilkins 461-62). This meticulous process echoes Mark Fisher's observation on hauntological artists:

> [They were] preoccupied with the way in which technology materialized memory – hence a fascination with television, vinyl records, audiotape, and with the sounds of these technologies breaking down. This fixation on materialized memory led to what is perhaps the principal sonic signature of hauntology: the use of crackle, the surface noise made by vinyl. Crackle makes us aware that we are listening to a time that is out of joint; it won't allow us to fall into the delusion of presence. (21)

Indeed, a crackle is audible throughout the series, particularly when Dan starts the recordings, signaling that the audiotape is running but also underlining the sense of foreboding. Qualities of the analog medium, particularly its materiality, thus become integrated into the digital streaming show, confronting the viewer with outdated and unfamiliar technology and, hence, uncanny mechanics. This causes the viewer to question Dan's grasp on reality because of his fascination with Melody's past.

Archive 81 gradually allows the past and present/future to collapse as Melody's memories and Dan's actions become entangled. While the promotional poster for *Archive 81* states, "[r]ewind to reveal the truth" (Tallerico), within the show, the academic urge to question and seek truths inadvertently leads to horror when Melody finds the answers for which she was initially looking. Uncovering their pasts, Melanie and Dan both become ghostlike as they travel through time and space through Dan's digitization of Melody's tapes. While Melody is brought back to the present, Dan seems to be trapped in the 1990s by the end of the show, waking up in a hospital in New York with the Twin Towers of the World Trade Center visible. In that way, Dan becomes a ghost, too—a supernatural creature, "an apparition, a specter, a phantom, often haunting a specific location" (*OED*)—who has traveled back in time via the found footage of Melody's tapes. Tellingly, Melody "thinks she's being haunted" by Dan as she sees his reflection in a telephone booth—a scene that is not captured on her tapes ("Through the Looking Glass"). Dan's fascination with Melody and the discovery of his father's involvement in Melody's disappearance underline his personal interest in the tapes. Rewatching the videos thus enables Dan to reach out to Melody, collapsing what Bartholomew noted on the early weird fiction, "the very boundaries of reality—the laws and limits of time, space, and matter" (9), and embedding this collapse of boundaries in the process of digitization, heightening the show's adaptation of the podcast for streaming audiences.

The interaction between Dan and Melody is seemingly a fabrication of Dan's imagination, challenging Dan's reliability as a narrator (Wilkins 462). The episode "Terror in the Aisles" starts with a segment of the same name discussing the horror movie "Satan's Carnival," with the two hosts divided on contemporary movies relying on "pseudo-religious" motives. The movie does not exist, but there is a similarly titled horror musical from 2012, *Devil's Carnival,* that takes place in hell. At the end of the episode, Melody is in the supermarket across the street with Anabelle. She suddenly starts talking to Dan through the screen, seeing him in front of her, reminding him of an earlier encounter. Why she would film this scene is not clear. Dan responds, confounded by this conversation, until Melody leaves to check on Anabelle. Then, apparently sensing the presence of Dan, Cassandra enters the supermarket. She scans the aisles until she reaches the spot that Melody has just left and warns Dan to "stay out." She reaches through the screen, choking Dan. The screen switches to black, and we see Dan waking up as if from a nightmare. What becomes clear is that Dan's restoration of the tapes allows him to reenter the past where inhabitants of the house are also enabled to interact with him. Still, both Dan and the viewer are unsure of whether the scene really took place, collapsing the perception of past and present. This maintains the suspense but also challenges Dan's reliability, heightening a feeling of eeriness that results from revisiting Melody's memories.

Dan's position as an archivist is a complex one. He is invested in restoring the material and preserving the memories but is also interested because of his late father's involvement and finding out what happened to him. Yet he is also directly endangered by being immersed in Melody's tapes. Derrida and Prenowitz's notion of archiving as housing the past, the title "mal d'archive" could be translated to "archive fever" but also possibly "the evil of the archive," thus hinting at something sinister waiting to be restored. Indeed, the show's intercutting of archive material and narrative storyline effectively situate the plot in a state of in-betweenness, collapsing the boundaries of past and present. Derrida and Prenowitz explain that archives always affect future events rather than past ones; they note that "if we want to know what this will have meant, we will only know in the times to come. Perhaps. Not tomorrow but in the times to come, later on, or perhaps never" (27). Dan and Melody's urge to "[r]ewind to reveal the truth" (Tallerico) reveals that the archive is a place of reckoning and of hopefulness with the past to understand the present/future. This way, the collapse of past and present allows for these secrets to be revealed, just as found footage in horror movies reveals a truth, painful or not, such as *The Ring's* tragic origin story of Samara. But this painful memory is needed to find enlightenment and for the show to find its conclusion. Found footage is archival material of a past, whether long gone or recent, that affects the present/future, revealing knowledge of what was not there before, the secrets and truth.

Playing with the notion of the archive as storing malicious intent through Dan's digitization, the show highlights the dangers of revisiting memories that can unleash evil powers. In episode 4, "Spirit Receivers," the link between past and present comes to a climax when a descendant of filmmaker William Crest, who recorded an earlier ritual to revive Kaelego, and other inhabitants gather at Cassandra's for a séance. Melody, at Cassandra's behest, calls for her mother. Telling her that she "do[es] not sense her presence in the realm of the dead," Béatriz, the medium, feels "someone else." The screen switches to Dan, who pauses the video, visibly scared, underlining the first-person perspective when watching the tapes; his reactions substitute the viewers from a seemingly safe distance. Melody appears behind him, asking him who the person in the video is and "what [he is] watching," unaware of her own role in the tapes. Dan does not tell Melody that he works on her tapes, instead saying that he is restoring "things that have been damaged, lost, or forgotten. I bring them back," signaling his reluctance to tell her that she is, in truth, dead. Melody recalls knowing the woman in the tape but then uses the past tense, "I knew her," unable to remember her name. What becomes more and more obvious is that she believes Dan lives at the Visser, although they are standing in Dan's cabin. The cabin works as another Derridean archive, where evil but also truth are stored. The conversation reveals that Melody's sense of time and space has collapsed as she neither realizes that she is talking to someone in the future nor recognizes people from her time. Thus, she resembles a ghost who is not tethered to a certain time (but space). Tellingly, Dan remembers a childhood conversation with his sister Emily when she told him that he doesn't need to be "afraid" of ghosts since they "are just lost." He reluctantly confesses to Melody that she's dead. Unsettled, Melody shouts, "I am not fucking dead," causing the lights to shut off before disappearing. The video stays on through the power cut, and the video starts on its own, with Béatriz reciting every conversation between Melody and Dan before she starts to scratch her own face and draws blood, cautioning Melody and Dan (and by that effect, the viewer) that calling on ghosts also means to remember the(ir) pain and that memories can be painful. The found footage thus bridges past and present and showcases not just a danger to Dan but also to people of the past, which breaks with earlier examples of the genre as only affecting the audience.

Underlining the show's use of digital methods, the better the technology, the more tangible the demon of Kaelego becomes; destroying the screening of Melody's video is the only way to stop Kaelego from passing through the veil. On the relationship between our modern society and ghosts, Sadeq Rahimi suggests that "the very space of everyday life is so filled with ghosts that nobody can avoid them—in fact, that the very experience of everyday life is built around a process that we can call hauntogenic, and whose major by-product is a steady stream of ghosts" (3). The found-footage trope in *Archive 81* plays with this notion as the demon Kaelego is tethered to Melody's tapes but needs Dan's digitization to escape. After the séance, Anabelle says "there's someone in there," and the camera switches to a recording of a painting on Dan's screen as static crackles set in, and the camera zooms in as the painting reveals a demonic face moving; as Dan left the room, the *viewer* is the only spectator of the demon reaching out ("Spirit Receivers"). When Melody rewatches the séance the next day in her room, trying to copy the video to a VHS cassette, the demon appears, as well, scaring her ("Through the Looking Glass"). This connects to another instance in episode 6, "The Circle," when Dan, while watching the tapes, encounters the demon Kaelego as the spirit breaks through the frequency of the tape and starts to materialize. Dan's only way to stop the demon is to break the screens. In effect, Kaelego is tied to the analog but needs modern technology to be restored, emphasizing the connection between past and present in the found footage and echoing Derridean notions of hauntology. Like the snapshots recorded on today's phones, which are restored but never truly destroyed, Kaelego survives through Melody's VHS tapes (Wilkins 462). Derrida and Prenowitz note, "One will never be able to objectivize [the archive] while leaving no remainder. The archivist produces more archive, and that is why the archive is never closed. It opens out of the future" (45).

Just like that, technology has created open-ended and endless archives, the files stored in the digital cloud could never be completely erased. Indeed, the show underlines modern technologies' possibilities to foray into the paranormal. At the same time, it also demonstrates the dangers that are attached to digitizing analog media. Rewatching the tapes, recycling fear and terror, gives power to memories, these ghosts of our past. Found footage here presents a gateway for both Dan and Melody, as well as the demon Kaelego to enter different realms.

Conclusion

Netflix's *Archive 81* became a hit on the streaming platform yet was canceled after its first season. Whether Dan's rescue mission was successful and how he returns to the twenty-first century are questions the viewer is now left to imagine. Basing its storyline on a podcast, the show tried to foray into new directions, following the found-footage horror genre to build a paranormal storyline over an entire season. Unfortunately, Melody's tapes and the aesthetics of 1990s video cassettes are only sparsely used, as Melody's storyline switches quickly to a third-person perspective shot on digital. The spectral (digital) apparition in *Archive 81* is created by human interference, the act of digitization. Just like Melody's mother's disappearance and Dan's father's death, some secrets are better left uncovered for us to stay sane.

Works Cited

Bartholomew, Henry. *Dangerous Dimensions: Mind-Bending Tales of the Mathematical Weird*. British Library, 2021.

The Blair Witch Project. Directed by Daniel Myrick and Eduardo Sánchez, Artisan Entertainment, 1999.

Botting, Fred. "Dark Materialism: Gothic Objects, Commodities, and Things." *The Gothic and Theory: An Edinburgh Companion*, edited by Jerrod E. Hogle and Robert Miles, Edinburgh University Press, 2019, pp. 240-59.

Cannibal Holocaust. Directed by Ruggero Deodato, United Artists Europa, 1980.

"The Circle." *Archive 81*, season 1, episode 6, Netflix, 14 Jan. 2022.

Clarke, Roger. *A Natural History of Ghosts: 500 Years of Hunting for Proof*. Penguin, 2013.

The Connection. Directed by Shirley Clarke, Milestone Films, 1961.

Derrida, Jacques. *Specters of Marx: The State of the Debt, the Work of Mourning and the New International*. Translated by Peggy Kamuf. Routledge, 2006.

Derrida, Jacques, and Eric Prenowitz. "Archive Fever: A Freudian Impression." *Diacritics*, vol. 25, no. 2, 1995, pp. 9-63. *JSTOR*, https://doi.org/10.2307/465144.

The Devil's Carnival. Directed by Darren Lynn Bousman, Empire Film & Entertainment et al., 2012.

"The Ferryman." *Archive 81*, season 1, episode 7, Netflix, 14 Jan. 2022.

Fisher, Mark. *Ghosts of My Life: Writings on Depression, Hauntology and Lost Futures*. Zero Books, 2014.

Freeman, Nick. "Haunted Houses." *The Routledge Handbook to the Ghost Story*, edited by Scott Brewster and Luke Thurston, Routledge, 2018, pp. 328-37.

"Ghost, n. and adj." *Oxford English Dictionary Online*, www-1oed-1com-1006 6f0at0e95.erf.sbb.spk-berlin.de/dictionary/ghost-story_n?tab=meaning_and _use#993151014. Accessed 29 Oct. 2023.

Kosofsky Sedgwick, Eve. *The Coherence of Gothic Conventions*. Methuen, 1986.

"Mystery Signals." *Archive 81*, season 1, episode 1, Netflix, 14 Jan. 2022.

Paranormal Activity. Directed by Oren Peli, Paramount Pictures, 2007.

Paranormal Activity: The Ghost Dimension. Directed by Gregory Plotkin, Paramount Pictures, 2015.

Powell, Marc, and Dan Solinger, creators. *Archive 81*. Dead Signals, 2016-2019, www.archive81.com/.

Rahimi, Sadeq. *The Hauntology of Everyday Life*. Palgrave Macmillan, 2021.

Ring. Directed by Hideo Nakata, Toho, 1998.

The Ring. Directed by Gore Verbinski, DreamWorks Pictures, 2002.

Sayad, Cecilia. *The Ghost in the Image: Technology and Reality in the Horror Genre*. Oxford University Press, 2021.

Segal, Douglas, et al., directors. *Lost Tapes*. Go Go Luckey Entertainment, 2008-2010.

Simms, Jonathan, and Alexander J. Newall, hosts. *The Magnus Archives*. Rusty Quill, 2016-2021, rustyquill.com/show/the-magnus-archives/.

"Spirit Receivers." *Archive 81*, season 1, episode 4, Netflix, 14 Jan. 2022.

Tallerico, Brian. "Creepy Archive 81 Wants to Be Your Winter TV Obsession." *RogerEbert.com*, 11 Jan. 2022, www.rogerebert.com/streaming/creepy-arch ive-81-wants-to-be-your-winter-tv-obsession.

"Terror in the Aisles." *Archive 81*, season 1, episode 3, Netflix, 14 Jan. 2022.

"Through the Looking Glass." *Archive 81*, season 1, episode 5, Netflix, 14 Jan. 2022.

Weinstock, Jeffrey Andrew. "The American Ghost Story." *The Routledge Handbook to the Ghost Story*, edited by Scott Brewster and Luke Thurston, Routledge, 2018, pp. 206-14.

"What Lies Beneath." *Archive 81*, season 1, episode 8, Netflix, 14 Jan. 2022.

Wilkins, Christina. "Beyond the Frame of the Past: Archive 81 (2022)." *Adaptation*, vol. 15, no. 3, Dec. 2022, pp. 460–63, https://doi.org/10.1093/ad aptation/apac012.

Wilson, Elizabeth. "Haunted Houses," *AA Files*, 2013, no. 67, 2013, pp. 113-18. *JSTOR*, www.jstor.org/stable/23595549.

Chapter 13

Body Horror and Disability in Video Games: The Fear of the Unknown and Different

Chayyim Holtkamp

Abstract

Horror games feature a specific type of ableism, or prejudice towards disability, through which video game developers use the body and the mind to make the game suspenseful and terrifying. These games frequently use the horror of the "other" by showing extreme examples of different bodies and minds than what is deemed normal. For instance, *Dead Space*, a survival horror game that takes place on a spacecraft with the constant threat of aliens and their technology, features many examples of how horror games use body and mind horror as a trope. In this game, an alien artifact turns humans into an undead enemy referred to as necromorphs, humanoid creatures that have a variety of human and arachnid combinations. The context of the horror game changes the necromorphs from being representative of disability due to body variations but rather due to revulsion and a sense of the "other." This chapter examines how horror video games use the fear of becoming disabled as part of the device that makes the games scary.

Keywords: ableism, disability, horror video games, "other"

* * *

Upon waking up in Castle Brennenburg, Daniel, the protagonist in *Amnesia: The Dark Descent*, finds himself following a bloody trail, being hunted by something or someone. The environment is dreadfully dark, eerie, and slimy. The castle itself is covered in grime, blood, and other fluids, while being poorly lit, making it difficult for the player to see.

Settings like this are intrinsic to horror video games, which utilize specific tropes in order to make the video game more frightening. Horror is a genre that is intended to frighten or scare the individual, often relying on particular tropes to achieve this goal. One such is the trope of using the disabled body and mind as a tactic to increase fear in the audience. Horror video games are no different from other media, such as cinema, television, or books, when it comes to the use of the disabled body and mind to create fear. These types of games feature a specific type of ableism (prejudice towards disability) or ablesanism (prejudice towards mental illness) through what the video game developers use about the body and the mind to make the game more suspenseful and terrifying (Costantino 11-12). These games frequently use the horror of the abject "Other" by showing extreme examples of different bodies and minds than what is deemed normal. This chapter will argue that horror video games utilize the disabled mind and body in order to scare or frighten the video game player. It will also look at four horror video games to specifically analyze their role in perpetrating ableist and ablesanist motifs in order to frighten video game players.

Horror Video Games

What makes a game fit the horror genre specifically? Carr describes survival horror as a game that "incorporates various conventions from horror cinema, and that succeed critically and commercially when they evoke feelings such as discomfort, anxiety, fear, and tension" (5). Similarly, Hand describes survival horror as "generally understood to be a game in which the player leads an individual character through an uncanny and hostile environment where the odds are weighed heavily against the avatar" (17). A main component of the horror game, therefore, is the antagonism of the environment, either through the introduction of enemies or the video game environment itself. This is not intended to frustrate the player but rather frighten them, as Carr mentioned.

Marak takes a similar approach to Carr, stating that horror's role is to terrify, unsettle, disgust, and discomfort its audience. Quoting Grixti, she states that horror is "irrespective of its medium or transition, a type of narrative which deals in messages about fear and experiences associated with fear" (Marak 8). It needs hints, clues, and motifs that scare the audience. Marak continues, arguing that one of the aspects that makes horror so terrifying is its apparent inability to be solved: "The fear characteristic of the horror genre would be the fear of what cannot be avoided, controlled, or conquered in any fashion" (10). I argue that the thing that cannot be "avoided, controlled, or conquered" *itself* is disability. Marak also discusses the abject Other and, by extension, the process of Othering. She argues that this process is necessary in American horror, that the Western abject relies on the Otherness of the enemy, the monster, or the frightening, and, in this case, the disabled.

Part of why horror sells is its scariness; thus, it needs to be genuinely scary in order to be considered a success. Clasen states, "Humans are fearful creatures. We fear getting killed, being assaulted, *contracting diseases*, losing loved ones, *going insane,* losing status, being humiliated... We fear monsters and *psychos*"

(26, emphasis added). Indirectly, Clasen has touched on the role that disability plays in horror: how we fear becoming disabled and disabled people themselves.

Marak suggests that conditions seem scary due to a cultural understanding. She explains:

> A ghost is scary because the audience shares an already existing comprehension of what a ghost is and all the cultural conceptual attachments connected with the figure of the ghost. Without that comprehension, a ghost would still be scary, but folklore, history, and culture allow the audience to become apprehensive even before the ghost appears… (Marak 7)

My argument is that disability acts in some video games in the place of ghosts; that is, disability has preconceived notions that cause it to be frightening for audiences and video game players, making the game more alarming to play because of the fear of disablement.

Horror video games often rely on monsters as the main enemy for the player-character to defeat. Gilmore argues that monsters "provide a convenient pictorial metaphor for human qualities that have to be repudiated, externalized, and defeated" (4). While he goes on to contend that these are psychoanalytic id-related qualities (such as sexual sadism), I would conjecture that disability be included in that, including deformity. Many people follow the medical model of disability, which suggests that disability needs to be cured or, in this case, defeated. Monsters, according to Marak, "suggest mutability, variability, and instability" and are "repulsive or at least deeply disturbing" (125). The focus here on monsters is that if they act as a metaphor for human qualities, as Gilmore suggests, why would those qualities not include that disability?

Horror video games also function differently than other forms of horror media due to their interactive nature. Video games require that people respond to stimuli in uncertain circumstances, such as whether monsters will appear, and then it requires the player to respond when the monsters come across them. Other forms of media, such as books, television, or film, do not require the person to actually respond to the stimuli and can instead remain passive in their commencement. Because of the need to respond in video games to progress the narrative, horror video games can be considered more frightening.

Disability, Disfigurement, and the Freak

There are several models of conceptualizing disability, but the most commonly used are the social model and the medical model. The social model, which is preferred by disability advocates and activists, "identifies [how] disability can be environmental (such as inaccessible buildings, services, languages), organizational (inflexible practices, procedures, people), or attitudinal (prejudice, stereotypes, and discrimination)" (Rodan 10). It places the onus of disability on society rather than the individual and argues that what is disabling is society itself. This is compared to the medical model of disability, which focuses on the illness, disease, symptoms, etc., from which the individual "suffers," arguing that it is the medical condition that is disabling ("Medical and Social Models of Disability").

Disability is an interesting category of identification because anyone can enter the category of being disabled at any time, as well as potentially exit it, too. According to the World Health Organization, one in six people experiences a significant disability. With that level of vulnerability comes fear. As Garland Thomson puts it, "Cast as one of society's ultimate 'not me' figures, the disabled other absorbs disavowed elements of this cultural self, becoming an icon of all human vulnerability and enabling the 'American Ideal' to appear as master of both destiny and self" (41). In short, able-bodied and neurotypical people fear disability because of an awareness that they could, at any time, lose that able-bodied and able-mindedness.

Garland Thomson includes the monstrous, the deformed, and the freakish as representations of disability (5). She states, "Stone Age cave drawings record the births of mysterious and marvelous bodies the Greeks and early scientists would later call 'monsters,' the culture of P.T. Barnum would call 'freaks,' and we now call 'the congenitally physically disabled'" (Garland Thompson 56). Freak shows, she argues, require people to think about the limitations of humanity and what makes one both human and normal (58). A "freak" is different from a non-disabled individual in that they are a person who "had a visible physical difference or an otherwise atypical body" (Garland Thompson 62). The monstrous, deformed, and freakish represent an anomaly meant to elicit a response out of the audience, including curiosity or fear. As Snyder and Mitchell state, "Quite simply put: *disabled bodies have been constructed cinematically and socially to function as delivery vehicles in the transfer of extreme sensation to audiences*" (162). In horror games, that extreme sensation is fear and fright.

Disability represents a lack of control over oneself and can be "discomforting" to those who are able-bodied: "These representations become discomforting to many individuals who prefer to believe they are in total control of their bodies, and by extension, themselves" (Rodan 8). According to Sontag, the most feared illnesses are the ones that are sudden and/or disfiguring. In video games, the player-character may suffer from a sudden bout of insanity, or they may become disfigured with deformities. Based on Sontag's most feared illnesses, the disabilities that are the scariest for audience members are the ones that threaten the player's livelihood suddenly (10). These are the disabilities that would change the player's life the most, such as insanity, paralysis, or bodily disfigurement.

In some ways, the portrayals of disability are internal or external, meaning they originate either within the body of the character or remain part of the external, non-playable characters. Fear of internalized disability is fear of becoming disabled and includes the fear of insanity and disease that become disabling. In contrast, the external loci of fear of disability is fear of the other disabled characters, such as monsters that represent mental illness or physical disability in their presentations to the video game player. These two loci of fear create interesting perspectives and patterns of how people may find disability frightening, whether they fear becoming disabled themselves or disabled people.

Analysis and Representations of Disability

This next section analyzes specific horror video games for their disability representation and content. This will provide information about the video games, gameplay, and how disability is featured in them to make the game more frightening for the players, even if unconsciously. This will feature spoilers for the endings of the games, as well.

Dead Space

Dead Space is a survival horror video game published by Electronic Arts that takes place in the twenty-sixth century on the USG Ishimura, a "planet-cracking" or space-mining ship that has had a total communication blackout. The player plays as Isaac Clarke, a systems engineer who accompanies a search and rescue team sent to the USG Ishimura and is searching for his girlfriend, Nicole Brennan. The ship is infested with Necromorphs, diseased humans with intense and violent deformities. The Necromorphs are caused by the Marker, an alien artifact that creates dementia-like symptoms that eventually culminate in the Necromorphs. Isaac is guided by Nicole to return the Marker to the nearby planet from which it came. Another one of the search and rescue team, Kendra Daniels, betrays Isaac by trying to escape with the Marker but ends up being killed by the Hive Mind. Isaac leaves on her shuttle as the planet, and the Marker are both destroyed.

There are multiple elements of disability in *Dead Space*. One is the Necromorphs themselves; because they are the result of the sickness caused by the Marker, they are, in essence, the most extreme form of disability possible in the game world. Carr has written extensively about the representation of disability in that the Necromorphs "are hardly straightforward depictions of disability, and yet the manner in which they function relative to Isaac, the deviance of their bodies, their association with medical research, and their spectacular 'freakishness' (Thomson 1996) certainly invoke resources of disability" (6). In this way, the Necromorphs themselves represent an ultimate version of disability, the most extreme version of the sickness that the Marker can cause. Carr quotes Synder and Mitchell, arguing that "What matters in horror, [Synder and Mitchell] go on to argue, is not that fact of bodies - or the fact of physical variability - as much as the 'social investment in certain bodies' presumed proximity to abjectness" (6). The Necromorphs function as abject, representing what could happen to the player character if they fail in their mission to eradicate the Necromorphs and the Marker itself.

Furthermore, disablement is a key feature of gameplay. The game prompts the user three times at the beginning of the game that the Necromorphs must be killed by removing their limbs, therefore disabling them. Removal of the head does not kill them. Disablement is necessary in order to successfully complete the game. It preserves what makes one the most human—the head— and one's identity to humanness. By removing the deformed limbs, the game seeks to "cure" or "fix" the Necromorphs of their deformities and disabilities. Deformities, while a type of disability, have many differences from other disabilities because of their visual distinctiveness. In the case of the Necromorphs, these deformities border on the grotesque, with mutated limbs that can slice or cut the player or the creation of bat-winged arms.

Another element of disability in *Dead Space* is Clarke's continual struggle with psychosis and hallucinations. As the player learns, Isaac experiences hallucinations of his revealed-to-be-dead girlfriend, Nicole. Another character, Kendra, informs Isaac that he has been experiencing hallucinations as a taunt, proceeding to call him insane over and over. In fact, the last scene of the video game has a cutscene with Isaac mourning Nicole, whom he discovers committed suicide in order to avoid becoming a Necromorph, and a hallucination of her attacking him. An element of this that makes the game more frightening is coming to the realization that the Marker is affecting the players themselves and that they are unable to trust their sensory information because what they see and hear could be hallucinatory. This harkens to the interactive narrative process of the video game that the game itself is more interactive than other media forms such as movies and television are, it relies on input from the player in order to progress the narrative.

Dead Space 2

Dead Space 2 also contends with disability. Isaac Clarke remains the protagonist and is mentally disturbed after the destruction of the Red Marker on Aegis VII. He is captured by EarthGov and taken to the Sprawl, which is a space station built on the remains of Saturn's largest moon, Titan. EarthGov scientists extract information about the Marker from his mind in order to build another one. Clarke is confined to the hospital on the Sprawl because he has developed an illness similar to dementia from the first Marker. It continues to utilize frightening hallucinations to disturb, confuse, and scare the player while playing the sequel. As Buday et al. state on the use of hallucinations in video games, "they are represented as audiovisual and the majority of them are portrayed as horror-like or otherwise fear-inducing" (5). There is a growing trend of video games using schizophrenia or hallucinations to make games scarier for the players, particularly relying on auditory and visual hallucinations to make this happen.

Amnesia: The Dark Descent

Amnesia: The Dark Descent is a survival horror game by Frictional Games. The player plays as Daniel, a man who wakes up in Brennenburg Castle in Prussia in 1839. All he can remember is his name, and that something is hunting him. Finding a note he wrote to himself, he learns that he deliberately erased his mind and is being hunted by a 'Shadow," a thing that reveals itself in the castle as acidic and fleshy growths. He is instructed by the note to find the Inner Sanctum of the castle and kill its baron, Alexander, as well. As Daniel and the player explore the castle, they encounter monsters, hallucinations, flashbacks about torture, and unsettling events, such as drilling into the head of a corpse to retrieve its blood. Daniel, and thus the player, discovered that he had found an orb that released the Shadow hunting him; he was contacted by Alexander about the orb and was told he could repel the Shadow by harvesting vital energy from tortured prisoners.

A main component of *Amnesia* is the sanity indicator, which functions alongside the health indicator. Managing Daniel's sanity primarily involves staying out of the dark. Thomas Grip, one of the designers of the game, stated that "the idea was basically that the darkness itself should be an enemy." Sanity is also reduced by looking at the monsters or witnessing unsettling events. Low sanity causes visual and auditory hallucinations as well as increased encounters with monsters. If Daniel's sanity gets low enough, the player will be unable to move the character or even die in higher difficulties, disabling the player-character themselves. The categories of sanity are "Crystal clear," "A slight headache," "Head is pounding and hands are shaking," and lastly, "...". The last category indicates the highest level of insanity, which, if unremedied, means the player-character will experience hallucinations and increased encounters with monsters. If the character is low on health and sanity at the same time, the screen becomes black around the edges and hallucinations in the form of bugs become visible.

This game relies on the fear of losing one's own sanity in order to make the experience more frightening for the player. At times, Daniel becomes so frightened when looking at monsters that the player is unable to move their character. The idea of losing one's own sanity, to the point that it interferes with the physical world, is terrifying, and the game harkens on this fear to make the game much scarier. As Clasen suggested, one of the fears that humans innately possess is the fear of going insane. *Amnesia: The Dark Descent* relies on this fear by making it near-to-impossible to retain sanity, ensuring that the game is scarier than just having monsters chase the player-character.

Eternal Darkness: Sanity's Requiem

Eternal Darkness: Sanity's Requiem, published by Silicon Knights, is an action-adventure game that features horror elements. The game follows several timelines in different eras from BC to 2000 AD. It begins in the year 2000 with the brutal murder of Alexandra's grandfather in his mansion, where she finds a tome bound in human skin and bone. The game then switches to 26 BC, where Pious Augustus, who is transported to an underground temple called the Forbidden City, receives an Ancient power at the cost of becoming undead. Continually, people encounter the Black Guardian, part of the ancient power, and are often killed by it. The main plot lines follow Alexandra Roivas and Pious, through which there is a long and eternal battle between them.

Like *Amnesia: The Dark Descent,* the game also utilizes a sanity indicator, which can decline when encountering too many enemies. Taylor covers the game mechanics and horror elements, stating,

> The insanity factor causes the internal game representations to blue and slide and allows enemies that are not actually there to be displayed. Such insanity factors even affect the interface itself. These include messages stating that the game controller is unplugged, that all of the saved game information is being erased, and so forth. These uses of the gaming interface question the relationship of the gamer to the game and the gaming interface as a mediator in that relationship. The majority of games use the interface as a functional means of allowing for gameplay to occur; survival horror games often use the interface to subvert typical play and to challenge conceptions of the game interface design and game design, questioning the materiality of the text itself. (52, as quoted in Perron)

By impacting the player's physical world, such as through having the controller itself be disrupted in its function, *Eternal Darkness* plays upon the same fears of insanity that *Amnesia* utilizes. It makes the game more frightening by tapping into the realness of the situation for the player by affecting the controller and controls of the game. This also plays into the interactivity of the game as part of what makes it scarier by impacting the player controls and almost the real-life situation for the player. Buday et al. studied video games and mental illness portrayals, finding that 75% of the games they looked at had representations of mental illness portrayed negatively. This creates cyclical stereotyping, encouraging people to garner and hold negative, ablesanist views about mental illness and mental health. *Eternal Darkness: Sanity's Requiem* can be seen contributing to this through the use of the sanity indicator, which causes negative reactions in the player when insanity is reached.

Silent Hill 2

Silent Hill 2, published by Konami, follows James Sunderland. James goes to the town of Silent Hill after receiving a letter from his wife, Mary, who had died three years earlier after suffering from an illness. As he explores the town, James meets several non-playable characters, most notably Maria, who is similar to his wife except for her more assertive personality and more promiscuous clothing style. James allows Maria to follow him into the town's hospital, where Maria is killed by the monster Pyramid Head. James finds Maria again, unharmed and having no recollection of their previous encounter, but she is aware of information that only Mary would know. James makes his way to the town's hotel, where he discovers a videotape of him killing his ill wife by smothering her with a pillow. He also learns that everyone he has encountered, sans Maria and a child named Laura, has killed or maimed someone before coming to Silent Hill. James begins to comprehend that the monsters were meant to punish him and are manifestations of his guilt and psyche. There are several endings, including James dying by suicide or leaving with Maria, who is shown to be sick herself.

Silent Hill 2 touches predominantly on themes of mental illness and guilt. James feels intense guilt over killing his wife, Mary, to the point of physical manifestation in the form of demented monsters. As the game progresses, the monsters become harder to defeat and are weaponized, symbolizing James's increasing guilt. Marak states, "The town gives the sin [of euthanizing his wife] tangible form - in fact, multiple forms - thus creating a nightmare that summons James and swallows him" (134). The focus on his increasingly deranged and guilt-ridden mind elevates fright as monsters become more frequent and increasingly difficult to defeat. The monsters themselves reveal different aspects of James's psyche, as well. For instance, the Flesh Lips monsters, which are strange creatures suspended from metal cages, represent confinement and sickness, according to Konami (Marak 136).

Silent Hill 2 monsters are much more humanoid than the Necromorphs of *Dead Space*. Beyond their representations of ideas such as confinement in the case of the Flesh Lips monsters, they also represent a fear of disability, deformity, and losing one's sanity. The monsters in *Silent Hill 2* rely on their deformities to be frightening.

The themes of mental illness and insanity are strong throughout the game. There are multiple memos and items that James can find that point to insanity.

For example, James finds what he calls "some gossip magazine" with the tale of Walter Sullivan, a man who killed two children brutally with an ax. The story continues to state that when he was arrested, Sullivan shouted, "He's trying to kill me. He's trying to punish me. The monster… the red devil. Forgive me. I did it, but it wasn't me!" A schoolmate of Walter's was quoted as saying, "I guess now that I think of it, he was kind of crazy." Sullivan's story pops up again in the hospital, making this a continuous theme of insanity and murder to scare players further by creating intrigue around the theme.

Other characters in the game, such as Eddie and Angela, also pertain to the trope of mental illness as frightening. Eddie is severely disturbed, often found muttering to himself, and the first instance the player-character finds him, he is vomiting into a toilet after seeing a brutally murdered dead body. He attacks James after he asks if he's "gone nuts," shooting him in the shoulder. Eddie also tells James that the town would not have called him to it had he had nothing on his conscience, bringing forth the message of guilt again. Angela is another mentally disturbed character who clearly suffers from post-traumatic stress and depression. She has attempted to die by suicide several times prior to her arrival at Silent Hill. Angela also likely suffers from body dysmorphic disorder, common in sexual assault victims such as herself; she was abused by her father and brother. She later kills them both and brings the knife with her to Silent Hill. Her story is twofold in its representation: she garners sympathy, which in a way transcends the trope of disability as frightening, yet she succumbs to other tropes about how society perceives disability as a tragedy, making her seem more volatile, unstable, and therefore frightening to the player.

Conclusion

Poor representation can create stereotyped views of disability and deformity that have harmful impacts on disabled people. While there is not much literature on how the representation of disabled video game characters impacts disabled and abled people's perceptions of disability, there is plenty of evidence to suggest that sexualized female video game characters have a negative impact on female players. Generalizing from this example, it is likely that negative and stereotypical representations of any minoritized population negatively impact that population of players, causing misunderstandings in the majority population (Norris 725-726; Behm-Morawitz and Mastro 819). Representations of disability that are intended to create fear in the player are likely to create real-life misunderstandings, fear, and stigmatization of disability. To remedy this, video game developers could include more disabled characters in horror settings that aren't representative of the fear of disablement, disfigurement, disease, or deformity. This would be a difficult task, admittedly, but would benefit horror video game players. It would allow video game players to see disability in a nonstereotypical light, helping end the cycles of stereotyping and stigmatization that hurt disabled people.

Works Cited

Amnesia: The Dark Descent. Frictional Games, 2011.

Behm-Morawitz, Elizabeth, and Dana Mastro. "The Effects of the Sexualization of Female Videogame Characters on Gender Stereotyping and Female Self-Concept. *Sex Roles*, vol. 61 2009, pp. 808-23, https://doi.org/10.1007/s11199-009-9683-8.

Buday, Jozef, et al. "Depiction of Mental Illness and Psychiatry in Popular Video Games over the Last 20 Years." *Frontiers in Psychiatry*, 2022, www.frontiersin.org/articles/10.3389/fpsyt.2022.967992/full.

Carr, Diane. "Ability, Disability, and Dead Space." *The International Journal of Computer Game Research* Dec. 2014, gamestudies.org/1402/articles/carr/#:~:text=In%20Dead%20Space%2C%20the%20contamination,affirmation%20of%20ability%20through%20play.

Clasen, Mathias. *Why Horror Seduces*. Oxford University Press, 2017.

Costantino, Jersey. "A Mad Trans Educational Scholar's Letter to Ablesanism of the Research Community." *Wordgathering: A Journal of Disability Poetry and Literature*, vol. 16, no. 1, 2022.

Dead Space. Electronics Arts, 2008.

Dead Space 2. Electronics Arts, 2011.

"Disability." *World Health Organization*, 2023, www.who.int/news-room/fact-sheets/detail/disability-and-health.

Eternal Darkness: Sanity's Requiem. Silicon Knights and Nintendo, 2002.

Garland Thomson, Rosemarie. *Extraordinary Bodies: Figuring Physical Disability in American Culture and Literature*. Columbia University Press, 2017.

Gilmore, David. *Monsters: Evil Beings, Mythical Beasts, and All Manner of Imaginary Terror*. University of Pennsylvania Press, 2003.

Grip, Thomas. "The Terrifying Tale of Amnesia." *The Escapist*, 2011, www.escapistmagazine.com/the-terrifying-tale-of-amnesia/.

Hand, Richard. "Profilerating Horror: Survival Horror and the Resident Evil Franchise." *Horror Film: Creating and Marketing Fear*, edited by Steffen Hantke, University of Mississippi Press, 2014, pp. 117-34.

Marak, Katarzyna. *Japanese and American Horror: A Comparative Study of Film, Fiction, Graphic Novels and Video Games*. McFarland & Company, Inc., 2015.

"Medical and Social Models of Disability." *Office of Developmental Primary Care*, 2018, odpc.ucsf.edu/clinical/patient-centered-care/medical-and-social-models-of-disability.

Norris, Kamala O. "Gender Stereotypes, Aggression, and Computer Games: An Online Survey of Women.' *CyberPsychology & Behavior*, vol. 7, no. 6, 2004, pp. 714-27, https://doi.org/10.1089/cpb.2004.7.714.

Perron, Bernard. "The Survival Horror: The Extended Body Genre." *Horror Video Games: Essays on the Fusion of Fear and Play*, edited by Bernard Perron, McFarland & Company, Inc., pp. 121-43.

Rodan, Debbie, et. al. *Disability, Obesity, and Ageing: Popular Media Identifications*. Routledge, 2014.

Silent Hill 2. Konami, 2001.

Snyder, Sharon, and David Mitchell. *Cultural Locations of Disability*. University of Chicago Press, 2006.

Sontag, Susan. *AIDS and Its Metaphors*. Farrar, Straus, and Giroux, 1989.

Chapter 14

Hollywood Mythology and *King Kong*

Kazım Tolga Gürel

Abstract

Monsters and giant creatures, frequently depicted in American cinema, are essential tools of postmodern narratives in terms of the violence they contain and in determining the limits of the social system. The phenomenon of the "monster" is a metaphor that includes psychoanalysis, political economy, and mythology in social sciences. In this chapter, these analyses of the monster phenomenon will be discussed through the character of King Kong in American mythology. After briefly describing the progress of American cinema on its way to becoming a giant industry and touching upon the mythology established, the relationship between this mythology and violence will be examined. In addition to describing the productions of both the 1933 and 2005 versions of *King Kong*, this chapter provides content analyses of the film's violent scenes and sexist approaches to heroic scenes.

Keywords: mythology, King Kong, violence, gender, power

* * *

Background on Mythology's Role in Hollywood

The phenomenon of myth comes from the Greek word "mythos," which means "word" or "story" (Brezezinski). Myths produce the values of social groups or communities that help keep people together, working as narratives that enable these subjects to act for the continuation of the community (Mills). As they evolve from community to society en masse, myths begin to reflect the dominant-oppressed relationship and conflict. With the history of civilization, this conflict and many phenomena, such as patriarchy and incest, can be read into myths.

   The first recorded myths, dating from the eighth to seventh centuries BC, are found in the poetry of Homer and Hesiodos, later appearing widely in Greek art (March 17). The primary sources for classical myths are literary texts and visual materials in various arts (Ateş 21). Claude Levi-Strauss, in his work "Myth and Meaning," states that history has replaced myth in contemporary societies. Attacking the whole philosophical and moral enterprise represented by

Socrates, Nietzsche argues in *The Birth of Tragedy* that the Socratic culture tried to solve myths and introduced morality to the world, the first nuclei of rational reason. In Nietzsche's belief, the spread of scientific culture could destroy art and, even worse, the original myth from which art is rooted (Megill 101).

Working on mythology beyond the predictions of Levi-Strauss and Nietzsche, Barthes used semiological concepts to interpret the myths and signs of modern society in his work *Mythlogies*. Based on Barthes's theories, Hollywood cinema is one of the contemporary mythologies. This mythology, which has many points where ideological abuses are evident, was initially under the intervention of the American State (Barthes). Myths push the man out of chronological time and place him in a qualitatively different time (Eliade 32). While myth presents archaic man with the story of his existence and conveys to him the ancient rules of his community and the rules of his ancestors about life (Eliade), contemporary myths instill the superstructural blocks of meaning produced by the economic system.

Mythic memory manifests itself with reproductions in every branch of art. This plane, which reveals a conscious transfer within the historical process, provides essential data at the point of showing the source of the new works produced and analyzing the context/change/renewal. Mythic repetitions, modeling, and exchanges between signs, which include many examples such as the similarities between the ancient Sumerian god July and Greek mythology's Adonis (both represent spring and revived nature), reveal the roots of narratives at every stage of the historical process. Myths also have an important place in the fictional universe of cinema, which is a much younger genre than other branches of art (Gariper).

The archetypes of many films stem back to mythological roots. In his work *The Hero with a Thousand Faces*, Joseph Campbell discusses the path followed and the result reached by the hero in myths. Trying to determine the characteristic lines of the hero motif, Campbell focuses on examining what the hero goes through and the adventures he experiences, that is, the hero's journey paradigm as a universal archetype (108). He defines the hero as the one who sacrifices himself for a greater purpose, which is to show a transformation by reaching a certain level of consciousness through the stages he goes through and the path he takes. With this transformation, the hero returns and teaches what he has learned. Campbell draws the triangle of separation-authorization-return as "the core unit of the monomyth":

> A hero leaves the ordinary world and travels into the realm of supernatural strangeness, where he encounters mythical forces. Sometimes, he fights them, or sometimes, he learns something from them and adds them to his development. When he returns, he wins a

decisive victory or sacrifices himself on the way and becomes a myth. (33-35)

Campbell's monomyth continues in the hero mythologies of Hollywood. The situation is repeated in Superman, Batman, X-Man, and many others. Locations change, and characteristics differ, but the same monomyth continues. The hero leaves a certain point, goes on a journey, and evolves and transforms himself and the audience as a result of what he experiences on that journey.

In the film *King Kong*, this monomyth continues. King Kong, the inhabitant of Skull Island, was born on an island and involuntarily embarked on a journey to a place he had never known: the civilized world. Along the way, the creature goes through various battles and suffers the wrath of an unknown, incomprehensible species. While following this monomyth, the film maintains the dichotomy between civilized and savage in its narrative structure. This dichotomy is rooted in the original script of the film. The King Kong narrative, directed and produced by Merian C. Cooper and Ernest B. Schoedsack in 1933, carries the prejudices of early anthropology, and the 2005 film *King Kong* perpetuates these stereotypes. The natives of the island are characterized as evil beings who want to sacrifice a beautiful woman to the gigantic hero, Kong; they carry primitive weapons and lack the positive aspects of civilization. The story of *King Kong* glorifies civilization and the West, implying that it is far away from the savagery of Skull Island. The film suggests that the *East*, the *foreign*, the *other*, and the *primitive* are the cause of the massacres, terror, and evils that occur while organizing the world for commercial purposes and continuing social engineering. The roots of this fascist idea, which continue today and form the ideological core of today's wars, can be traced back to the geographical discoveries of Europe on other continents. However, Hollywood mythology has repeated this ideology throughout time and in different forms.

This general ideological attitude of Hollywood cinema can be seen in the sacrifice scene of the film. In savage societies, sacrifice is not something to be judged but rather a valuable phenomenon to be admired. However, it is seen that this anthropological fact is reproduced differently in *King Kong*. In the early tribes, the sacrifice is usually the creature most valued by the tribe, and this creature represents birth, abundance, and re-creation. However, the sacrifice in *King Kong* mythology is "civilized" and has a protective hero, which is a reversal of the traditional sacrificial ritual. In this way, civilization is transformed into a phenomenon that needs to be protected; it represents life with its purity and cleanliness. The reality of blood and massacre, which is hidden and hidden just beneath civilization, is veiled.

Rene Girard's and Lévy-Bruhl's accounts are two of the most salient and fundamental anthropological insights into the sacrifice ritual in so-called "savage" societies. The sacrifice scene in the movie *King Kong* repeats the myth of the native community killing the modern white man, a common myth in early Hollywood mythology. Girard states that the sacrifice usually chosen is always the most valuable in terms of its utility, the sweetest in terms of its motives and habits, the most innocent, and the one most in contact with man. According to Girard, sacrifice is a symbol used to appease the anger of the other tribe or the gods (4). However, the savages in *King Kong* act with unconscious and senseless behaviors. They do not have the prelogical mind mentioned by Lévy-Bruhl, which he describes as a mind that is meaningful in itself and has deep knowledge in its field. According to Lévy-Bruhl, the "savage" mind is mystical. This mentality does not connect events to physical phenomena and cause-and-effect sequences; for savages, the physical and the supra-physical coexist. The savage mentality cannot perceive any object as a form; the object is perceived in a magical quality and a mystical sense. It cannot determine the succession of rules and sequences between events (Lévy-Bruhl). According to Lévy-Bruhl, the prelogical mind is not infantile and pathological. On the contrary, the savage mind can respond to its conditions and is highly complex and capable of developing within these conditions (Lévy-Bruhl 32-33). Lévy-Bruhl's anthropological information is related to the mythologization of the scene in the film through the opposite of reality. The natives on the island are depicted in *King Kong* are childish and even crazy, which is completely disconnected from anthropological realities, thus producing a myth that reinforces the audience's judgment of the superiority of the modern world, perpetuating a dangerous trope. The tribe shown in the film gives the impression of being made up of wild people whose sole purpose is to kill, as often seen in early Hollywood films.

To put it more simply, mythology reflects a culture in a complex and layered way, as Mircea Eliade puts it (258). The slogan "beauty killed the beast" appears before the audience as a phenomenon that reproduces the beauty of civilization killing the beast with a woman-centric metaphor. Eventually, civilization wins, but this victory reproduces savagery and destroys the real beauties within a power struggle.

The mythological world of *King Kong*, like the oral myths of the past, contains complex and intertwined pieces of reality. However, unlike past examples, it produces an ideological dimension in which this reality is inverted, thus transcending tropes. The giant ape threatening civilization, the white woman representing the "beauty" of civilization, and the savage tribe acting wild and childlike: unlike the mythology of oral culture, this is the inverted ideological perception of "reality" in the world.

The narratives of oral culture listened to by the fire are perhaps the first consumption points of "safe fear," which keeps people in the tribe without causing physical or psychological trauma and teaches them to fear those outside the tribe, thus strengthening the unifying mortar of the community. The narratives show what is familiar and what is not, combining differences with demonic and mystical powers. Safe fear is the type of fear experienced in sterile modern life's fear-free and safe spaces, as the comfort of modern life has moved away from the natural and relatively dangerous life of bygone eras. Thus, thrills have become a commodity offered for sale in the consumer society. Amusement parks, houses of horror, horror cinema, images of brutality in cinema, bungee jumping, rafting, etc., enable the secretion of fear hormones such as adrenaline and cortisol in safe environments. The production of fear and excitement in Hollywood mythology can also be read from this perspective. Movies like *King Kong* are reminiscent of horror stories told around a fire, just like in ancient times. These safe horror narratives, like the social rites of their audiences, have become "weekend movie rituals" and produce intersections with ideological myths.

Walter Ong, who works in the field of oral culture related to storytelling, discusses the qualities of modern cinema rituals:

> Since its physical structure consists of sound, the spoken word contains many qualities of human beings. It connects people as conscious internal structures, as persons. It creates clusters of people tightly bound to each other. When the speaker addresses a community, the listeners become a whole, both among themselves and with the speech. Suppose the speaker distributes a text and asks the audience to read it. In that case, each person who begins to read the text retreats into his or her world, and this unity dissipates until the speaker retakes the floor—writing and printing isolated. (93)

Like other films, *King Kong* connects the cinematic audience to its own mythology and focuses the audience on a single whole; this is the power of the cinematic stage. Just like in savage societies, the audience becomes one with the narrative. Unlike reading a book or watching television alone, the audience members come under the ethos of collective power.

Cinema has the power to become immortal. Painting and sculpture are created to continue existence (Bazin 15). The freezing of the image, and therefore of time, is one of the human endeavors for immortality. To this point, in his novel *Immortality*, Milan Kundera describes dealing with permanent elements as follows:

> The immortality Goethe speaks of has, of course, nothing to do with believing in the immortality of the soul. It is a different, non-religious

immortality, an immortality that exists for people who will remain in the memory of future generations after death... People are not equal in the face of immortality. It is necessary to distinguish between "small immortality," which means the memory of a man in the minds of those who knew him (the immortality dreamt of by the village headman in Moravia), and "great immortality," which means the memory of a man in the minds of those who did not know him. There are professions that bring a person face to face with the great immortality, which may be doubtful, or even, in all likelihood, unquestionably possible: These professions are art and statesmanship. (64-65)

Immortality is linked to birth and cosmogony. In a sense, the agents in the mythologized story become immortal by becoming independent from the rules of cosmogony imposed on ordinary people. Photography, which is involved in a film, is like a rebellion against immortality and the rules of existence. The invention of photography and its depiction of beings in a manner close to the way the eye sees has taken the phenomenon of myth to a completely different dimension. Myths persist, but the reality is known in parallel with the secularization of life. The vast majority of the world knows that King Kong is not alive. However, the images reflected on the screen carry mythical qualities regarding sub-meanings that can distort reality. Sontag emphasizes that photography is a "liar" (52).

Although it is known that King Kong did not live and is not accurate, the stereotypes about the tribe in the narrative may seem real to the vast majority who do not know anthropology. In this sense, myths continue to take shape around the unknown and make them known or reinforce what people think of as the norm. Due to the illusion created by the photo frame and its animated state, the immortality of the film producers and the heroes has penetrated an area and a mass that perhaps no other art has spread.

King Kong Film and Scenario

A central element in the critical analysis of a film is to address its historicity. The film's meaning and signifiers reflect the cultural milieu of its time and place and interact with the meanings of that milieu. Being aware of the historicity of a particular film, then, requires grasping and studying the various aspects (social, political, economic, psychological, etc.) of the hegemony that dominated the life of artists and audiences at the time of its creation and initial presentation.

Many versions of *King Kong*, from films to comic books and other pop-culture iterations, have been interpreted from various angles in cultural studies. In this sense, *King Kong* has transcended cinema or pop culture, becoming a ritual of academia and writing on cinema. It has been the subject of dozens of articles in many fields ranging from racist politics to transnational enemy metaphors, from Lenin-Stalin dynamics to Nazism, from criticism of heteronormativity to state violence and modernism. There is a large academic corpus that identifies *King Kong* with fears such as the depression of 1929 and the clash of civilizations or the specter of communism (Schleier, Sexton; Hansbury; Combe and Boyle).

King Kong is arguably the most famous fictional character ever on the big screen. The 2005 version is the closest to the original 1933 film (Sorenson 11). In both theatrical versions (1933 and 2005), King Kong is modeled on the narrative of an exploration film: the monster appears in wild and colonizable lands and is later discovered by human (European) "heroes"; its "terrifying" presence is seen, and the film ends with a fight to the death between man and the "monster" (colonialism) (Carroll 99). In a sense, the element of fear in *King Kong* is similar to the colonizers' fear of the other. If he cannot control and exploit it, he kills it, which is what the history of Eurocentric capitalism is based on (Galeano).

Each of these interpretations can be said to reflect the faces of power that *King Kong* carries. It should not be forgotten that the film was popularized in a time of social depression when people were subjected to violence and marginalized because of their skin color amid the degeneration processes of capitalism. It should be remembered that only five years after 1933, when the film was shot, the most horrible years of fascism the world has ever known would begin. The film is an icon reflected on the screen when many fears, class conflicts, and state terror peaked. For this reason, it is one of the films in which physical and symbolic violence is at its peak and shown at its most extreme points with the technology of the time. In this sense, *King Kong* contains many horror components.

King Kong is not a white male hero like Batman or James Bond. The film is an exotic tale of monstrosity, also representing marginalization outside the system. It shows the victory and power of civilization over a monster, controlling, colonizing and excluding fears of the unknown that King Kong represents. Just like in the film, the "civilized one" wants to explore the unknown but also control it. This is the contradiction of the exotic also seen in the script of the movie.

The team sets sail on a ship called Venture, symbolizing the colonial entrepreneur, and despite their fear of King Kong, they want to control and sell him. They turn Kong into a commodity to be viewed in a showroom. The colonial entrepreneur wants to exhibit the exploited, just like the human gardens across Europe in the nineteenth century. When it becomes impossible to profit from the exploited, the colonial entrepreneur destroys it. When Kong was captured, the crew leader, in a clear expression of this endeavor, stated that "in a few months, his name will be on all the Broadway signs, and they will run to see him." The exotic object, which up to that moment had inspired fear, is now advertised on signs as ' the eighth wonder of the world."

The dangerous, uncanny, unsafe, and exotic object is transformed into an object of consumption as an "other"; Kong is exhibited in Broadway theatres as a "safe fear." The captured Kong is transformed into a commodifiable and monetizable product as long as it is controlled. Colonialist reflexes are still visible in the lower layers of the film's narrative line. However, Kong gets out of control and breaks his chains; the "exotic object" transforms from a "beast" consumed by being watched into a horrible monster. What makes him a horrible monster is that he acts according to his existential qualities and to be liberated. As seen at the end of the movie, Kong will be destroyed.

The threat to civilization by an unknown, incomprehensible, and irrational outsider, along with his taming of a woman, strengthens the argument that King Kong is a sub-self of parallel Hollywood heroes. The character is depicted as uncanny, disgusting, ugly, and out of the norm. Kristeva emphasizes that disgust towards the ugly and monstrous is limited and ambiguous. "Disgusting" separates the subject from what threatens him and reminds him of the uncertainty of the system, that everything does not go in a particular order (Kristeva 22).

The white male hero resembles an ego that can control itself, acting together with the police and the military against a danger that threatens the system, as seen in many examples. However, King Kong acts as a pure id and controls this id in his love for a single woman. Kong is a giant ape who represents the primitive side of man. He is the opposite and, in a sense, the "other" of civilization. Our marginalized animal side has to be suppressed by the "white male hero" (ego) supported by society (superego). The marginal and exotic giant ape is the id that civilization excludes, but it constructs the entire civilization by repressing it. Freud attributes the production of civilization to the principles of repression, which is the primitive reflex that enables the marginalization of the marginal.

King Kong, a giant ape coming from a mysterious island not shown on the maps, being an uncivilized creature with wildness and strangeness, represents the alter ego of civilization. The most crucial character in the film is a white and beautiful woman opposite the monster. Susan Buck Morss saw the representation of modernity in the 1933 film *King Kong* and interpreted modernity through the representations in the film.

Kong also symbolizes the marginalized and repressed aspects of civilization in general and different fears at the time of its cinematic projection. His era is a time of economic crisis, full of uncertainty and fear. Mayne states that *King Kong* was inspired by the economic depression of 1929. He notes similarities between the economic conditions that could not thoroughly analyze the crisis conditions of capitalism, which suddenly burned and destroyed everything in *King Kong*, and that the giant gorilla is a reflection of the ideology of capitalism.

King Kong is the reflection on the screen of the fearful years of the economic crisis based on uncertainty (Mayne).

Since the film's release in 1933, one of the most common arguments about it has been the representation of racism through the "black gorilla." *King Kong* exhibits the fear of white workers. The fear of unemployment, especially during the economic depression and the widespread idea that Blacks, who are the "other" in depression times, are held responsible for the depression strengthen the ideas that the film reflects this point of social memory. It is thought that Black citizens took over the jobs of whites in times of severe economic depression. In addition, the film reflects the feelings and fears that render non-white people invisible, shows the desires and fears of repressed sexuality, and associates it with death symbolized by Blackness, in short, deepening differentiation and social exclusion; to the cinematographic universe, this echoes the ideology of the patriarchal, colonialist, and racist system in the cinema (Dines; Hairston; Hund; Carcel).

To understand how *King Kong* embodies these ideals, consider the plot. While filming and researching on the mysterious Skull Island north of Sumatra, the American crew, hearing rumors of a strange demonic force worshipped by the natives, are shocked one night when the beautiful Ann is kidnapped from the ship. Ann is to be presented to King Kong, a giant gorilla, to appease his wrath. The giant animal comes to the young woman as she struggles in her restraints. The demonic power, a creature with an eye for beauty who is attentive and affectionate despite his size, will love this beauty but will not be able to make her accept his love. Then, he is caught, imprisoned and taken to New York. According to the most superficial capitalist logic, he is put on display to make money. However, his incredible strength will enable him to break the bars and everything else and embark on a glorious adventure that will take him to the skyscrapers of New York. His main goal is to find peace with the always beautiful and charming Ann.

Violence and *King Kong*

One of the ways to use content analysis in film is to analyze it by dividing it into scenes and sequences. Of the 228 scenes in the 2005 *King Kong*, 23 contain direct violence and horror. The other scenes also contain tension-raising images, but this is the number of unquestionably violent scenes. Stone discusses violence in film as such:

> No film has iconic power, but the repetition of similar images in films weaves these images into the fabric of the everyday life of its society. It influences everything from clothing styles to accepted behavior. Filmic conventions, of which most viewers are never consciously aware,

cumulatively affect people's self-esteem, expectations, attitudes and behavior in relationships. It can be argued that they have an impact on the normalization of violence and the acceptance of violence.

Because people of the past were not used to images of violence as much as society is today (Bryan-Wilson), a parallel can be drawn between the consciousnesses accustomed to violence and the fact that the whole world watches while Israel massacres civilians in Palestine in the path opened to it by Hamas, which was founded against socialist organizations and directed the people of the region towards an Islamic structure, and the fact that many people support this massacre by justifying it. Films containing intense mass violence produce consciousnesses accustomed to the violence of states and their affiliated organizations against the masses.

In the part of the film that takes place on Skull Island, it is seen as an unknown and surreal place. However, its qualities provide facts about the perspective of the savage society, reflecting a point of view that makes civilization superior and labels those outside of civilization as barbarians. This freedom also reflects the ideological perspective. At this point, the scriptwriter can move away from reality as much as they wish. The viewer who does not have experiences with this place cannot reach any judgment of abnormality. This part of the film carries the main ideological structuring. The tribe on the unknown island has common similarities with pre-civilized anthropological tribes yet is depicted as wild and barbaric.

The American Indians described in Columbus's diaries, or as anthropologists such as Malinowski, Lévy-Bruhl, and Levi-Strauss have shown, the natives far from civilization are not savages. They have learned violence from civilized people with the touch of civilized people. After entering into the system of exploitation of civilized people, they turned to violence to rebel against colonialism. In its early stages, European capitalism exploited Africa and the Americas to an extent unprecedented in history. The birth of Western capitalism is based on blood and violence. In early film scripts, this violence was inverted in a sense and presented as a metaphor for a threat to civilization, as in *King Kong*.

When Columbus arrived on the main continent, he wrote that the concepts of "honor" and crime were very different from civilization (Sanchez et al.). The Inquisition morality of Christianity and state laws brought crime and sin to those regions (Ferro). However, in the movie *King Kong*, the tribe, rather than society, is seen to have these negative qualities. They exhibit brutality in a way that is far from meaning and reason. The basic script of the film, which was written in the 1930s, reflects the stereotypes that people had developed against the concept of foreigners. However, although it tries to position itself as sterile, innocent, and democratic today, this civility is a civilization built on blood.

The violent scenes of such films raise the thresholds of the masses for violence, accustoming them to these images. This increases the acceptability of wars in the world. It is understood from the chronicles of Columbus and the stories of many anthropologists that the tribal life shown on the island in the film is not accurate. However, the reality (the ideological part) that the *King Kong* series builds is the opposite.

Scenes in the film were coded into categories of violence. "Least" referred to scenes of violence where no blood was seen; "medium" designated parts where no blood was seen but people were dying; "quite a lot" were scenes with people dying and direct blood; "maximum level" included scenes such as body dismemberment and blood splattering.

In data analysis, the scenes in which brutality is used "quite a lot" have the highest rate, showing that scenes of violence are produced more in terms of their importance and effectiveness for the film. One of the three points where the film exhibits the highest level of brutality is when the natives on the island attack the group arriving on the island. The others are the scene in which King Kong and three dinosaurs fight as well as the battle between the group who fall into a dark well and strange insect-like organisms.

A study of violence, initiated in the late 1960s by George Gerbner and his colleagues at the Annenberg School, aimed to provide an analysis "of the extent and nature of overt violence in television plays" (Gerbner et al. 30). Gerbner et al. did not analyze the act of violence or its consequences in physical detail. Instead, they looked at the social identities of the characters and their interactions with violence. They created the first analytical paradigm by introducing analytical elements: frequency, seriousness, physical consequences, and the program format on the screen. Seriousness is opposed to the comic, while consequences indicate the presence or absence of injury without specification (Gerbner et al.). In *King Kong*, the main character is social only because of his love for the white woman. In this sense, he has no social character. He is *other*. The identification of the other with violence and its presentation as an element of fear is repeated at various points in the film.

According to Gerbner et al.'s famous cultivation theory approach, the messages constantly presented to the viewers on the screen affect the viewers' ideas and attitudes about reality. Gerbner and his colleagues stated that television is constantly sowing the dominant ideas in society. Therefore, the perception of reality of people who watch much television is formed directly by television messages. From this point of view, Gerbner et al. emphasized that the excessive violent content on the screens causes many people to fear the outside world and stated that these people evaluate the world as a more insecure environment than its natural state (Erdoğan; Özkan; Kaya).

In this sense, the character of King Kong increases the viewer's fear of the outside world and especially of the other, sowing fear and avoidance instead of recognizing it. The fear of the outside world reinforces the need for the state and its institutions and reinforces the consciousness that trusts all kinds of discourse and propaganda of the state. This situation justifies state terror and produces large fascist masses who are far from questioning the reasons for any anti-system movement. The violence presented in various programs and film formats normalizes violence in real life. Exposure of the representation on the screen to violence breaks its power of empathy for the situation of encountering actual violence. Violence is reduced to a simple element of consumption, consumed like a snack without fear or empathy.

In total, 34 minutes of the 2005 *King Kong* are devoted to scenes in which blood is seen clearly and intensely. This length of time strengthens the argument that violence in the film is consciously used to make the audience tense and increase their interest in the film. Intensive studies on color psychology at the Oxford School of Architecture show that red increases tension much more than blue and green. Our historical relationship with fire and blood causes the perception of danger signals and increases focus and interest (Mikellides). For this reason, the adornment of violent scenes with blood also increases the interest in the film.

The facts that the perpetrator of the violent act is not a civilized person in the scenes with intense images of violence and that in the few scenes where a civilized person is the perpetrator, he does it for defense purposes are related to the "myth of superior civilization," which purports that violence and brutality come not from civilization but from the other: the disgusting, the uncivilized, and the barbaric. This narrative, which is constantly repeated in Hollywood cinema, unites a consciousness that makes it difficult to question the causes of violence in real life. Today, the roots of this consciousness can be seen in the wars caused by capitalism. The causes of violence based on injustice are not questioned. While the violence of the oppressed is considered terrorism, the violence of states is rendered "legal" and "legitimate." Hollywood mythology produces or reinforces a consciousness based on the barbarian-civilized distinction.

Another element seen in *King Kong* is the concentration of violence on women. It is known that popular culture within the scope of visual entertainment plays a vital role in shaping people's mentality. A parallel can be drawn between nature and women, especially how these two beings are oppressed (Suresh). This is precisely what is seen in the film: the suppression of the relationship between King Kong, who represents nature distortedly, and the woman by the state apparatus and the partnership of civilized consciousness.

In the years when the basic script of the film was written, the effects of the economic depression of 1929 had just been experienced. Therefore, there is a kind of anti-civilization anger in the screenwriters. We can accept the analysis of the message "Beauty killed the beast" as an outcome of this depression. The inability to consume the commodity drove the system into a crisis, and the Fordist accumulation and production in the last years ensured the perfection of the commodity for that period. This period is one of the triggering factors for the shaping of the script in this way.

Kong is the hero in most of the scenes. However, in some scenes, the screenwriter, the captain, and the captain's assistant are the heroes. Justifying the feminist criticisms directed at the film from various angles, it can be seen that the female figure is ineffective in the film, and the representation of "in need of protection" is repeated as she is constantly protected by changing male protectors and heroes. Moreover, with the film's motto, the responsibility for all problems and all kinds of violence is placed on a woman.

Conclusion

Just like architecture, cinema is an expensive art and therefore depends on commercial resources. This situation brings about the commercialization of this art and the ideological structuring of many of the works produced. Moreover, if discussing an industrialized production center like Hollywood, there are not only substantial economic resources allocated for the film but also state interventions, such as the Hays Code, which was created to determine what kind of entertainment was appropriate for the audience (Maltby). In this way, films were assigned a cultural role, ideologically regulated, and acceptable boundaries were set. Like many secret practices in the United States, it is an anti-democratic censorship law.

The cinema industry is a severe carrier of ideology. For this reason, it is essential that the cinematic film is watched and attracts attention, both as a focus of profit and as a means of propaganda.

The problematic production of cinema stems from two reasons. First, the art of cinema depends on technology and, therefore, on capital. Second, cinema is an art that transcends the individual. In other words, it is produced by a group. The fact that it has become the most capital-based art after architecture has blunted its avant-garde status to some extent; it has turned into a conformist structure and, in a sense, a pop commodity. Films, which are visual extensions that create mass consciousness and numb the minds of human communities, have mostly become factory products rather than artistic products with a free and distinct point of view. The fact that their scripts end predictably by watching only the first fifteen minutes of the film strengthens the argument that the products of this factory have ceased to be art.

King Kong, as one of the most prominent icons of this factory, bears all the faces of power. It glorifies masculinity, legitimizes violence, puts forward civilization as a pure and clean ideal, and labels everything else as "savage." Moreover, the fact that a film with a violence rate of 30% of its total duration can be watched in prime time and can be shown in all cinemas shows that the myth of "civilization," which is glorified today and is economically very productive, has long ago been destroyed by capitalism. If anthropology that glorifies human rights presents a film to the masses with a violence rate of 30%, this point should be viewed with skepticism.

King Kong is an iconic film that embodies all the qualities of the society and period in which it was produced. Considering the point that violence and war have reached today, the symbolic violence and oppression with which today's world is burdened, *King Kong* is a myth that reflects the period and way of life in which it was produced and reveals the point reached by capitalist civilization. The *King Kong* myth and the infrastructural installations of its violence indicate that the choice that results from Rosa Luxemburg's important slogan, "Socialism or Barbarism," is barbarism itself (Meszaros).

Works Cited

Ateş, Mehmet. *Mitolojiler ve Semboller* [*Mythologies and Symbols*]. Milenyum Yayınları [Millenium Publications], 2018.

Barthes, Roland. *Çağdaş Söylenler* [*Mythologies*]. Translated by Tahsin Yücel, Metis Yayınları [Metis Publications], 2023.

Bazin, Andre. *Sinema Nedir?* [*What Is Cinema?*] İzdüşüm Yayınları [İzdüşüm Publications], 2000.

Bryan-Wilson, Julia. *Art Workers: Radical Practice in the Vietnam War Era.* University of California Press, 2011.

Buck-Morss, Susan. *Rüya Alemi ve Felaket* [*Dream World and Catastrophe*]. Translated by Tuncay Birkan, Metis Yayınları [Metis Publications], 2004.

Campbell, Joseph. *Kahramanın Sonsuz Yolculuğu* [*The Hero with a Thousand Faces*]. Translated by Sabri Gürses, İthaki Yayınları [Ithaki Publications], 2017.

Carroll, Noël. *The Paradox of Suspense.* Routledge, 1996.

Combe, Kirk, and Brenda M. Boyle. *Masculinity and Monstrosity in Contemporary Hollywood Films.* Springer, 2013.

Dines, Gail. "King Kong and the White Woman: *Hustler Magazine* and the Demonization of Black Masculinity." *Violence against Women*, vol. 4, no. 3, 1998, pp. 291-307.

Eliade, Mircea. *Mitlerin Özellikleri* [*Myths*]. Translated by Sema Rıfat, Alfa Yayınları [Alfa Publications], 2018.

Erdoğan, İrfan. "Gerbner'in Ekme Tezi ve Anlattığı Öyküler Üzerine Bir Değerlendirme" ["An Evaluation of Gerbner's Dissertation and the Stories He Tells"]. *Kültür ve İletişim* [*Culture and Communications Journal*], vol. 1, no. 2, 1998, pp. 149-80.

Ferro, Marc. *Sömürgecilik Tarihi* [*History of Colonization*]. Translated by Muna Cedden, İmge Kitabevi [İmge Publication], 2017.

Freud, Sigmund. *Uygarlığın Huzursuzluğu* [*Civilization and Its Discontents*]. Translated by Haluk Barışcan, Metis Yayınları [Metis Publications], 2019.

Galeano, Eduardo. *Open Veins of Latin America: Five Centuries of the Pillage of a Continent.* Monthly Review Press, 1997.

Gariper, Kağan. "Mitten Sinemaya Olympos'tan Hollywood'a Göstergelerarası Düzlemde Tanrilarin Göçü" ["The Migration of the Gods in the Intersemiotic Plane from Myth to Cinema, from Olympus to Hollywood"]. *Millî Folklor* [*National Folklore*], vol. 17, 2022, pp. 92-105.

Gerbner, George, et al. "Dimensions of Violence in Television Drama." *National Commission on the Causes and Prevention of Violence*, 1968.

Girard, Rene. *Kutsal ve Şiddet* [*Violence and the Sacred*]. Translated by Necmiye Alpay, Kanat Kitap [Kanat Publication], 2003.

Hairston, A. "Lord of the Monsters: Minstrelsy Redux: King Kong, Hip Hop, and the Brutal Black Buck." *Journal of the Fantastic in the Arts*, vol. 18, no. 2, 2007, pp. 187-200.

Hansbury, Griffin. "King Kong & Goldilocks: Imagining Transmasculinities through the Trans–Trans Dyad." *Psychoanalytic Dialogues*, vol. 21, no. 2, 2011, pp. 210-20.

Hund, Wulf. D. "Racist King Kong Fantasies: From Shakespeare's Monster to Stalin's Ape-Man." *Simianization: Apes, Gender, Class, and Race*, edited by Wulf D. Hund et al., 2015, pp. 43-73.

Kaya, Büşra. "Televizyonda Şiddet Gösterimi: George Gerbner ve Kültivasyon Analizi Üzerine" ["The Representation of Violence on Television: George Gerbner and Cultivation Analysis"]. *Journal of International Social Research*, 2019.

King Kong. Directed by Merian C. Cooper and Ernest B. Schoedsack, RKO Pictures, 1933.

King Kong. Directed by Peter Jackson, Universal Pictures, 2005.

Kristeva, Julia. *Korkunun Güçleri* [*Powers of Horror*]. Translated by Nilgün Tutal, Ayrıntı Yayınları [Ayrıntı Publications], 2018.

Kundera, Milan. *Ölümsüzlük* [*Immortality*]. Can Yayınları [Can Publications], 2002.

Lévy-Bruhl, Lucien. *İlkel Toplumlarda Mistik Deneyimler ve Simgeler* [*The Mystic Experience and Primitive Symbolism*]. Translated by Oğuz Adanır, Doğu Batı Yayınları [Doğu Batı Publications], 2020.

Levi-Strauss, Claude. *Mit ve Anlam* [*Myth and Meaning*]. Translated by Gökhan Yavuz Demir, İthaki Yayınları [Ithaki Publications], 2018.

Malinowski, Bronislaw. *Magic Science and Religion.* Kessinger Publishing, 2005.

Maltby, Richard. "The Production Code and the Mythologies of 'Pre-Code' Hollywood." The Classical Hollywood Reader, edited by Steve Neale, Routledge, 2010.

March, Jenny. *Klasik Mitler* [*Classic Myths*]. Translated by Semih Lim, İletişim Yayınları [İletisim Publications], 2014.

Mayne, Judith. "'King Kong'" and the Ideology of Spectacle." *Quarterly Review of Film & Video*, vol. 1, no. 4, 1976, pp. 373-87.

Megill, Allan. *Aşırılığın Peygamberleri [Prophets of Extremity]*. Translated by Tuncay Birkan, Ayraç Kitabevi [Ayraç Publication], 2021.

Meszaros, Istvan. *Ya Sosyalizm Ya Barbarlık [Socialism or Barbarism]*. Translated by Irfan Mehmetoğlu, Epos Yayınları [Epos Publications], 2004.

Mikellides, B. "Colour Psychology: The Emotional Effects of Colour Perception." *Colour Design: Theories and Application*, edited by Janet Best, Woodhead Publishing, 2012, pp. 105-28.

Mills, Jon. "The Essence of Myth." *Journal of Indian Council of Philosophical Research*, vol. 37, 2020, pp. 191-205.

Nietzsche, Friedrich. *Tragedyanın Doğuşu [The Birth of Tragedy]*. Translated by Mustafa Tüzel, Türkiye İş Bankası Yayınları [Türkiye İş Bankası Publications], 2019.

Ong, Walter. *Sözlü ve Yazılı Kültür [Orality and Literacy]*. Translated by Sema Postacıoğlu Banon, Metis Yayınları [Metis Publications], 2014.

Özkan, Selfiye. "A Research on Television News Content in the Context of Gerbner's Theory of Cultural Signs." *Abant Journal of Cultural Studies*, vol. 2, no. 4, 2017, pp. 129-41.

Sanchez, J. P., et al. *Bibliografia Colombina, 1492-1990: Books, Articles and Other Publications on the Life and Times of Christopher Columbus*. National Park Service, Spanish Colonial Research Center, 1990.

Schleier, Merrill. "The Empire State Building, Working-Class Masculinity, and 'King Kong.'" *Mosaic: A Journal for the Interdisciplinary Study of Literature*, 2008, pp. 29-54.

Sexton, Jared. "The Ruse of Engagement: Black Masculinity and the Cinema of Policing. *American Quarterly*, vol. 61, no. 1, 2009, pp. 39-63.

Sontag, Susan. *Fotoğraf Üzerine [On Photography]*. Translated by Osman Akınhay, Agora Kitaplığı [Agora Books], 2008.

Sorenson, John. *Ape*. Reaktion Books Ltd., 2009.

Stone, Bryan. "Religion and Violence in Popular Film." *Journal of Religion & Film*, vol. 3, no. 1, 1999.

Suresh, Jhansi. "Popular Culture as an Entrenching Agent: A Postcolonial Ecofeminist Analysis of *King Kong, George of The Jungle* and *Epic*." *Anveshana's International Journal of Research in Education, Literature, Psychology and Library Sciences*, vol. 3, no. 4, 2018, pp. 45-49.

Chapter 15

No One Is Coming to Save Us: Government Inadequacy in Large-Scale Horror

Andrew Wilczak

Abstract

There is a subset of horror cinema where terror has spread beyond the immediate surroundings of the main characters and now represents a national, if not global, threat. In these films, the horror the main characters experience is compounded by the state's wholesale inability to confront the problem, if not the state's immediate and total collapse. In these stories, the characters are truly alone, with no hope of a cavalry charge coming over the hill to save them. Drawing on the work of Marxism, specifically the field of critical criminology, and focusing on films including the original *Godzilla, The War of the Worlds*, and George Romero's *Night of the Living Dead* franchise, this chapter argues that this trope is still absolutely necessary.

Keywords: Marxism, critical criminology, white collar crime, sociology of revolution

* * *

It is a simple trope in any horror film featuring widespread disaster: the state is wholly unprepared to deal with it, leaving the cast of characters to fend for themselves. Whether the source of the horror is some external attack (aliens, giant monsters, aliens bringing giant monsters), disease (such as a zombie outbreak), or the corruption of the state itself, characters in these films quickly learn that they are on their own. They must rely on their own wit, ingenuity, and resilience to survive in the brave new world into which they have been thrust. That this trope—near immediate total government collapse—is so prevalent across generations of filmmakers speaks to an unfortunate reality of our lives: when faced with far less catastrophic crises, the state is just as incompetent as depicted on screen.

Drawing on the field of critical criminology, the purpose of this chapter is to examine horror films featuring either widespread government collapse or widespread government corruption in the face of some cascading horrific event, comparing the usage of this trope in these films to real-life instances of widespread government collapse and/or corruption in the face of real-world problems. For better or worse, the reality for the characters in these films is frequently the same one we all must confront: no one is coming to save us.

Theoretical Background

The work in this chapter is largely derived from critical criminology. Critical criminology began as the Marxist branch of sociological criminology that has evolved into a crucial component of the discipline encompassing 15 or more subfields, united by a critical viewpoint of more mainstream criminology (DeKeseredy 10). Classical critical criminology argues that the state is just as criminal as the people it is prosecuting and that, in fact, the criminal justice system exists as a shield deployed by the state to deflect attention from its own crimes (Quinney). As Walter DeKeseredy argues, critical criminology focuses on the relationship between social stratification and crime, specifically the unequal distribution of power across racial, ethnic, gender, and social class lines (12). Moreover, critical criminology focuses on the flaws of society rather than the flaws of the individual and expands the definition of crime to include those systematic processes that unjustly harm, disadvantage, or otherwise oppress people within society (i.e., racism, imperialism) (DeKeseredy 13). For the purpose of this chapter, the ways we see the state perform incompetently in large-scale disaster horror are criminal; it is, both on-screen and in real life, a dereliction of duty.

The theoretical underpinnings in the sociology of revolutions also add an interesting perspective to this discussion. Here, the role of theory is to help find some commonality across major social and political revolutionary events—both those that work, meaning there is some significant change in a given society as a result and those that fail, meaning the status quo eventually wins the day. Theda Skocpol approaches sociopolitical revolutions from a Marxist standpoint, drawing on the events of the French, Chinese, and Russian revolutions to argue that all major change ultimately stems from economic growth and transformation that renders the present structure of the state irrelevant, inadequate or both. She writes:

> Social revolutions are set apart from other sorts of conflicts and transformative processes above all by the combination of two coincidences: the coincidence of societal structural change with class upheaval and the coincidence of political with social transformation. In contrast, rebellions, even when successful, may involve the revolt of subordinate classes – but they do not eventuate in structural change. Political revolutions transform state structures but not social structures, and they are not

> necessarily accomplished through class conflict. Processes such as industrialization can transform social structures without necessarily bringing about or resulting from sudden political upheavals or basic political-structural changes. What is unique to social revolution is that basic changes in social structure and political structure occur together in a mutually reinforcing fashion. And these changes occur through intense sociopolitical conflicts in which class struggles play a key role. (Skocpol 4-5)

This perspective provides a useful addendum to DeKeseredy's description of critical criminology as a field focusing on societal injuries as a form of crime; here, Skocpol argues that these forms of oppression, disproportionately experienced by the underclasses in a given society, become the engine for future revolution. Skocpol argues the sociology of revolution should put the organization of the state front-and-center and consider how the state behaves at the intersection between international pressure and conflict on one hand and economic pressure and political actors on the other (32). Skocpol's work provides a new framework for the protagonists in many of the films discussed in this chapter: they are sociopolitical actors at this intersection of localized class structure and international conflict, sometimes acting as vanguards of change, swept up in the tides of massive structural change.

   Another reason to draw on the theoretical work produced by the sociology of revolutions is the functionalist perspective championed by Chalmers Johnson. Johnson views revolution as a failure of the state, though not purely an economic one. As functionalism views social structures and institutions the way a biologist may view the evolutionary processes that render some organs obsolete, Johnson argues that revolutions occur because the state is no longer performing the basic functions with which it has been charged by its population, namely, providing food and shelter, safety and security. There is a ready application of Johnson's perspective to large-scale horror. When faced with some horrifying conflict, whether on screen or in reality, there is an expectation that the state will rise to the challenge to protect all of us. On-screen, the state inevitably and spectacularly fails to meet this challenge. In reality, as implied by the very existence of the sociology of revolution, the truth does not always appear to be much different.

   On that point, it is important to discuss what, exactly, the federal government has done in the past century in terms of any large-scale federal policy designed to mitigate or eliminate complex social problems. Simply put, there is one tool in the federal government's toolbox: war. The United States has declared war on poverty, war on crime (twice), War on Drugs, war on terrorism, and war on Covid-19. The United States has gone winless in these imagined conflicts. Michelle

Alexander and Elizabeth Hinton have each written extensively on the catastrophic effects of mass incarceration and the policies underpinning the war on crime and the War on Drugs. The argument Alexander makes in *The New Jim Crow* is that the current system of mass incarceration is an extension of Jim Crow-era policies, which in turn were a modification of the system of chattel slavery that resulted in the American Civil War. Elizabeth Hinton's work in *From the War on Poverty to the War on Crime: The Making of Mass Incarceration in America* goes deeper into more recent history, outlining the policy processes at the presidential level, beginning with President Kennedy, and demonstrates how mass incarceration developed from a deeply racist belief system that targeted African Americans in urban areas. DeKeseredy's definition of critical criminology would surely consider this criminal.

The losses from the War on Drugs alone are staggering. It has cost over a trillion dollars—including over 39 billion in federal money—and incarcerated people for an incalculable amount of time that likely extends well beyond tens of thousands if not hundreds of thousands of years (Chinni). As a result of this 50-plus-year war, it is just as easy to get drugs today as it was when President Nixon declared drugs a major crisis in need of a federal response.

The list goes on. Despite the fact that the federal government has transformed the U.S. into one of the most punitive nations in the world, not only do we have crime, but mass violence has become so common that other countries issue travel warnings to their citizens thinking of visiting the U.S. The war on terror brought with it a massive expansion in federal power, yet terrorism is no closer to eradication globally than it was before 9/11, as evidenced by the surprise attack launched by Hamas on Israel in October 2023. To Johnson, this could be evidence of the state no longer functioning as well as it should. To Quinney and DeKeseredy, these policy failures should be viewed as either desperate attempts to distract the public from crimes committed by the state or as criminal acts unto themselves; likely, they are both.

To demonstrate how these theoretical perspectives apply to large-scale horror, this chapter is divided into three sections: external threats, covering those films that exist at the intersection of horror and science fiction, wherein non-human, largely unknowable entities unleash violence on the Earth; internal threats, when the state must somehow protect society from itself, largely focusing on the work of George Romero; and lastly, those films where the state itself is the problem, and the story centers on characters first discovering this betrayal and then attempting to retake control of their world.

External Threats: Monster and Alien Attacks

The first category of films includes those where the state collapses in reaction to the introduction of some external threat. Major urban centers have been pounded flat by monsters, aliens, and alien monsters for generations, from the original *Godzilla* in 1954 to *Independence Day* in 1996 to *Nope* in 2022. The original radio broadcast of *War of the Worlds* by Orson Welles in 1938 and its subsequent film adaptations in 1953 and again in 2005 also fit this description. *War of the Worlds* is notable because of the legend of its initial radio broadcast. Because it aired without commercial interruption, many in the listening audience believed that what they were hearing was true. Brad Schwartz from the *Smithsonian Magazine* writes,

> Some listeners mistook those bulletins for the real thing, and their anxious phone calls to police, newspaper offices, and radio stations convinced many journalists that the show had caused nationwide hysteria. By the next morning, the 23-year-old Welles's face and name were on the front pages of newspapers coast-to-coast, along with headlines about the mass panic his CBS broadcast had allegedly inspired.

Though there is some debate over how widespread those beliefs were, the fact remains that while these kinds of science fiction disaster epics may not be traditionally considered true horror films, the ramifications of their stories certainly are horrifying and can inspire the same psychological and emotional reactions in the audience. That there was a backlash against the original *War of the Worlds* broadcast because at least a portion of the listening audience believed it was genuine is evidence of that.

The typical method of operation in these films is that the state is presented with an external crisis of unknown origins or intent but with clear destructive power. The evidence is oftentimes presented by a lone whistleblower, usually someone so far down the bureaucratic chain that they are easily dismissed by the powers that be; this person may also be the one with the so-crazy-it-just-might-work solution to the crisis that leads into the third act of the film. Shortly after the state is presented with this potential threat, it becomes actualized, unleashing absolute carnage and destruction on a massive scale. As the state's go-to response in real life to any crisis is rapid militarization, their fictional protégés follow the same logic, to no effect: the external force(s) are impervious to traditional weaponry. Someone will likely advocate for a nuclear option, which is also unsuccessful. The day is saved when the unlikely heroes, thrust into leadership because the state has no other solution, discover some unexpected Achilles' heel, which they're able to exploit near-perfectly on the first try, saving the day.

Godzilla is clearly a reaction to the real-life horror of its times. It is important to remember that the film was released nine years after the United States dropped the first nuclear bombs on Hiroshima and Nagasaki to accelerate the end of the Second World War. In the original *Godzilla*, the scariest, saddest part of the film is when the characters are seeking shelter and pass an older gentleman who laments that he can't believe this is happening again. This is why *Godzilla* and films like it deserve a place in the horror lexicon. The audience is engaging with very real horror via the monster on screen.

While *Godzilla*'s sequels tended more towards camp, the 2016 film *Shin Godzilla* follows a similar pattern to the original, only shifting the focus away from nuclear war and towards climate change. Here, the monster is mutated and driven to violence by pollution, emerging from the ocean as a sort of enormous gecko and growing quickly into a version of the monster fans have come to love. What makes *Shin Godzilla* so effective is the combination of dizzying cinematography and crushing bureaucracy, as the film cuts from scene to scene of meeting after meeting at such a breakneck pace that it begins to mimic the feel of a high-octane action movie, but government incompetence prevents anything from happening. This has the effect of making the audience feel the same disorienting desperation as the main characters, who need the agents of power to leap to action to save them from this threat but instead have a front-row seat to the irrationality of bureaucracy.

The United States government has handled major external threats in ways that have been widely criticized. Most recently, the War on Terror launched in response to the September 11th terrorist attacks perpetrated by Al-Qaeda on the World Trade Center and Pentagon provides a multi-pronged example. The federal government ignored evidence of a possible attack, doctored evidence of weapons of mass destruction in Iraq where there were none, invaded Iraq and murdered hundreds of thousands of Iraqis (Costs of War), continued an economic and military partnership with the country actually responsible for the attacks, hold a significant military presence in both Iraq and Afghanistan even after two decades of military surges and drawbacks, and, lastly, reshaped domestic policy to allow for a tremendous expansion of federal power in name only of fighting terrorism while wasting billions (if not trillions). Why, then, would we expect the federal government to respond to a fictional alien monster invasion with any more sophistication?

The failure of the state in these films, especially as evidenced in *Shin Godzilla*, mirrors the arguments made by both Johnson and DeKeseredy. To Johnson, revolution happens when the state fails to fulfill its basic functions, including protecting the environment. While the monster Godzilla is a clear environmental threat, the real threat here is its cause, whether nuclear war or climate change. Critical criminology would argue the same and would point to a recent legal case where a court ruled that there is a constitutional right in the United States to a clean environment (Kuta).

Disease and Disaster: Threats from Within

The most obvious avatar for this genre of large-scale disaster-horror is the zombie apocalypse. Zombie films either show us the beginning of the outbreak or drop us into it after the apocalypse is in full swing. The films of George Romero encompass both events. In the original *The Night of the Living Dead*, the viewers experience the outbreak from the perspective of Barbra (played by Judith O'Dea) after she and her brother are attacked in a cemetery, and she flees to a nearby farmhouse. As Barbra meets other survivors in the house, the crux of the story centers on whether they should stay inside or look for other survivors and where in the house they should stay. While the plot centers on which part of the house is more defensible, the important factor here is the characters' automatic and understandable assumption that they need to stay close to a television or radio for any communication from the government about what to do. By the end of the film, without anyone in a position of authority to provide direction, the entire cast except one man (Ben, played by Duane Jones) dies, consumed by the undead. The sole survivor meets his fate at the hands of the police, who mistake him for a zombie and shoot him in the head. No one saved them, and the people who were supposed to do the exact opposite.

The sequels to *Night* also grapple with this trope of state collapse in their own fascinating ways. The original *Dawn of the Dead* in 1978 is possibly the most well-known horror commentary on capitalism, as the bulk of the film is set in a shopping mall. The main characters are two SWAT team officers, a helicopter pilot, and a television news reporter. Early in the film, viewers see the police raiding a public housing project looking for zombies. The characters are mortified at the incredibly racist behavior of some of their fellow officers, whom the audience will believe have been tasked with protecting and serving the community. After executing one racist officer, they decide to flee the scene altogether, abandoning their posts in the name of survival. As the characters fly their helicopter over the Pennsylvania countryside looking for shelter, they pass a mob of people out hunting the undead, making sport of it. Rather than landing the helicopter and joining them, and perhaps lending their tactical expertise or usage of the helicopter for scouting, they essentially turn their noses up at the crass behavior of these common people trying to survive. While this dereliction of duty is perhaps the most obvious example of state agents flatly refusing to serve in a time of crisis, there is a large section of the second act of the film where viewers watch them live out a sort of child's escapist fantasy wherein they run wild in the mall, doing whatever they want. To critical criminologists, this is clear-cut negligence; this inaction is criminal (DeKeseredy).

In *Day of the Dead*, the story begins at an underground government lab on a remote island. Some of the characters believe they may be the only people on Earth left alive. They are a joint military-civilian operation that is supposed to be dedicated to finding a solution to the outbreak, but clearly, their isolation plus the stakes have driven them to break. The head scientist, nicknamed Dr. Frankenstein by the military, is more interested in domesticating the undead than finding any sort of explanation for why this all happened in the first place. The head of the military side, Colonel Rhodes, played by Joseph Pilato, has had enough of trying to save the world through (mad) science and, frankly, enough of everything. When tensions finally reach their breaking point, and the zombie horde breaches their underground base, the military runs, individual soldiers turning on one another, while the remaining civilians manage to escape in the helicopter and flee to the safety of an uninhabited tropical island.

Romero's original trilogy has its own depictions of the state. In *Night*, the state is very much in the background but ultimately ineffective at best and criminal at worst when the sole surviving character is shot in the head. In *Dawn*, we see representatives of the state shirk their responsibility to go play out their adolescent fantasies in an abandoned mall. In *Day*, the state is violently inept, its project an abject failure.

Diary of the Dead, Romero's attempt to bring a found-footage style film into this universe, showcases a failure of the government to provide support. Here, a group of college students and their film professor shoot a horror film when the outbreak begins and chronicle their attempts to find safety. There are two key scenes in *Diary* that are worth discussing: First, they go to a hospital; second, they are ambushed by the military. In the former, the students go to a hospital after an encounter with the undead that leaves one of them suicidal; it is natural they would seek help there, as this is part of the social infrastructure designed to help in emergencies. The hospital is, of course, abandoned and overrun by zombies, who attack one of the students, Gordo, who is eventually killed by his girlfriend, Tracy. The second incident comes later in the film when the survivors are stopped by members of the National Guard. Rather than helping shepherd the survivors to safety, the National Guardsmen rob them of all of their food and water. This is a direct contrast to what one should expect of agencies in real life, as their role is to swoop into these emergency situations to provide food, water, and medicine for those in need. In *Diary*, the National Guard acts in the complete opposite role, a blunt example of the trope in action.

Romero's stories are mirrored by real-life equivalencies. Two recent examples demonstrate the state's complete inability to handle these sorts of internalized threats to its well-being. First, the HIV/AIDS epidemic beginning in the early 1980s was a monumental disaster wherein government inaction (and, indeed, deep-seated homophobia) led to the deaths of thousands in the first decade. A 1991 CDC report estimates that over 100,000 people died between 1981 and 1990 from HIV/AIDS in the United States, with gay or bisexual people constituting 80% of those deaths and one-third of those deaths happening in 1990 alone ("Current Trends Mortality"). This only happened because of government inaction. Not only did President Reagan's administration slash the budgets of public health agencies, but there is some question as to how the Reagans handled the speculation that their long-time friend and Hollywood superstar Rock Hudson tested positive for HIV and was denied (what Hudson believed to have been) crucial treatment in France that he might have been able to receive if only the White House had called (Tumulty). Tumulty argues that perhaps the Reagans withheld their support because, had they helped their rich and famous friend, they might have been criticized for not helping the poor and indigent, which emphasizes the point made in this chapter: no one is coming to save us.

Further underscoring that message is the global response, specifically the American reaction to the ongoing Covid-19 pandemic. As of this writing, two Presidential administrations have mismanaged the federal reaction to a virus that has killed over 1.1 million people in the United States. The early days of the pandemic under the Trump White House were especially troubling as the President advised a variety of dangerous solutions to the virus up to and including injecting disinfectant, i.e., bleach, as one possible cure, using the same press conference to brag about his intellect ("Coronavirus: Outcry after Trump Suggests Injecting Disinfectant as Treatment"). After achieving victory in the 2020 presidential election and inheriting a fraught federal Covid program, the Biden administration declared in March 2022 that the work done by their administration meant that Covid-19 was "no longer in control of our lives" ("Remarks by President Biden"). Within 18 months after President Biden made that statement, a new variant has emerged, vaccine skepticism remains high, and mask mandates threaten to return. The overwhelming message from early 2020 has been that it was worth the loss of over a million people plus the heretofore unknowable long-term health consequences that Covid survivors may experience if it means that the status quo, such that it is, is allowed to grind on. This may be somewhere remotely understandable if Covid-19 was an unknowable, impenetrable disease, but it was not. The world shut down for two weeks in the initial period of lockdown to try to prevent the spread of the disease, and then the state gave up. Who is to say the world would not be a healthier place today if we had locked down for a month? Put differently, were there to be an outbreak of some sort of zombie-apocalypse-level virus, which scenario seems more likely: the world coming together to change to make things safer or Donald Trump speculating that a combination of sunlight and bleach will kill zombies?

Further still, we can view the War on Drugs as another example of the state failing to solve an internal problem. *If* we accept President Nixon's assumption in June of 1971 that drugs were a problem worthy of federal attention, indeed, worthy of a declaration of war ("Public Enemy Number One"), *then* we can frame the state's response here in terms of reacting to an internal threat. The War on Drugs has been a failure of immeasurable proportions, wherein state and local police, through federal incentives, effectively destroyed urban communities across the country in the name of the War on Drugs. Survivors of this war— friends and family of people in the grips of vicious substance abuse—are cut down and treated as collateral damage in the state's ruthless effort to behead the zombies and drug dealers in its midst.

Across Romero's films, the audience sees the state in various stages of collapse. Even in *Land of the Dead*, when it appears that some new order has risen and the existence of the undead has become part of a new normal, it still falls under the weight of its corruption. In his work in the sociology of revolution, Johnson argues there are basically two paths that the state follows when threatened existentially: reform, where the state changes itself just enough to placate the revolutionary vanguard or intransigence, doubling down on the dysfunctional practices that created a revolutionary sentiment in the first place. In the world Romero has created, especially in *Day of the Dead* and in *Land of the Dead*, intransigence is at work, in a way. Though viewers don't know the cause of the zombie apocalypse, they see power endeavoring to carry on as if nothing has changed, in terms of social stratification in *Land*, in terms of hegemonic masculinity—the need to control through violence—in *Day*.

The System Is Working Exactly as Designed: The State as the Problem

An interesting addition to this category of films focusing on state collapse are those in which the state is the source of the problem itself. Perhaps most famously depicted in John Carpenter's *They Live*, star Roddy Piper, as Nada discovers aliens have infiltrated the U.S. and are forcing people to subconsciously conform, consume, and obey. The narrative thrust of this style of filmmaking is that the state has been co-opted and is the source of all manner of horror being visited upon society. Here, the horrors are less visually compelling—there are no Kaiju crushing cities underfoot, no zombie hordes shambling through the ruins of a city—but may be viewed as more psychologically terrifying, especially to the conformists in the audience. In other words, in a society where we are socialized to trust the government to confront any serious threats on our behalf, what happens when those agents of the state are the problem themselves? Certainly, this is nothing new to people in the U.S., especially those with historically marginalized and minoritized identities. In fact, in communities across the country, American history is exactly that: one where the threat of violence and destruction hangs over everything, explicitly or implicitly.

Like *Dawn of the Dead*, the anti-consumerism (and arguably anti-capitalist) theme of the film is very blunt. As the film progresses, Nada is able to get close to the heart of the conspiracy only to discover one of the allies he made along the way was secretly a human collaborator who kills Nada just as he destroys the transmitter, blinding humanity to the aliens in their midst. What makes *They Live* especially poignant and relevant to people trying to do reform or justice work or who otherwise want to affect change in their community is not the extremely overt anti-capitalist/anti-conformity messaging in the story but rather that betrayal at the end, which shows how countless other nascent civil rights organizations failed to launch: betrayal from the inside. The United States ran a program specifically targeting civil rights organizations, the Counter Intelligence Program (COINTELPRO), that systematically decimated many efforts to create a more equitable society. That Nada is able to lift the veil and reveal to humanity the truth of their situation before he dies could also arguably speak to the number of civil rights leaders who were themselves assassinated precisely because of their ability to speak truth to power; that Roddy Piper is white while all of the civil rights leaders who were assassinated are Black is also worthy of discussion.

Another film that excellently depicts the state as the source of terror is the 1978 remake of *Invasion of the Body Snatchers*. Unlike *They Live*, where the state is already corrupted, in *Invasion* we watch as the main characters fight against and inevitably succumb to the takeover of the state and society at large. While *They Live* shows ordinary people living out their lives as mindless sheep under the control of the alien presence, the goal of the invaders in *Invasion* is to replace the entire population. The terror here then comes from not knowing who has been turned already. Where *They Live* brings the human collaborator angle to the forefront at the end (as opposed to people who are collaborating because they don't know any better). *Invasion* makes the "are they or aren't they" component central to the tension of the story. Further, while the aliens invading in *They Live* are humanoid, the force in *Invasion* is plant-based: a literal invasive species that grows human replicants in large pods. As the story of *Invasion* continues, the characters, led by Donald Sutherland as Matthew, find their odds of survival rapidly decreasing as the number of pod-people grows at an exponential rate. In the end, Matthew is able to burn down a building full of pods in one last burst of defiance; however, viewers learn in the final shot of the film that he, too, has been replaced by a duplicate.

Taken together, *They Live* and the remake of *Invasion of the Body Snatchers* excellently detail the need for this specific version of the "no one is coming to save you" trope. Both films show a society overtaken by an insidious force that is masquerading as the state itself. In both cases, the main characters want to turn to the authorities instinctively for help, but when they realize the authorities are not on their side—that "protect and serve" is quite literally fiction—it is far too late to do anything about it. Further, it demonstrates the importance of working together in communities to build our own networks for survival. In *They Live*, Nada is a loner and a vagrant, and while he is able to convince a few people of the alien takeover, he is ultimately hindered and destroyed by his disconnectedness. The main characters in *Invasion* are of a higher social class and have some degree of social capital but are not oriented towards helping; they are the stereotypical "good liberals" who are all too happy to cede authority and responsibility to the powers that be at the first sign of a crisis. The way this trope is deployed in *Invasion* clearly makes the point that this mindset is just as useless in the face of disaster as Nada's apparent self-imposed isolationism. This is an important trope given the multiple cascading crises currently facing humanity, all of which the state has effectively punted on.

In his definition of critical criminology, DeKeseredy argues that the various forms of oppression that exist in a given society should be considered criminal; if we accept that a function of the state is to promote the safety and well-being of *all* of its people, then Johnson's argument that revolution happens when the state is no longer performing its basic functions frames Nada's behavior as revolutionary acts taken against a criminally negligent apparatus.

Conclusion

The purpose of this chapter was to examine the various ways that the state is presented as an incompetent collective in large-scale horror films and showcase how this on-screen incompetence mirrors the multitude of ways the federal government in the United States has failed, time and again, to do its job. By examining films covering both external threats (i.e., *Godzilla*) and internal threats (i.e., *Night of the Living Dead*) and by comparing these to how the state has responded to real-life external and internal threats (terrorism, disease), it is clear that this trope has a useful function. By depicting the state at its worst in fictional crises, we should not be surprised that it is just as useless when real emergencies arise. Further, there exists a subgenre of films where the state itself is the problem, presented here by *They Live* and *Invasion of the Body Snatchers*, again reflecting widespread corruption, negligence, and malfeasance that defines the modern American state.

As a storytelling trope, the absence of the state as a sort of knight in shining armor to rush in and save characters from whatever crisis they are in is important because it forces agency upon characters who may not be used to making real choices for themselves. Without being able to defer to any authority figure or allow some outside agency to step in and take control, the characters in these films have to figure things out for themselves. This should be instructive, if not aspirational, for audiences. How many people have talked, jokingly or otherwise, about whether and how they would survive a zombie apocalypse? Is this just a thought experiment, or is it a collective understanding that no one is coming to save us?

Works Cited

Alexander, Michelle. *The New Jim Crow: Mass Incarceration in the Age of Colorblindness.* The New Press, 2012.

Chinni, Dante. "Costs in the War on Drugs Continue to Soar." *NBC News*, 2 July 2023, www.nbcnews.com/meet-the-press/data-download/costs-war-drugs-continue-soar-rcna92032. Accessed 5 Oct. 2023.

"Coronavirus: Outcry after Trump Suggests Injecting Disinfectant as Treatment." *BBC.com*, 24 Apr. 2020, www.bbc.com/news/world-us-canada-52407177. Accessed 28 Sept. 2023.

Costs of War. "Iraqi Civilians." *Watson Institute for International and Public Affairs*, watson.brown.edu/costsofwar/costs/human/civilians/iraqi. Accessed 8 Jan. 2024.

"Current Trends Mortality Attributable to HIV Infection/AIDS -- United States, 1981-1990." *Centers for Disease Control and Prevention*, 25 Jan. 1991, www.cdc.gov/mmwr/preview/mmwrhtml/00001880.htm#:~:text=From%201981%20through%201990%2C%20100%2C777,deaths%20were%20reported%20during%201990. Accessed 28 Sept. 2023.

Dawn of the Dead. Directed by George A. Romero, Laurel Group, 1979.

Day of the Dead. Directed by George A. Romero, United Film Distribution Company, 1985.

DeKeseredy, Walter S. *Contemporary Critical Criminology.* 2nd ed., Routledge, 2022.

Diary of the Dead. Directed by George A. Romero, Artfire Films, 2008.

Godzilla. Directed by Ishiro Honda, Toho Film Ltd., 1954.

Hinton, Elizabeth. *From the War on Poverty to the War on Crime: The Making of Mass Incarceration in America* Harvard University Press, 2016.

Independence Day. Directed by Roland Emmerich, 20th Century Fox, 1996.

Invasion of the Body Snatchers. Directed by Philip Kaufman, Solofilm, 1978.

Johnson, Chalmers. *Revolutionary Change.* 7th ed., Stanford University Press, 1982.

Kuta, Sarah. "Montana Youths Win Key Climate Lawsuit on Their Right to a 'Clean and Healthful Environment.'" *Smithsonian Magazine*, 15 Aug. 2023, www.smithsonianmag.com/smart-news/montana-youths-win-key-climate-lawsuit-on-their-right-to-a-clean-and-healthful-environment-180982734/.

Land of the Dead. Directed by George A. Romero, Universal Pictures, 2005.

The Night of the Living Dead Directed by George A. Romero, Image Ten, 1968.

Nope. Directed by Jordan Peele, Universal Pictures, 2022.

"Public Enemy Number One: A Pragmatic Approach to America's Drug Problem." *Richard Nixon Foundation*, 29 June 2016, www.nixonfoundation.org/2016/06/26404/. Accessed 10 Oct. 2023.

Quinney, Richard. *Class, State, and Crime: On the Theory and Practice of Criminal Justice*. David McKay Company, 1977.

"Remarks by President Biden on the Status of the Country's Fight Against COVID-19." *The White House*, 30 Mar. 2022, www.whitehouse.gov/briefing-room/speeches-remarks/2022/03/30/remarks-by-president-biden-on-the-status-of-the-countrys-fight-against-covid-19/. Accessed 28 Sept. 2023.

Schwartz, A. Brad. "The Infamous "War of the Worlds" Radio Broadcast Was a Magnificent Fluke." *Smithsonian Magazine*, 6 May 2015, www.smithsonianmag.com/history/infamous-war-worlds-radio-broadcast-was-magnificent-fluke-180955180/.

Skocpol, Theda. *States and Social Revolutions*. Cambridge University Press, 2015.

Shin Godzilla. Directed by Hideaki Anno and Shinji Higuchi, Cine Bazar, 2016.

Tumulty, Karen. "Nancy Reagan's Real Role in the AIDS Crisis." *The Atlantic*, 12 Apr. 2021, www.theatlantic.com/politics/archive/2021/04/full-story-nancy-reagan-and-aids-crisis/618552/.

They Live. Directed by John Carpenter, Alive Films, 1988.

War of the Worlds. Directed by Byron Haskin, Paramount Pictures, 1953.

War of the Worlds. Directed by Steven Spielberg, Paramount Pictures, 2005.

Index

Milton Keynes UK
Ingram Content Group UK Ltd.
UKHW022227130524
442669UK00015B/173/J

9 798881 900038